CULTURAL
PEDAGOGY

Critical Studies in Education and Culture Series

Education and the American Dream: Conservatives, Liberals and Radicals
Debate the Future of Education
Harvey Holtz and Associates

Education and the Welfare State: A Crisis in Capitalism and Democracy
H. Svi Shapiro

Education under Siege: The Conservative, Liberal and Radical Debate over
Schooling
Stanley Aronowitz and Henry A. Giroux

Literacy: Reading the Word and the World
Paulo Freire and Donaldo Macedo

The Moral and Spiritual Crisis in Education: A Curriculum for Justice and
Compassion
David Purpel

The Politics of Education: Culture, Power and Liberation
Paulo Freire

Popular Culture, Schooling and the Language of Everyday Life
Henry A. Giroux and Roger I. Simon

Teachers As Intellectuals: Toward a Critical Pedagogy of Learning
Henry A. Giroux

Women Teaching for Change: Gender, Class and Power
Kathleen Weiler

Between Capitalism and Democracy: Educational Policy
and the Crisis of the Welfare State
Svi Shapiro

Critical Psychology and Pedagogy: Interpretation of the
Personal World
Edmund Sullivan

Pedagogy and the Struggle for Voice: Issues of Language,
Power, and Schooling for Puerto Ricans
Catherine E. Walsh

Learning Work: A Critical Pedagogy of Work Education
Roger I. Simon, Don Dippo, and Arleen Schenke

CULTURAL PEDAGOGY

Art/Education/Politics

DAVID TREND

CRITICAL STUDIES IN EDUCATION AND CULTURE SERIES

EDITED BY HENRY A. GIROUX AND PAULO FREIRE

Bergin & Garvey
New York • Westport, Connecticut • London

Library of Congress Cataloging-in-Publication Data

Trend, David.
    Cultural pedagogy : art/education/politics / David Trend.
        p.   cm. — (Critical studies in education & culture)
    Includes bibliographical references and index.
    ISBN 0–89789–256–9 (hb.:alk. paper) — ISBN 0–89789–257–7 (pb.: alk. paper)
    1. Arts and society—United States.   2. United States—Popular
culture.   3. Arts—Political aspects—United States.   I. Title.
II. Series.
NX180.S6T7   1992
700′.1′03—dc20   91-32090

British Library Cataloguing in Publication Data is available.

Library of Congress Catalog Card Number: 91–32090
ISBN: 0–89789–256–9
    0–89789–257–7 (pb.)

First published in 1992

Bergin & Garvey, One Madison Avenue, New York, NY 10010
An imprint of Greenwood Publishing Group, Inc.

Printed in the United States of America

∞™

The paper used in this book complies with the
Permanent Paper Standard issued by the National
Information Standards Organization (Z39.48–1984).

10 9 8 7 6 5 4 3 2 1

Contents

Series Foreword: Education, Pedagogy, and the Politics of Cultural Work

During the last decade, numerous scholars in a variety of disciplines have increasingly focused on the notion and practice of pedagogy. Refusing to reduce the concept to transmission of knowledge and skills, the new work on pedagogy instead views the practice as a form of political and cultural production deeply implicated in the construction of knowledge, subjectivities, and social relations. The shift away from pedagogy as a form of transmission is increasingly accompanied by attempts to engage pedagogy as a form of cultural politics. Both inside and outside the academy this has involved analyzing the production and representation of meaning and how these practices and the practices they provoke are implicated in the material and ideological dynamics of social power. Increasingly, the link between education and cultural work has been viewed in light of recent developments in feminism, cultural studies, postcolonialism, deconstruction, and the new historicism.

Unfortunately, while the conception of pedagogy as the systematic production of knowledge, identities, and values has moved out of its ghettoization within the established discourses of schooling, the new discourse on pedagogy has not been able to develop a theory of articulation that links the work of cultural workers in a variety of public spheres. That is, the new discourse on pedagogy and culture lacks a theory for addressing how the relationship between pedagogical practice and cultural production can be taken up as part of a political and ethical project which links education in the broader sense to the relevancies shared by diverse cultural workers. David Trend's book admirably demonstrates how a cultural pedagogy might provide the theoretical signposts for creating a shared forum for cultural workers without denying the specificity of their work.

Currently there is no book which addresses the relationship between cultural work and critical pedagogy in the arts while simultaneously offering a theoretical discourse for establishing the basis for such a project. There is a need for a text(s) to provide a new discursive space to begin to make apparent the relevancies that teachers, artists, and other cultural workers share in their analyses of pedagogy and their engendering practices. *Cultural Pedagogy* fills this gap.

As a practicing artist, writer, and former editor of *Afterimage*, Trend has been researching artists who think of themselves as educators deeply interested in how politics and power inform dominant perceptions of the relationship between art and culture. Central to his work have been questions such as "What politics inform accepted understandings of art and culture? Whose interests are served by such cultural conventions? How is culture made, and for whom is it made?"[1] In *Cultural Pedagogy*, Trend performs an invaluable theoretical service. First, he examines the issue of cultural production and its relationship to texts, economies, institutions, audiences, and communities and how these social forms and the practices that inform them can be understood within and across the different circuits of power that characterize the wider society. He does this by focusing on pedagogy as an articulatory concept that provides a discourse of unity, one in which differences are not erased but linked within a set of unifying principles. Second, Trend does more than offer the reader a new understanding of how artists, educators, and other cultural workers can produce new cultural zones and public spheres, can engage in new forms of art making, and can address the challenges provided by multiple audiences. He also attempts to provide an innovative political discourse in which the concept of critical pedagogy informs and is informed by the concept and practice of radical democracy. *Cultural Pedagogy* offers a new vision for rewriting not only the relationship between culture and power, between art and pedagogy, but also between cultural work and the project of democratic renewal.

The discourse of art/education/pedagogy which informs Trend's book is situated in a theoretical and historical context that serves to rewrite the relationship among cultural and pedagogical production as part of a broader vision that extends the principles and practices of human dignity, liberty, and social justice. In this view, the task of pedagogy is to deepen diverse democratic struggles which extend the ideological and material possibilities for self- and collective determination across a broad range of economic, social, and political spheres. In part, this means taking up pedagogy as a form of cultural politics that addresses how art gets produced, and how it comes to function in the broader community. Trend wants art and pedagogy to refigure a variety of human experiences within a discourse in which diverse political views, sexual orientations, races, ethnicities, and cultural differences can coexist amid social relations that support free expression and uninhibited debate. For Trend, cultural pedagogy is inseparable from cultural democracy. On one level this means deepening the political aspects of the pedagogical by providing equal access for cultural workers to the educational and cultural institutions that organize daily life; on another level, it means making the pedagogical more political by reconstructing the very concept of pedagogy as a social practice that generates new knowledge, opens up contradictions, and challenges all hierarchical structures of power that demand reverence at the expense of dialogue and debate. Art and pedagogy in this sense do not point to a romanticized notion of the cultural worker who can only function on the margins of society, nor do they refer to a notion of teaching/cultural production in which methodological reification erases the historical, semiotic, and social dimensions of pedagogy as the active construction of responsible and risk-taking citizens.

The concept of cultural worker in its narrower definition has generally been understood to refer to artists, writers, and media producers. Trend's book provides the theoretical groundwork for extending the range of people associated with this term to those working in professions like law, social work, architecture, medicine, theology, education, and literature.[2] By expanding the concept of cultural work to include issues related to public philanthropy, media reception, town meetings, and popular education, Trend makes a vital contribution to rewriting the cartography of innovation and struggle that such work involves, and in doing so expands the spaces/locations and potential alliances from which the production of knowledge can be interrogated and reconstructed within the primacy of the political and pedagogical.

The pedagogical dimension of cultural work refers to the process of creating symbolic representations and the practices within which they are engaged. This includes a particular concern with the analysis of textual, aural, and visual representations, and how such representations are organized and regulated within particular institutional arrangements. It also addresses how various people engage such representations in the practice of comprehension and significance. As a cultural practice, pedagogy both contests and refigures the construction, presentation, and engagement of various forms of images, text, talk, and action which results in the production of meaning, through which students construct their individual and collective futures. Pedagogy in this sense represents both a discourse of critique and a project of possibility.[3]

Crucial to Trend's book is his recognition that the political dimension of cultural work recognizes that the symbolic presentations which take place in various spheres of cultural production in society manifest contested and unequal power relations rooted in discursive and nondiscursive social forms. As a form of cultural production, pedagogy is implicated in the construction and organization of knowledge, desires, values, and social practices. It also serves to contest dominant forms of symbolic production. Cultural work, in this sense, informs a project whose intent is to mobilize knowledge and desires that may help to significantly reduce the degree of oppression in people's lives. At stake is a political imaginary which extends the possibilities for creating new public spheres and alliances in which the principles of equality, liberty, and justice become the primary organizing principles not only for structuring relationships between the self and others, but also for creating new social movements.

Cultural Pedagogy avoids pedagogy as a form of cultural politics that refuses to engage its own sense of purpose and meaning. There are no claims to a discourse of origins, authenticity, or master narratives in this work. In fact, Trend is at pains to expand the multi-accentuality of cultural work and critical pedagogy to broader public arenas. At the same time, he offers the broadest parameters for redefining and reworking a cultural politics in which the notion of the pedagogical is subject to self-criticism, constantly reworked in order not to be appropriated and depoliticized, and made practical without being paraded as a recipe book. I use the term practical in a cautionary sense. The notion of the practical is not defined in Trend's book in a merely instrumental sense; on the contrary, it is linked to a political imaginary that "suggests potential alliances and collaborations across divisive boundaries, and 'community' because in spite of internal hierarchies within [and between various groups], it nevertheless suggests a significant, deep commitment to what Benedict Anderson, in referring to the idea of the nation, calls 'horizontal comradeship.' "[4]

The range and depth of *Cultural Pedagogy* brilliantly redefines the relationship between cultural work and pedagogy. It helps to reconstruct and illuminate diverse forms of pedagogical practice. Similarly, it addresses how the pedagogical as an organizing practice can serve to articulate a politics of solidarity within and among various cultural workers who engage in assorted forms of material and symbolic production in a number of critical public spheres.

This book will give teachers access to a new language and range of pedagogical practices. At the same time, it will offer cultural workers in other public spheres an opportunity to deepen their understanding of what they have in common with those educators who work in schools. Trend's attempt to redefine and expand the relationship between pedagogy and cultural work will bring together within and outside of the schools groups of cultural workers who can join in a new movement to deepen and extend the relationship among pedagogy, democratic culture, and the reconstruction of public life. This invaluable book needs to be read and reread by all those cultural workers interested in addressing the broad intellectual, social, and economic challenges facing us as we approach the twenty-first century.

Henry A. Giroux
Miami University

NOTES

1. Group Material, "On Democracy," in *Democracy: A Project by Group Material* (Seattle: Bay Press, 1990), p. 1.

2. The attempt to redefine the relationship between critical pedagogy and cultural work is also discussed in Henry A. Giroux, *Border Crossings: Cultural Workers and the Politics of Education* (New York: Routledge, 1992) and Roger I. Simon, *Teaching Against the Grain: A Pedagogy of Possibility* (New York: Bergin and Garvey, 1992).

3. This notion of pedagogy comes from Roger Simon, *Teaching Against the Grain: A Pedagogy of Possibility* (New York: Bergin and Garvey, 1992).

4. Chandra Talpade Mohanty, "Cartographies of Struggle: Third World Women and the Politics of Feminism," in Chandra Talpade Mohanty, Ann Russo, and Lourdes Torres (eds.), *Third World Women and The Politics of Feminism* (Bloomington: Indiana University Press, 1991), p. 4.

Acknowledgments

Thanks are due to Richard Bolton, Lorraine Kenny, Patricia Lester, and Matthew Sommerville for content reading of selected chapters and to Aimée Ergas, Laura Marks, and Nadine McGann for additional editorial advice. Support for much of this project was provided by the Visual Studies Workshop in Rochester, NY, under whose auspices significant portions of this manuscript were generated. Credit should also be given to the Capp Street Project in San Francisco for affording me time to complete the essays. Funding for the initial research came from the Electronic Media and Television Arts Program of New York State Council on the Arts. I am particularly grateful to Henry A. Giroux for his encouragement and help throughout this effort.

Introduction: Radical Epistemologies

Percentage of U.S. population who rate the arts a "very important" part of life: 89.[1]

Percentage of population who visit museums, art galleries, or alternative spaces: 5.[2]

Percentage of population who feel that art making is a leisure activity in which they can participate: 6.[3]

Rank of TV viewing, eating, and shopping among activities Americans spend the most leisure time engaged in: 1, 2, 3.[4]

Number of companies that produce and distribute 98 percent of television seen in the United States: 4.[5]

Change since 1980 in the percentage of income paid in taxes by the richest 1 percent of U.S. citizens: −15. [6]

Change since 1980 in the percentage of income paid in taxes by the poorest 20 percent: +19.[7]

Number of 16-to-24-year-olds who drop out of high school and college each year: 4.3 million.[8]

Percentage of teachers who say that they would choose teaching again if given the chance: 38.[9]

Percentage of population who oppose artistic and intellectual censorship: 94.[10]

Number of U.S. universities that have instituted restrictions on free speech since 1988: 137.[11]

Percentage of citizens who voted in the 1988 presidential election: 22.7.[12]

Clearly the United States is in a state of cultural schizophrenia and democratic crisis. Discrepancies abound between wealth and poverty, "high" and "low" culture, civic participation and apathy. Nowhere are these issues more pronounced than in battles over education and culture. Debates over canonical values, multiculturalism, artistic censorship, and freedom of expression have moved from the margins of public debate to its center. Increasingly, those on both the Left and the Right recognize the pedagogical role of the arts and humanities in shaping human identities and influencing politics. In a post–cold war era lacking in superpower conflicts, ideological debate has become internalized as it did in the 1950s. Once again battles that were waged with guns and bullets are now fought with ideas and symbols. And once again access to the debate is a crucial issue, as attempts are made to exclude voices that would contest the status quo. This is the legacy through which all dominant regimes work to reproduce their supremacy. In some societies repression is achieved through violence; in modern Western nations it lives in the manufacture of consent.

As recent events have demonstrated, these struggles for consent are not fought on the traditional grounds of political conflict. Rather than materializing in direct appeals for campaign support or votes, such new contests are waged over the texts, institutions, and practices through which subjectivity is formed. The terms of the debate are well characterized by columnist Patrick Buchanan, who urged his fellow conservatives "to wage a cultural revolution in the 90s as sweeping as the political revolution of the 80s."[13] Because understandings of social position are culturally acquired, these are profoundly pedagogical issues.

Artists and teachers have an important role to play in explicating the relationship of power to its representations. Power, especially as deployed in contemporary capitalist nations, is discontinuous and therefore open to subversion. But it is always represented as uniform, unchanging, and invincible. Because of such representations people come to feel weak and ineffectual in the face of ruling regimes. Agency suffers as a consequence. Cultural workers can help reverse this pattern by encouraging ways to break this representational facade. One approaches this arena of cultural education by examining how learning is institutionalized and politicized. This entails a broadening of conventional definitions of art, literature, taste, "quality," and school itself to examine them within the fullest contexts of daily experience.

If culture is the ensemble of stories we tell ourselves about ourselves, it is useful to realize that such stories are never neutral, but are always constructed, delivered, and received in specific historical encounters. For this reason they are political by definition. A pedagogy of culture entails analyzing these stories, tellers, and their times—and encouraging this analytic spirit in others. The practice involves the study, not merely of particular objects or classroom practices, but of the range circumstances in which cultural forms are produced and received. It cuts across boundaries between amateurs and professionals, students and teachers, and among practitioners in various academic disciplines.

For obvious reasons, the task of discussing cultural pedagogy gets more complicated as its range broadens. Such expansive methodologies can totalize their objects of study within particular paradigms. Some argue that all such "generalized" theoretical discussions inevitably foreshorten the complexities and contradictions of particular circumstances as they are reduced for linear discussion. This book employs two strategies to sidestep such epistemological traps. First, it incorporates a broad sampling of theoretical approaches, attempting to appropriate *critically* the most useful elements of Marxist, feminist, deconstructionist, and postcolonial theories. Chapter 1 reviews certain ways cultural work and pedagogy intersect within these discourses. The term *critical* should be emphasized here because it is a recurrent theme throughout this book. A critical approach to learning asks one to question and reevaluate the legitimacy of knowledge forms, theoretical positions, ideological postures, and the presumed grounds on which arguments are based. It strives to be a dynamic attitude that searches for new and better ways to function by continually reexamining its own assumptions.

Second, and perhaps more important, I've tried to use actual examples of cultural practice as it is applied both inside and outside the classroom by teachers, parents, artists, writers, administrators, labor organizers, social workers, and others. By citing specific applications of cultural theory this book seeks to demonstrate the necessarily reciprocal character of ideas and actions. It proposes to evoke the ethical imperative of applying idealized thought to material relations.[14] Cultural workers have a responsibility to do more than simply think and talk about human injustice. Social change requires action as well as philosophy.

At the same time, I hope that by virtue of the number of examples cited, these principles are never reduced to prescriptive generalizations. Because theories are themselves texts and therefore subject to varying interpretation and use, they must be reevaluated in the context of each new application. A theory written for one community may be meaningless to another. In a similar fashion, individualized gestures of activism such as those described in these pages must be viewed as the historically specific and local phenomena they are. To presume the existence of "global" solutions to social problems is to arrogantly reduce difference to equivalence in a narrative of a universal subjectivity.

Every story embodies a range of theories. All too often both academics and artists discount the theoretical character of seemingly "simple" books and movies. By combining a multiplicity of viewpoints with examples of their concrete application, one can break down the debilitating boundary that separates critical theory from everyday life. While complicated ideas often require an esoteric vocabulary, theories are meaningless unless they can be used. The ability of people to apply theoretical ideas is especially important in an age of diminished public discourse. A regrettable consequence of modern

life is that the public forums of critical exchange so important to civic well-being
have largely passed into oblivion. Prior to the positivist age of disciplines and
specializations, it was not uncommon for people to convene spontaneously in
cafés, social clubs, and public watering holes for the common analysis of social
or political issues. Indeed, within the United States, the town meeting existed as
a discursive form into the early decades of this century. Although the decline of
"organic society" has been perhaps overly romanticized in recent years by many
on the Left, the absence of such spaces has frustrated the formation of positive
alliances.[15] Writing in the 1930s, British critic F. R. Leavis ascribed an ethos
of cultural alienation to this loss, a distancing of people from the traditions and
rituals of daily life:

> What we have lost is the organic community with the living culture it
> embodies. Folk-songs, folk-dances, Cotswald cottages and handicraft
> products are signs and expressions of something more: an art of life,
> a way of living, ordered and patterned, involved in social arts, codes
> of intercourse and a responsive adjustment, growing out of immemorial
> experience, to the natural environment and the rhythm of the year.[16]

Leavis was not lamenting decline in cultural nationalism of the sort currently
promoted by the Right. He was referring to the increasing distance people feel
from common rituals—and thus from social and political instrumentality. As the
citizens lose touch with each other they become more susceptible to mythological
representations of authority that place them "outside" the realm of power. In this
manner, the populace becomes less and less capable of recognizing the partial,
fragmentary, and therefore potentially productive character of such control.

Part of the blame is attributable to the growth of "professional" expertise in the
sciences and the humanities. This has rendered much discourse the domain of the
specialist, perpetuating divisions between intellectual subjects who speak and the
citizen objects spoken to (or about). Ultimately this has resulted in an erosion of
democratic practice—a situation exacerbated by the mass media. However, this
is not to say that all discursive arenas have been supplanted by Roseanne and
Channel One. People continually devise new ways of making culture of their
lives—whether it is through a CB radio or a card game. Pedagogical cultural
workers can encourage this positive articulation of civic voice. All too often
artists, writers, or teachers cast themselves as experts to whom others should
look for answers, inspiration, or insight. As useful as this can be in mobilizing
students or audiences, cultural workers must realize that it can contribute to
oppressive subject/object relationships. Teachers and artists need to recognize
their responsibility to create dialogues with their readers. This implies a continual
interrogation of the positions one occupies and of the visible and hidden political
implications of one's actions. It means recognizing the necessity of considering
how one's very role as a radical intellectual is framed within an institutional
matrix of power and privilege. By extension, the exercise of critical pedagogy

also suggests that cultural producers should encourage this attitude of scrutiny in others.

This critique of cultural subjectivities and institutions will return repeatedly to the contradictory construction of "art" across a range of discursive spaces—from the school book to the museum. As the Right has intensified its assertions of the timeless value of canonical masterworks, the distance continues to widen between these mythic narratives and the experience of most people. This is particularly true of the growing sector of the population held at the low end of the economic scale. One of the most pernicious myths that modernism foists on the children of working-class parents or people of color is the promise of escape from material hardship through the aesthetic transcendence of high culture. While denying the comparable utopian dimensions of television and movies, institutionalized modernism denies these people access to and appearance within high culture. In this scheme "great art" is construed as an array of objects that exists beyond the lives and productive capabilities of ordinary people. Indeed a recent poll conducted by the Survey Research Center revealed that less than 6 percent of respondents viewed art making as a leisure activity in which they could participate.[17] Sanctified within the hallowed halls of its enabling institutions, high culture is diametrically opposed to the popular culture of daily life.[18] Posing as a means of escape from the humdrum experience of the everyday, art degrades the very genuine and nurturing aspects of culture that people create as they work and play.

Regrettably, the Left has often been complicit in this valorization of elite expression. One need look no further than the pages of publications like *The Nation* or *In These Times* to find an objectified view of culture as a substance set apart from political reality. As explained by former *In These Times* cultural editor Pat Aufderheide, "Although there is widespread consensus on the Left that cultural expression is empowering, the notion that art offers a way to envision other ways of being is less common than the notion that art is something pleasant and extra at the end of a hard day."[19] Indeed, this narrow view of culture among educated leftists has itself been a major stumbling block in the formation of a broader progressive coalition. Whether we all like it or not, the closest thing to a culture we hold in common is popular culture.

It is time for the Left to recognize the political potential of such culture, not merely as a vehicle of ideological resistance, but also as a means of nourishing popular grassroots activism. Upon artists and cultural workers rests the important job of encouraging and facilitating forms of citizen-based cultural production. This task will necessarily entail the dismantling of old forms of art, arts institutions, and art patronage. For this reason we must contest at every opportunity pedagogies that deny the very real ways that we all both consume and *produce* culture.

This is particularly important in an era in which conservative pressures to promote singular, unchallengeable definitions of quality are on the ascent. Chapters 2 and 3 analyze processes of cultural reification at the levels of text and material apparatus, respectively. The discussion identifies ways that activists have responded to such circumstances. In this regard text entails the stories we find in books and movies, as well as those that emanate from such spaces as the shopping mall and the home. Material apparatus comprises the range of institutional production and delivery mechanisms that mediate textual flow. Indeed, the conservative program discourages the multiplicity of opinions so necessary to a functioning democracy by asserting an essential hierarchy of discourses. This argument delegitimizes difference by theorizing the so-called American "melting-pot." It asserts that through a process of mixing and strife, particular peoples have "naturally" gained preeminence and that the resulting hierarchy constitutes the common heritage by which all people should live. It argues that an immutable set of shared values and objects is necessary for social coherence. Those excluded from its higher register see the self-serving character of this position, but it is often difficult to recognize by those it privileges.

By placing itself at the center of all value, this conservative attitude toward culture not only excludes other perspectives, but ultimately ignores its own self-justifying tendencies.[20] Although this phenomenon restricts those on both the inside and outside of the dominant regime, it is structured to discredit any attempt to reveal these deficiencies. Therefore the challenge facing us entails a public analysis of this negative program as well as an explication of the ways human diversity functions as a positive element in social organization. Rather than discouraging multiple viewpoints and dissent, we should demonstrate the necessity for difference in the maintenance of a functioning democracy.

In sketching its interwoven political and pedagogical agendas the Left should organize its work within the framework of a radical imaginary that speaks in the tradition of history's great emancipatory struggles. Such a practice rejects the conservative deployment of "liberty" and "freedom" as excuses for exploitation and self-interest, and restores their meaning as values of collectivity and mutual respect.[21] Chapters 4 and 5 outline the specifics of this task. Moving from a reactive to a proactive stance, Chapter 4 addresses the interface of identity and community. In doing so it describes the creative ways that cultural workers and citizen groups have utilized existing institutional resources. Emphasis is placed on practices that support the production of diverse knowledge as a prerequisite for an egalitarian civic order. Yet, while honoring difference, efforts are made to resist romanticizing difference into equivalence. Such a program acknowledges that identities shift and are often shaped in asymmetrical power relationships and that the resultant conflicts give democracy its dynamic character. In the context of cultural struggle, this involves a critical reexamination of the way textual signification is constructed, as well as an acknowledgment of the frequent indeterminacy of narrative representations.

Ultimately cultural producers need to articulate a "language of possibility"—a set of positive manifestations of the construction of a new political imaginary.[22] Chapter 5 builds on the strategies for working within existing social structures described in Chapter 4 to propose a series of recommendations for new discursive spaces. Perhaps the word *new* is a misnomer here, because many of the communicative networks and relationships described have existed for some time—from the institutional alternatives of artists organizations to the technological innovations of satellite television networks. By demonstrating ways that artists, writers, and school people can come together, one recognizes other forms of alliances that can dislodge the rigid compartmentalization of public life. All too often leftist writing is framed in the debilitating vocabulary of response to the imperatives of a "dominant" order. Necessary as such critiques are, we need to move forward. Otherwise, we may find ourselves in the condition George Orwell attributed to the postwar British Left, when he said that "there is little in them except the irresponsible carping of people who have never been or never expect to be in a position of power."[23]

With this caveat in mind, the book closes with a discussion of two principles that bind cultural workers together: pedagogy and democracy. Here pedagogy is regarded as an instrument through which people locate themselves, analyze their environments, and formulate plans for the future. It is a method for reaching beyond individualism, competition, and consumption—and is therefore a profoundly political gesture. A radical democracy continually reevaluates and produces new forms of civic life. The vehicle for accomplishing this is culture in all of its many forms, whether they are found in the library, the museum, or the street. Critically applied in the context of this volume, this pedagogy also represents a means to forge alliances without insisting upon totalizing dogma, ineffectual pluralism, or binary exclusion.[24] The platform it supports is grounded in an ethical commitment to social justice. This type of democratic impulse exceeds the liberal ethos of "equal rights" by assuming an activist posture that is aggressively antiracist, antisexist, and antihomophobic. In this, it is also not content to passively respond to the mandates of a given order. Paulo Freire has said that we cannot enter the struggle as objects in order to later become subjects.[25]

NOTES

1. C. Richard Swaim, "Introduction," in *The Modern Muse: The Support and Condition of Artists*, ed. C. Richard Swaim (New York: American Council for the Arts, 1989), p. 3.

2. Ruby Lerner, *Comprehensive Organizational Assistance for Artists' Organizations* (Washington, DC: National Association of Artists' Organizations, 1988).

3. John P. Robinson, "Assessing the Artist's Condition: Some Quantitative Issues," in Swaim, *Modern Muse*, p. 33.

4. "Harper's Index," *Harper's*, Dec. 1990, p. 15.

5. Ben Bagdikian, *The Media Monopoly* (Boston: Beacon Press, 1990).

6. "Harper's Index," *Harper's*, Jan. 1990, p. 41.

7. Ibid.

8. Branda Miller, *Talkin' 'bout Droppin' Out* (Boston: Madison High School, 1988, videotape).

9. C. Emily Feistritzer, *The Condition of Teaching: A State by State Analysis* (Princeton, NJ: Princeton University Press, 1986).

10. *The American Public's Perspective on Federal Support for the Arts and the Controversy over Funding for the National Endowment for the Arts* (Washington, DC: People for the American Way, 1990).

11. "Harper's Index," *Harper's*, Aug. 1990, p. 13.

12. Brian Wallis, ed., *Democracy: A Project by Group Material* (New York: DIA Art Foundation, 1990), p. 5.

13. Patrick Buchanan, "In the War for America's Culture, the 'Right' Side Is Losing," *Richmond News Leader*, June 24, 1989.

14. The ethical mandate to act upon critical insight is discussed in Michel Foucault, "Politics and Ethics: An Interview," trans. Catherine Porter, in *The Foucault Reader*, ed. Paul Rabinow (New York: Pantheon, 1984), p. 373.

15. As an argumentative student of Leavis, Raymond Williams has noted that to a certain extent all such organic communities exist in the past, as a form of nostalgia.

16. F. R. Leavis and Denys Thompson, *Culture and Environment* (London: Chatto and Windus, 1933), pp. 1–2.

17. John P. Robinson, "Assessing the Artist's Condition: Some Quantitative Issues," in *The Modern Muse*, ed. Swaim (New York: American Council for the Arts, 1989), p. 33.

18. See Paul Willis, *Common Culture: Symbolic Work at Play in the Everyday Cultures of the Young* (San Francisco: Westview Press, 1990).

19. Pat Aufderheide, "Charting Cultural Change: The Role of the Critic," in *Reimaging America: The Arts of Social Change*, ed. Mark O'Brien and Craig Little (Santa Cruz, CA: New Society Publishers, 1990), p. 359.

20. Gayatri Chakravorty Spivak, *The Post-Colonial Critic: Interviews, Strategies, Dialogues*, ed. Sarah Harasym (New York: Routledge, 1990), p. 19.

21. Chantal Mouffe, "Radical Democracy: Modern or Postmodern?" in *Universal Abandon? The Politics of Postmodernism*, ed. Andrew Ross (Minneapolis: University of Minnesota Press, 1988), p. 42.

22. See Henry A. Giroux, *Schooling and the Struggle for Public Life* (Minneapolis: University of Minnesota Press, 1988).

23. George Orwell, "England Your England" (1941), in *A Collection of Essays* (New York: Harvest/Harcourt, Brace, Jovanovich, 1953), p. 274.

24. See Donna J. Haraway, "A Cyborg Manifesto," in *Simians, Cyborgs, and Women: The Reinvention of Nature* (New York: Routledge, 1991), pp. 149–80.

25. Paulo Freire, *Pedagogy of the Oppressed*, trans. Myra Bergman Ramos (New York: Continuum, 1970), pp. 27–57.

1

Culture and Pedagogy: Theories of Oppositional Practice

Despite their many affinities education and culture are usually considered separate issues, with the former functioning as the delivery mechanism for the latter. The reasons for this derive from divisions established by academic disciplines, routines of professional certification, and a fair amount of good old-fashioned intellectual bias. Regrettably, this separation of artists, writers, and critics from school teachers, technical instructors, and college professors is part of a broader scheme of social fragmentation that compartmentalizes public life. Set in place by the bureaucratic impulses of modernity and the economic drives of the corporate state, the resulting divisions frustrate dialogue and the formation of positive alliances. This difficulty in finding common ground has been a persistent impediment to the advancement of progressive politics. Recent critical theory has further exacerbated the problem by introducing broad-based suspicions of totalizing paradigms.

This chapter discusses some of the reasons that cultural practice and teaching have been held apart and proposes the benefits of considering them together. It seeks to establish a broadened definition of cultural "writing" that encompasses all efforts to produce, transmit, and organize subjectivity. It also resuscitates the term "cultural worker" from the lexicon of the 1960s to unite those on the Left involved in the making and sending of texts. This terminology would intentionally frustrate the identification of culture with "art" to extend its definition in sociological and political terms. Although produced in differing circumstances and regimes of legitimization, the generalized substance we call culture is something that all of us fashion in the course of our daily lives as we communicate, consume, and build the world around us. We make it as it makes us.

To contextualize the more practical chapters that follow, this analysis addresses a series of general topics that have strongly influenced recent thinking about education and culture: Marxism, postmodernism, cultural studies, and identity politics. Due to the breadth of each area, these discussions will be necessarily schematic and partial, for rather than providing definitive prescriptions, they are intended to provoke questions about pedagogical culture and its possible applications. By drawing connections among a variety of discourses in the humanities and social sciences this chapter proposes that the most effective strategies for critical analysis incorporate a wide range of interpretive approaches. If we are to be successful in establishing a truly integrated revision of the social order, we will need to consider the breadth of historical circumstances, economic conditions, linguistic formations, institutional structures, personal subjectivities, community affinities, and ideological formations that make up the civic domain. Accomplishing this calls for a willingness to suspend epistemological boundaries and polar oppositions. It takes the courage to admit one's incomplete understanding of the world and to accept the need for collective vision.

Scrutiny of these issues binds cultural workers together in a common project of emancipatory dialogue. As recent court cases and congressional debates have demonstrated, the health of a functioning democracy depends on the ability of its citizens to openly communicate. This is not an easy process. Free societies are by definition clamorous affairs in which dissent and agreement ebb and flow in continual negotiation. This makes the civic order responsive to the citizens who rule it.

The Left can stand united in an imaginary of radical democracy. Its common vision projects a diverse and egalitarian social order in which citizens engage actively in their mutual governance. Achieving these goals hinges on three objectives.[1] The first entails an analysis of oppressive conditions as they currently exist, including their enabling historical and subjective contexts. The second requires negations, revisions, and alternatives to unsatisfactory relations and institutions. (It is necessary to remember that these plans can never be imposed from outside the social environments they would change, but must always grow from within.) Last is the means of producing action from the theoretical and activist models of the first two. This is the pedagogical link among people demanding change.

MARXISM AND HISTORY

Although contested and fraught with factional infighting, Marxism has provided many significant analyses of education and art. From an early emphasis on economic conflict to its increasingly complex cultural inquiries, Marxism has lent a unity to disparate critiques by bridging the gap between abstract philosophy and concrete instrumentality. Its broad-based address of human oppression has allowed Marxism to be adapted to the needs of many groups. At the same time, Marxism's universalizing implications have evoked criticism. Orthodox Marxism is often equated with paternalistic attitudes of social engineering that analyze society strictly in terms of work and class. This "crude" Marxism has been accused of ignoring the distinctive (and overlapping) social configurations of women, people of color, lesbians, and gay men, among others, who contend that its theoretical ends could be satisfied without altering the oppressions they suffer.

As a consequence, Marxism has fractured and changed in the post-Enlightenment era. By the 1930s it grew apparent that the working-class revolution Marx predicted was not going to occur. Instead Europe witnessed the horrors of fascism, Stalinism, the holocaust, and, ultimately, a cataclysmic war—events that cast doubt on prior theories of bureaucratic utopianism. As technology reshaped ideological transmission, Marxists began to reevaluate their rigid economism and reconsider the complexities of culture. The work of Frankfurt School thinkers applied Marxist theory to these evolving sciences of communication and mass production. With such innovations as radio, audio recording, halftone photographic reproduction, and high-speed publishing, commentators on both the Left and Right lamented the triumph of "mass culture" over local or high culture.

Max Horkheimer and Theodor Adorno, among others, described a system in which the masses were systematically duped into lives of servitude and consumption. Within such apocalyptic logic, cultural objects functioned as propaganda, and the citizenry was incapable of resisting the seduction of the dominant "culture industry." Although useful in the broad mapping of ideological reproduction, this totalizing position refused to grant makers or audiences any autonomy whatsoever. It also was unabashedly elitist in its views of "the masses." The resulting "reflection theory" readings of art and entertainment produced somewhat predictable evidence of existing class inequities. But as overgeneralized as these attitudes were, they yielded important critiques of cultural commodification. By drawing attention to the way ideology is embedded in signification, this work prompted forms of subversive analysis.[2]

Alternatives to reflection theory date to the 1940s, although until recently many were unknown to wide audiences.[3] Some of these works emphasized the independent character of cultural practices, apart from the presumed overdetermination of the economic base. Others focused on audiences. Louis Althusser's work in particular sought to undo myths of unproblemmatized transmission and reception. In his paradigmatic essay "Ideology and Ideological State Apparatuses (Notes Toward an Investigation)" he argued that subjectivity is socially inscribed in the relationships *between* individuals and organizations.[4] Institutions like the school and museum construct systems of meaning that install people in imaginary relations to the real situations in which they live. Identity becomes a fictional text upon which various forces exert influence.

More significantly, Althusser proposed a revision of reflection theory that assigned a quasi-autonomy to cultural works. No longer mere superstructural manifestations of the economic base, culture was recognized to operate in a complex dialectic with the market. In other words, a space was acknowledged between the oppressive institutions of the state and the consciousness of individuals. Within this space, resistances could form that were capable of destabilizing ruling power structures. These sentiments were echoed in the writings of Herbert Marcuse, who likewise argued against the classical Marxist doctrine that material relations alone were responsible for producing consciousness. Emphasizing the role of human agency, Marcuse said that "radical change in consciousness is the beginning, the first step in changing social existence: emergence of the new Subject."[5]

A further refinement of Marxist cultural theory came in 1970 when Hans Magnus Enzenberger proposed in his "Constituents of a Theory of Media" that the Left had been misguided in its understandings of how culture actually works. He suggested that instead of tricking the masses into a web of false desires, media actually found ways of satisfying real (but often unconscious) desires. This position was later elaborated upon by poststructuralist Marxists like Frederic Jameson and Roland Barthes, who further considered the negotiable possibilities of signification. If cultural signs could be interpreted variously, their meanings assumed a "floating" character as individuals assigned them different readings. From an understanding of the contingency of meaning has evolved a complex discourse on the many forces that struggle to influence it. The very way we see the world becomes a matter of strategy. For this reason issues of cultural "reading" and "writing" are explicitly pedagogical concerns. Texts need not necessarily be interpreted as intended by their authors or manufacturers. They can be revised, combined, or contested within the framework of the reader's capabilities. Use is a factor of knowledge.

This has led to broadened considerations of the many issues that contextualize interpretation. As a consequence, Marxist critics have begun addressing factors hitherto subsumed within base/superstructure objectivism. In its contemporary applications, "traditional" Marxist territories of history, social formation, class struggle, and revolution are being examined in relation to language, identity, pleasure, representation, technology, and power. Ultimately, this discursive expansion challenges strictly aesthetic definitions of culture by reading into the very fabric of all political and social relations.[6] Because texts are subject to multiple readings, meaning becomes a matter of contest on the broad terrain of politics. For cultural producers in the school or the gallery this widened analysis presents new challenges. It invites practitioners to question the institutional and discursive structures in which they find themselves and encourages them to reinvent the world in more humane, less exploitative, ways. At the same time, it asks them to be troublemakers in challenging the circumstances in which they work, exhibit, or teach.

THE POSTMODERN CONDITION

The evolution of postmodernism during the last 15 years has had a profound impact on education and the arts, signaling a radical reconsideration of long-held philosophical traditions. Debates over "pluralism," "historicism," "appropriation," "representation," and the "canon" all result, at least in part, from a theoretical iconoclasm that would topple modernist paradigms of universal knowledge and progress. Throughout the world the failure of grand master narratives is apparent—from the nations of the Eastern bloc to the urban centers of the United States. Still, modernism weighs heavily on cultural pedagogy in both positive and negative terms. This reciprocal relationship is important to bear in mind in an era when modernism's most useful elements are often jettisoned. As Jürgen Habermas has noted, there are severe problems with this reactionary aspect of postmodernism, not the least of which involve the resultant difficulty in formulating strategies that are proactive rather than reactive.[7]

Postmodernism's emphasis on language argues that what we know about the world is limited to what we say about it. All knowledge is a matter of "representation." Yet, too often the postmodern critique of absolute meanings, totalizing narratives, and social engineering leaves nothing behind but an alienated nihilism. Postmodernism quite correctly rejects the universalizing scientism of structuralism, but quite incorrectly overlooks structuralism's important critiques of essentialism. One can more productively approach modernism by appropriating its most useful elements and discarding others. Doing this requires an acknowledgment that modernism is divisible into at least two historical camps. These nonsynchronous and politically disparate modernisms part their ways in philosophical traditions dating to Kant and Hegel. The former tradition celebrates the transcendental character of "pure" aesthetics and intellectual inquiry; the latter would assimilate these areas into practical experience to dissolve the art/life dichotomy.

Both views foster utopian speculation based on generalized premises of social planning. Since the Enlightenment, Western philosophy presumed the feasibility of direct knowledge of reality—a faith that nature could be improved by reason. These attitudes became manifest in the nineteenth-century developments of secular humanism, particularly as espoused by Matthew Arnold. In the face of religion's declining influence as an instrument of social and moral cohesion, abstract notions of intellectual excellence were promoted as universal ideals to which citizens might aspire. In Arnold's view, this high-minded intellectualism would be delivered through an educational apparatus that would level social differences and eliminate class antagonisms. He encouraged a belief that the sciences and humanities could solve the problems of humanity through a self-reflexive organization of knowledge into discrete categories and hierarchies.

This program of human unity and singularity of purpose assumed greater poignancy after the turn of the century as World War I physically splintered and brutalized Europe. Within this atmosphere the need for a stabilizing imaginary became even more pronounced. Thus evolved a vision of history arranged in grand master narratives, with social evolution flowing forward in linear sequences of change and modernization. These narratives were rarely seen as the limited constructions that they were. Instead they were promoted as pure visions of progress. In this sense, modernism's claims of self-reflexivity (in almost all of the many modernisms) were mistaken. It failed to recognize that histories and social theories are written by people already inscribed within a range of interests.

In the artistic realm modernist formalism produced extraordinary investigations into the mechanics of language and the physicality of perception. In the arenas of art, architecture, theater, and performance, movements ranging from constructivism to the Bauhaus sought to perfect the social order through an enhanced philosophy of aesthetics and design. In the postwar years these ideas took an ideological spin. Writers like Clement Greenberg and Harold Rosenberg promoted minimalism and abstract expressionism as democratic practices of "pure seeing" accessible to all viewers. By plumbing the very essences of human communication they argued that representations could democratically edify even the most unschooled citizen.

The flaw in this logic lay in modernism's denial of its enabling politics. It gradually became apparent that aesthetic formalism purporting to serve every citizen was actually produced and consumed by a rather small minority. Moreover, in seeking to educate the populace with examples of highly polished form, the value of other cultural expressions was implicitly denied. Despite its egalitarian impulses, modernism eventually came to reinforce a stratification of culture into high/low, center/margin registers. Fundamental to this program was a systematic purification of knowledge and elimination of thinking deemed incorrect. This resulted in a central massing of power around a particular set of ideas and people.

But modernism's demise was more than a matter of culture alone. In recent decades we have witnessed the horrifying consequences of the rationalist program, as industrial superpowers decay from the inside and the world remains poised at the brink of environmental disaster and nuclear war. From Europe to the United States it has become evident that the historical grand recits of reason are not enough. The near-universal failure of master narratives—whether in art or politics—has created a suspicion of totalizing paradigms. This has produced two distinct actions: a movement to unseat the unified modernist establishment, and an effort to efface modernism's protective boundaries, particularly those that separate it from mass culture.[8] The latter tendency is characterized by a frenetic splintering of discourses that frustrates an easy understanding of postmodernist principles, especially for the nonacademic observers it often claims to serve. This new postmodern discourse that evolved during the 1970s and 1980s generated a terminology that exhausts itself as soon as it is deployed. As Dick Hebdige has ironically put it, postmodernism encompasses

> a process of cultural, political, or existential fragmentation and/or crisis, the "de-centering" of the subject, an "incredulity towards metanarratives," the replacement of unitary power axes by a plurality of power/discourse formations, the "implosion of meaning," the collapse

of cultural hierarchies, the dread engendered by the threat of nuclear destruction, the decline of the university, the functioning and effects of the new miniaturized technologies, broad social and economic shifts into a "media," "consumer" or "multinational" phase, a sense (depending on who you read) of "placelessness" or the abandonment of placelessness, or (even) a generalized substitution of spacial for temporal co-ordinates.[9]

As set forth in the writings of Jacques Derrida, Jean-François Lyotard, Frederic Jameson, Gayatri Spivak, and others, postmodernism signifies not so much an assault on the old truths of modernism (as it is often accused of being) as a pondering of whether we can recognize truth when we see it. Rather than an objective reality, the world becomes a constellation of signs. Everything we perceive is a part of this narrative. In the academic realm such textual diversification opened all manner of inquiries into territories formerly considered beneath (or outside) respectable scholarship. Within the past decade academics and artists have become increasingly interested in vernacular culture. As one might expect, photographic media have figured prominently in these endeavors—particularly in the fields of film studies and communications. As linguistic currency of both high and low culture, photography has been used by academics to make critical commentaries on the character of its own functioning and of broader social phenomena.

None of this has been lost on the art world. Avant-gardists with strong linkages to the academy quickly adopted poststructuralist theories. In the fall of 1977 an exhibition entitled "Pictures" appeared at the lower Manhattan alternative gallery Artists' Space. Although the show itself attracted little attention, its explanatory catalog essay by curator Douglas Crimp made history. In what has since become a postmodern manifesto, Crimp said that the "Pictures" artists operate from the assumption that "we only experience reality through the pictures we make of it. To an even greater extent our experience is governed by pictures, pictures in newspapers and magazines, on television and in the cinema. Next to these pictures, firsthand experience begins to retreat, to seem more and more trivial."[10] Much of the work on display recontextualized images from mass media sources (and occasionally from high art). By reproducing the Marlboro man in an art gallery, the artists intended to dramatize the arbitrary character of aesthetic value. These "stolen," "scavenged," or "appropriated" pictures sought to make viewers question the institutional practices that assign images to high and low culture. The obviously "copied" quality of the works raised questions about authenticity, originality, authorship, genius, creativity—and by implication, art history, art criticism, and the art market.

Or at least that was the plan. By now the failures of postmodern art are as famous as its utopian intentions. Ironically, because these postmodern artists staged their critiques within the gallery, their activist photographs were often commodified just like other art objects. Many analysts argue that the art world's tendency to aestheticize dissent limits the extent to which genuine political change can be effected. As Richard Bolton suggests, the capitalist art world almost always co–opts radicalism in this way.

> This is now the case with postmodernism—this once promising critical practice, posed against the mass media, has become a media version of critical practice. The analysis of the politics of aestheticization has been transformed into an aestheticized version of politics. And the criticism of commodification has become an advanced form of this commodification—the "progressive" forms of the commodity and the progressive structure of late capitalism.[11]

Yet, as valid as such critiques of postmodernism are, they fail to adequately acknowledge its importance in destabilizing dominant regimes of meaning. As Hal Foster has pointed out, even though transgressive works may eventually be swept into the realm of capital, they often succeed in demonstrating the arbitrary character of signification, nevertheless. For Foster, the radical implications of this exceed the specifics of individual gestures. This practice differs from the "countercultural" arts activism of the 1960s and 1970s in that it "recodes cultural signs rather than poses a revolutionary program of its own."[12] Within this logic the ultimate disposition of a sign is less significant than the critical awareness put in place through its manipulation.

The radical potential of postmodernism to destabilize regimes of meaning and instill agency has been recognized by conservatives, particularly within the university. Postmodern theories are now part of much larger political struggles waging over censorship, canons, and curricula. In an age in which the real and imagined influence of Western colonial power is on the decline, in which multiethnic urban populations are placing whites in the minority, in which lesbian and gay communities are gaining visibility and strength—the beneficiaries of established order are increasingly put on the defensive. The decentering and dehierarchizing of society is cast as a threat by such thinkers as Allan Bloom, Lynne V. Cheney, Dinesh D'Sousa, Roger Kimball, Hilton Kramer, and Diane Ravitch. That postmodernism appears to be such a danger is perhaps the best evidence of its impact.

THE CULTURE OF CULTURAL STUDIES

In recent years growing numbers of academics and artists have become preoccupied with vernacular forms of culture—fascinated, if you will, with the ways "ordinary" people construct and consume the world around them. Brought about by critiques of modernism and the dissolution of old-fashioned disciplinary boundaries, intellectuals have found new ground for inquiry in what they find outside the university. No longer restricted to high culture's ivory tower, academics have eagerly embraced the exotic (and pleasurable) "other" discourses of advertising, movies, pop music, and fashion.

Prior to the evolution of the cultural studies movement, scholarly assumptions about popular culture tended to err in either of two directions. In a narrow sense, popular culture was defined as high culture's vulgar opposite: it was not the art of museums, the music of symphonies, or the literature of the language department. Instead, it was the commercially produced and antieducational material of entertainment, escape, fantasy, and fun. The other view romanticized popular culture as the only true expression of social values, arguing that TV and movies gain appeal because they accurately convey human wants and needs. The market simply validates citizen desire. Of course, both positions represent parts of the story, but their fragmentary accounts cannot explain the construction of meaning in the transactions *between* people and the things they use.

The more integrated field of cultural studies began to emerge in Great Britain in the 1960s as a response to the generalized inability of humanistic disciplines to account for the complexities of everyday life. Influenced by the earlier social criticism of Richard Hoggart, F. R. Leavis, and Raymond Williams, the cultural studies movement specifically sought to reconcile rifts between high and low culture. It argued that culture is not so much a value that inhabits a particular commodity or sign but an event that occurs as such things are used. For this reason it is both a site of perpetual struggle and political possibility. As with the Frankfurt School movement, cultural studies represented a response to perceived social and political shifts, in this instance changes brought about by crises in British colonial hegemony and the resultant internal restructuring of British society. As recounted by Stuart Hall,

> cultural studies really begins with the debate about the nature of social and cultural change in postwar Britain. An attempt to address the manifest break-up of traditional culture, especially traditional class cultures, it set about registering the impact of the new cultural forms of affluence and consumer society on the very hierarchical and pyramidal structure of British society. Trying to come to terms with the fluidity and the undermining impact of the mass media and of an emerging mass society on the old European class society, it registered the cultural impact of the long-delayed entry of the United Kingdom into the modern world.[13]

In examining the changing character of nationhood, cultural studies borrowed liberally from anthropology, sociology, history, economics, literature, and philosophy, in effect criticizing these disciplines for their individual inabilities to adequately explain social phenomena. At the heart of this analysis lay a deconstruction of the often self-serving perpetuation of specific knowledge forms, texts, and institutions. It undertook

> the task of unmasking what it considered to be the unstated presuppositions of the humanist tradition itself. It had to try to bring to light

the ideological assumptions underpinning the practice, to expose the
educational program (which was the unnamed part of the project), and
to try to conduct an ideological critique of the way the humanities and
the arts presented themselves as parts of disinterested knowledge.[14]

Not surprisingly, cultural studies was rejected as a bastardized discourse by
most recognized scholars within those disciplines. Failing to gain a foothold
among the elite academics of Oxford and Cambridge, its practice grew within
the faculties of the polytechnics.[15] Rather than addressing culture as a coherent
assemblage of received knowledges handed down from generation to generation,
the movement underscored the fragmentary, partial, and often contradictory
functions of cultural forms and institutions.

Particularly of interest were the cultural habits and artifacts of groups typically
excluded from academic analysis. In Britain, cultural studies initially focused on
teenagers (primarily boys), whose rebellious attitudes toward clothing, music,
sexuality, and schooling generated affinities among comparably rebellious academics. These early subcultural inquiries yielded significant insights about the
abilities of young people to resist authority and remake culture in their own
image.

Despite its academic underpinnings, cultural studies aspired to reach beyond
the university. Unfortunately the promise of fields like cultural studies and
media studies has been undercut by their lack of genuine contact with the
constituencies under analysis. Attention has focused on the movies, music, or
fashion accoutrements of young people as objects for scholarly discourse—but
little on young people themselves. This is especially true of the brands of
cultural studies emerging outside Great Britain in such countries as the United
States. Despite its high-minded intentions, cultural studies has been criticized for
contributing to the very academization it seeks to combat. As Judith Williamson
observes,

> To study a culture presumes to some extent that one is outside it,
> though it is fashionable to "slum it" culturally . . . among the masses.
> It is extraordinary but true that a recent proud admission among some
> left-wing academics was to have cried at *ET*. There is a perverse
> contradiction whereby the higher up the educational scale you are, the
> more fun is to be had from consuming (while criticizing) the artifacts
> of mass culture.[16]

This intellectual distance also has been accused of indirectly harming those
studied. Besides exploiting disadvantaged communities, academics have at times
exaggerated the ability of "the people" to outsmart capitalist manipulation.
By romanticizing this ability to escape material reality, cultural studies has
underplayed the significance of "real" racism, sexism, homophobia, or economic
injustice.[17]

With this in mind cultural workers must be constantly attentive of their own affective investments in groups they address. Writers, teachers, and artists are never disinterested observers and can easily project their own agendas upon those they study, teach, or depict. For new interdisciplinary fields like cultural studies to achieve what they promise, their practitioners must recognize the difficulties inherent in the discursive and political locations they inhabit. Regardless of how progressive a scholarly text might be, its effectiveness is undermined if framed within an oppressive method of address.

REPRESENTING DIFFERENCE

Needless to say, there is a need to theoretically account for diversity in the constitution of human subjectivity. In recent years many of the most far-reaching analyses of power, identity, and representation have come from those outside the realm of white male heterosexuality. As recent controversies over "multiculturalism" and "political correctness" have demonstrated, this thinking has not always been welcome within the precincts of traditionalism. Yet, not all of these critiques are necessarily new. As Paula A. Treichler has noted in discussing feminist theory, "the history of feminism is in part a history of theory."[18] Indeed many of the ideas discussed elsewhere in this chapter derive from fundamental premises emerging from the women's movement. As both a philosophical and political enterprise, feminism anchored its critiques of work, sexuality, and social organization in the experiences (both oppressive and liberating) of women.[19] As with Marxism, this initially exclusive inquiry led some to criticize feminist theory for an overly narrow approach. However, almost from its earliest stages feminist theory has been characterized by efforts to establish relationships rather than boundaries between diverse approaches to knowledge.

Most genealogies of feminism identify at least two discursive sites of feminist contest: language and the body.[20] From ontological analyses of linguistic formations (Jacques Lacan's theories of paternal "naming") to their contemporary visual manifestations (Laura Mulvey's formulation of the male cinematic "gaze"), language has been recognized in feminist theory as a highly politicized instrument. Far from being a "neutral" carrier of ideas and images, language establishes hierarchies in form as well as content. It shapes the acquisition of culture. Vocabularies, semantic conventions, speech acts, and specific inflections all have a bearing on who can speak and how. The pedagogical implications of language are particularly significant for women, who, as a group, have often been denied entrance to literary canons or have been written out of literature by men. For feminism, history itself is a site of erasure and oppression. As a consequence it is subject to continual revision.

Issues of the body range from the literal to the symbolic. Biological determinism, reproductive politics, homosexuality and heterosexuality, physical regulation and measurement, phallic presence or "lack," issues of "beauty" and appearance, food and eating, nature and ecology—all of these debates have roots in feminist inquiries into the role of the body in the public and private sphere. Indeed, as they intersect in the body, feminism has demonstrated the inseparability of these two worlds and, by extension, the epistemological continuum between most bipolar oppositions. This position has lent a continual emphasis on cooperation, collectivity, and decentered authority to the movement.

The "postcolonial" era described in recent writings by Homi K. Bhabba, Teshome H. Gabriel, Audre Lourde, Edward Said, Trinh T. Minh-ha, Gayatri Spivak, and Michelle Wallace, among others, is marked by an acknowledgment that changing knowledge forms and social configurations have created a crisis in power, patriarchy, authority, identity, and ethics. These changes are but representations of broader demographic shifts placing "white" people in the minority in one-third of the nation's 50 largest cities.[21] Global population statistics indicate that only 25 percent of the world is inhabited by people of European descent, a figure expected to drop precipitously in the next century.[22] Despite the efforts of Reagan/Bush policymakers to dismantle social programs and reverse civil rights advances, ethnic and racial groups formerly considered "other" are advancing from the social margins to the center. From the international arena to the local neighborhood, traditional narratives are being fragmented, challenged, and replaced.

Perhaps the most dramatic shift in recent years, and the one most aggressively fought by the Right, has been the increased visibility of the nation's 25 million lesbians and gay men. Although carefully phrased in generalized concerns over obscenity and "artistic quality," the unifying theme of nearly every recent fundamentalist assault on artistic expression was homophobia. The cultural wars over art and funding constitute symbolic contests over the day-to-day rights of lesbians and gay men. In an age in which such symbolic struggles can influence issues of housing, employment, and health, the role of culture is foregrounded.

Whether the topic is gender, race, or sexual orientation, debates typically divide over views of human "difference." The Right seeks to suppress differences in the interest of civic versimilitude. Herein lies the construction of the mythic "mainstream" that the Right claims to represent. Rather than acknowledging the vast diversity of interests that make up the nation, conservatives promote an illusion of common values and unproblematized patriotism. Although this imaginary mainstream purportedly includes a majority of people, in fact it excludes everyone. Rather than functioning as a marker of the civil middle ground, it works as a mechanism to naturalize social hierarchies. When stripped of its mystifying pretensions, the mainstream can be seen as an abstract representation that at best describes a rather small minority of people. Nevertheless, its primary referent of male, European heterosexuality marks the coordinate around which Western language and culture are organized. This structural hegemony frames efforts to contest, infiltrate, or subvert it as acknowledgments of its dominance. In this manner the relation of margin to center has been maintained.

Questions of difference produce several additional polemics. One pits "assimilationists" against "separatists." The former argues for a single culture to which all groups should subscribe; the later would develop and maintain many distinct cultural identities. This opposition creates an important dynamic between the general needs of the nation and the specific rights of constituent bodies. The assimilationist view has held sway in most school programs, and it is the attitude conservatives now press in the cultural realm. Its ethos dates to the early days of the republic, as typified in the words of an eighteenth-century French immigrant, Hector St. John de Crevecoeur: "He is American, who, leaving behind him all his ancient prejudices and manners, receives new ones from the new mode of life he has embraced, the new government he obeys, and the new rank he holds. . . . Here individuals of all nations are melted into a new race of man."[23] From the reasonable assertion that social cohesion is formed through shared values and compromise, this position can deteriorate into a rigid extremism. The result is an ossified traditionalism that asserts a single culture over all others. Typically this conservative position claims that "special interests" wrongly seek preferential treatment in a system that already provides equal opportunities to all. Such assertions are defended most strongly by those who have benefited from existing arrangements. The assimilationist position has become difficult to rationalize in an era in which the universal applicability of the so-called common culture is increasingly called into question. As U.S. demographics grow more multiracial, it becomes apparent that Eurocentric traditions constitute a culture by a few and for a few.

Reacting against the oppressive implications of assimilation, some groups move to consolidate constituent identity. Educational separatism replaces dominant knowledge with group-specific knowledge. The approach may even extend to the pedagogies through which meaning is exchanged and subjectivities formed. As with conservative "common culture" extremism, separatism can essentialize itself by asserting exclusive relationships to particular knowledges based on social location. Such an attitude refutes the presumption that anyone can possess an adequate knowledge of the needs and placement of other groups.

Beyond arguments over assimilation lie issues of tokenism, solipsism, and homogenization. Identified by civil rights activists in the 1960s, tokenism is the now familiar liberal strategy of redressing representational imbalances through cosmetic means. In the 1990s tokenism takes more subtle forms, as pronouncements of "equality" and "empowerment" have become fashionable in the art and education worlds. Even though marginalized artists and scholars are appearing in exhibitions, securing book contracts, and gaining academic appointments, the overall numbers of such success stories are relatively few. For example, in the arts, although women make up 45 percent of the professionally trained workforce, they receive fewer grants than men (27% of those awarded), hold fewer academic jobs (20% of faculty positions), and receive fewer reviews in publications (15% of those in newspapers and magazines). Also, their work is represented less frequently in textbooks (3.3% of material published).[24]

By solipsism, I am referring to the tendency of groups absorbed in one struggle to overlook others. As Catherine Lord has characterized the situation within the women's movement,

> much of "feminism"—that is, the academic discourse now institution-alized in publications, textbooks, course offerings, and departments—has been a white, heterosexual, mainly middle-class movement, pitched to reform a world imagined to consist primarily of white, heterosexual, mainly middle-class men. Doubtless, this is largely unconscious: despite straight white feminism's talk about "difference," adverse racism, eco-nomic privilege, homophobia, and male identification run deep. The erasure of particular, other, subcultural issues is predictable.[25]

Stuart Hall used the term "homogenization" in discussions about the British "Black" community.[26] This practice views all members of a group as alike, their identities interchangeable, and their struggles equivalent. It fails to recognize partial affiliations or multiple subjectivities.

To avoid these conceptual pitfalls, the Left needs to acknowledge that groups are both defined by what they have in common and what they do not share. No community is composed of identical bodies, and often these constituencies have different needs and desires. We also need to recognize the relationship between identity and representation, for within language and images all differences are, in a sense, constructed. In acknowledging the extent to which stereotypical portrayals of woman, man, black, brown, yellow, gay, lesbian are indeed fictions about lived circumstances, we should be conscious of the conditions through which these representations have been made. We might consider, for example, the authors of various characterizations and, by extension, in whose interests they have functioned.[27] We need to recognize the contested character of such representations, the need for new representations, and the multiple and fragmentary character of representations once thought to be singular. After all, it is through such devices of communication that we come to know our world and develop opinions about it. Subject positions and political locations evolve from the form of such communications. This is where pedagogy is of utmost importance in helping to dismantle romantic (and debilitating) notions of identity.

In theorizing a democracy that acknowledges the complexities of these cir-cumstances, we must incorporate an acceptance of groups' different needs and a recognition of the contested character of a healthy democracy.[28] This type of democracy admits the struggle that results from difference, but counts it as a positive force in the continual testing and reevaluation of political arrangements. As Kobena Mercer notes, "What is at issue is to acknowledge differences without necessarily ending up in a divisive situation, how to enact an 'ethics of disagree-ment,' as Hall says, without recourse to rhetorics that cut off the possibility of critical dialogue."[29] No single set of ideas is privileged over others because no one method can satisfy the needs of a diverse people.

PEDAGOGY AND POLITICAL STRATEGY

Cultural workers on the Left can stand united in the principles of democracy and pedagogy—if, and only if, we can reclaim these values in our own terms. The brand of democracy currently touted by conservatives, which would suppress (or neutralize) difference and dissent, is a common threat to all disenfranchised groups. It offers a model of an unchanging social order that perpetuates existing hierarchies of power and privilege. Similarly, the Right's program of education reform reintroduces bureaucratic control, measurement, and ranking in the service of a capital-driven curriculum of basic skills. It promotes an unquestioning view of authority and cultural heritage. These neoconservative efforts to maintain order and enforce traditions reveal the anxiety of a dominant regime faced with instability. It is the sign of the monoculture coming unglued.

At a similar historical juncture 25 years ago, when elements of diversity and social change were gaining momentum, such circumstances were termed "an excess of democracy" by the Trilateral Commission. Largely forgotten today, the Trilateral Commission was assembled by a corporate confederation led by David Rockefeller in the wake of another era of activism by students, women, and people of color. Its infamous report by Samuel P. Huntington entitled "Crisis of Democracy" argued that unbridled freedom breeds anarchy, loss of common purpose, and, more to the political point, economic decline.[30] Couched in terms of social moderation and cooperation, the report presented a program to perpetuate the rule of the corporate elite.

Two decades later the cultural right has resurrected these dusty arguments again. As Allan Bloom points out, "democracy liberates from tradition, which in other kinds of regimes determines the judgment."[31] To conservatives like Bloom this democratic liberation from regulation throws the rules of civic reason in jeopardy. "Since very few people school themselves in the use of reason beyond the calculation of self-interest encouraged by the regime, they need help on a vast number of issues—in fact, all issues," Bloom asserts.[32] Rather than acknowledging the democratic potential in multiple, conflicting viewpoints, the conservative program's pessimistic view of human agency brands such diversity a danger to social coherence. Due in part to the economic scapegoating applied to liberal social and educational programs following the Vietnam War, this conservative program has held sway over the major institutions of the United States.

Clearly steps need to be taken to reconstitute alliances among progressive groups inside the academy and outside. Doing this requires a radical democratic imaginary that speaks in the tradition of history's great emancipatory struggles. Such a political philosophy requires a pedagogy that supports the production of diverse knowledge as a prerequisite for an egalitarian civic order. While honoring difference, a radical democracy resists the temptation to romanticize difference into equivalence. It recognizes that identities are often shaped in asymmetrical power relationships and that the resultant conflicts give democracy its dynamic character. In the context of cultural struggle, this involves a critical reexamination of the way textual signification is constructed, as well as an acknowledgment of the frequent indeterminacy of narrative representations.

Given the mutable politics of representation, the questions that remain are ones of strategy. This is where pedagogy comes in. Some primary answers can be found in the writing of Antonio Gramsci, who formulated a range of practical applications to the theories developed by Marx. Gramsci saw social change as a process of learning in which the masses come to form a new social order. Unlike Lenin, Gramsci believed that working people possessed the intellectual capability to articulate this vision without the guidance of a vanguard. Indeed, it was extremely important that the principles of revolution would emerge from the oppressed themselves.

For Gramsci, "every relationship of 'hegemony' is necessarily an educational relationship."[33] In this context he was not simply referring to the forms of teaching that one commonly associates with the classroom. Gramsci was describing the profoundly political process through which citizens are socialized to recognize and validate state power. This process infuses all components of the social apparatus: the office, the church, the museum, and particularly the school. If we think of these situations as sites of potential ideological persuasion, then Gramsci's theory of education becomes significant. Obviously we are nearly always in a process of learning. Therefore pedagogies can encompass such diverse activities as parenting, filmmaking, architecture, and storytelling.

Opinions vary about how these various pedagogies actually work. Following the liberal school reform movements of the 1960s, a brand of educational analysis emerged based on economic theories of social reproduction. Manifest primarily in the work of Samuel Bowles and Herbert Gintis, this functionalist position said that schools teach people ways of adapting to the civic order. Its purpose was to create happy workers. Students were thought to be relatively powerless in relation to institutionalized education, and for that reason the apparatus (schools, curricula, texts, examination, requirements, etc.) became the primary site of contest for reformers. Later this thinking was modified by Pierre Bourdieu, who elaborated on the role of culture in reproducing relations of domination and subjugation. Although the sphere of politics was broadened to include culture, again the role of the institution was foregrounded.

With the evolution of relativist theories of knowledge and power came a distrust of functionalism and a new consideration of subjective autonomy. Taking cues from reader response theorists, leftist educators recognized that not all parties respond to ideological transmission in exactly the same way.[34] Students reject what they are told as often as they accept it. But rather than a purely negative attribute, this willful ignorance was recognized as a positive manifestation of students' desire for power. From this realization evolved a range of "resistance" theories, emphasizing the ingenious ways that suppressed student energy found release: vandalism, drug abuse, sexual promiscuity, radical dressing, and gang violence. Teachers were to seek ways to harness this often self-destructive power. Largely a reaction to the rationalist monolith, the early resistance theory movement often locked itself into a debilitating polarity. In emphasizing student response to authority, it failed to adequately consider the complex ways that students make culture of their own. Later work began to address the formation of student identity, as suggested in the title of Dick Hebdige's 1979 book *Subculture: The Meaning of Style*.[35] However, most of these efforts focused on the culture students made outside of school. As useful as this thinking was in suggesting ways that education could be considered wherever it is found, it went too far in neglecting the issue of institutional formations. It also largely left unaddressed the ways that adults and young people, teachers and students might constructively engage each other in an educational dialogue.

An effort at synthesis was made in the "critical pedagogy" movement, an amalgam of educational philosophies originating among oppressed peoples of the developing world. During the 1970s and 1980s, the philosophies of critical pedagogy were adapted within Western industrialized nations, and much of its vocabulary of "empowerment," "dialogue," and "voice" has entered the lexicon of contemporary social reform movements. The principles of critical pedagogy have been modified to adapt them to the needs of contemporary technocratic societies. They have also provoked criticism.

Because critical pedagogy stresses the importance of human agency, it is sometimes faulted as a "motivational" practice that exaggerates the importance of education in political life. Its emphasis on subjective empowerment has been accused of romanticizing political struggle, while doing little to alter power imbalances within school itself. While such claims identify the problems of pitting determinism against agency, very little current work carries the emphasis on motivation to such an extreme. As it has evolved in the 1980s and 1990s, critical pedagogy locates itself in a dialectical relationship between such overdetermined influences as capitalism, sexism, racism, and homophobia and the subjective autonomy of the individual.[36] Meaning and ideology are fashioned in quasi-autonomy by historical subjects, who always retain the baggage of their lived circumstances. Stanley Aronowitz and Henry A. Giroux's *Education under Siege* exemplifies the balance that can be maintained between these two potentially consuming positions. At the same time, the work demonstrates ways that critical pedagogy can bridge disparate knowledge forms. This is effected through a series of analytical categories that cut across disciplinary, even interdisciplinary, boundaries.[37] While not a schematic approach to current theoretical dilemmas, Aronowitz and Giroux's four categories provide a useful model for framing issues that will repeatedly reappear in the following pages: a broadened vision of the political, an effort to link "languages of critique and possibility," a view of teachers and cultural workers as transformative intellectuals, and a reconsideration of the relationship between theory and practice. Because these ideas offer a framework in which to synthesize many of the issues discussed above, I will discuss each as it makes connections between education and cultural production.

A broadened notion of the political entails more than simply recognizing the implications of everyday actions. It means admitting that many areas that claim neutrality in our lives are in fact sites of profound ideological struggle. Television newscasts, school curricula, art museums, scientific breakthroughs, "great" works of literature—these are not "objective" phenomena that somehow exist outside the realm of ideology. They are forms of representation invested with specific interests in every manifestation. Through these texts dominance strives to replicate itself, often disguising its actions in the process. It is the common experience of all readers to forget what lies outside the text. We may be aware of the violent suppression of certain dissenting voices, yet we often don't consider those consigned to the "structured absences" of discourse. In this sense every act of writing, of film production, of curriculum design, of institutional organization is an act of inclusion and exclusion. Therefore these and other social forms must be continually scrutinized for what they represent.

Because it intrinsically challenges the status quo, much critical education is consigned to the margins. School teachers who question the legitimacy of knowledge forms, writers who refuse to respect the canon, artists who would dismantle the institutions of the art world—these are not the type of people who curry favor with those in power. For this reason they often find themselves outside the "basic" curriculum. Not so coincidentally these are the exact areas that are viewed as irrelevant or illegitimate by conservative educational reformers. Media studies is a case in point. As an interdisciplinary field largely devoted to popular culture, media studies is often dismissed by school administrators as an educational frill. Thus, although it is highly popular among students and teachers, media studies has difficulty gaining a foothold in many schools. Such circumstances demonstrate the difficulty of critiquing institutions or discourses that would define themselves as "above" politics. They also point out the consequences that sometimes result from direct confrontation with a powerful institution. While such strategies can be very effective in some circumstances, they can also polarize both sides of a debate. For this reason, there are tactical reasons for considering a "language of possibility" to accompany or replace a practice of pure critique. All too often, Left culture has consigned itself to a reactionary posture in which the very terms of its struggles are defined by the opposition. This locks progressive activists into a one-dimensional paradigm of response, casting them as the voice of a marginalized and subordinate Other. Such an attitude precludes the articulation of a positive agenda that might define the terms of an argument.

Of course, on an epistemological level it is impossible ever to escape the contextual frames of language, power, and desire. For this reason we must acknowledge that we are always operating within the parameters of received subjectivity. However, at the same time it is equally important to recognize our abilities to reject and exceed subject positions as received. This is accomplished through the active investigations of alternative narratives, revised histories, and newly coded meanings. Simply put, it is pointless to dismantle one mechanism without another to take its place. In the art world this paradox is demonstrated in the relationship between postmodern appropriation and more instrumental practices of viewer repositioning. Although some argue that it is impossible to step outside the realm of representation, it is equally true that material relations are an integral part of any politics of representation and not, as some would have it, a metaphoric corollary. With this in mind, we can no longer simply reveal the underpinnings of the dominant order by subversively fetishizing its codes. Besides its easy cooptation as an endorsement of commodity aesthetics, this strategy typically fails to offer alternatives. Moreover, it can replicate harmful hierarchies of expertise that divide political activists and the broader publics they would serve.

This is not to say that cultural workers cannot assume leadership functions, only that such leadership needs to be facilitative rather than prescriptive. It means engaging the project described by Gayatri Spivak of "unlearning our privilege as our loss" by realizing that positions of dominance often are accompanied by blindness.[38] The "transformative" intellectual is one who provides the catalyst for change. This might involve encouraging a community to look into its own past to resuscitate lost narratives of emancipation. Certainly this is the case with current efforts to combat the systematic erasure of the labor movement from textbooks. In other instances activists in school districts are engaging in local campaigns to rewrite the struggles and gains of African-American, Asian, and Latino peoples into school curricula. Similar motivations have brought together dozens of groups to celebrate the diversity of immigrant peoples through community mural projects.

Beyond these practices in the classroom or the exhibition hall, cultural workers need to recognize the importance of establishing political alliances among themselves—both within institutions and among like-minded groups. In this transformative activity activists support each other to establish coalitions for breaking down the debilitating separation that occurs in the workplace and between workplaces. Ultimately the university and the community are not segregated realms for theory and practice, but integrated components of a single system. Theory has to be redefined as the everyday instrument that it is—a tool that is only as good as its uses make it. The rest of this book is dedicated to such an enterprise—to an explication of the ways theories of materialism, modernity, difference, culture, democracy, and pedagogy intersect the lived world of students, teachers, gallery goers, TV watchers, etc. This is not to imply anything like a unified set of answers to the questions that have plagued society for generations—only to suggest that strength and empowerment derive from seeking them out.

NOTES

1. These objectives are outlined in Stephen T. Leonard, *Critical Theory in Political Practice* (Princeton, NJ: Princeton University Press, 1990), p. 4.

2. Significant reflection theory analyses of mass culture continue to be written by such people as Ben J. Bagdikian, John Berger, Stuart Ewen, Todd Gitlin, and Herbert Schiller.

3. Important writings of Louis Althusser, Walter Benjamin, Ernst Bloch, Bertolt Brecht, Antonio Gramsci, and Georg Lukacs remained untranslated or unpublished until the late 1960s and 1970s.

4. Louis Althusser, "Ideology and Ideological State Apparatuses (Notes toward an Investigation)," in *Lenin and Philosophy and Other Essays*, Ben Brewster (London: New Left Books, 1971), pp. 121-73.

5. Herbert Marcuse, *An Essay on Liberation* (Boston: Beacon Press, 1969), p. 21.

6. Marxism's contemporary interpreters are as diverse as its field's applications, and they include such individuals as Perry Anderson, Stanley Aronowitz, Chantal Mouffe, Terry Eagleton, Julia Lesage, and Cornell West, to name but a few.

7. Jürgen Habermas, "Modernity versus Postmodernity," *New German Critique* 22 (1981): 3014.

8. Frederic Jameson, "Postmodernism and Consumer Society," in *The Anti-Aesthetic: Essays on Postmodern Culture*, ed. Hal Foster (Port Townsend, WA: Bay Press, 1983), pp. 111-25.

9. Dick Hebdige, *Hiding in the Light: On Images and Things* (New York: Comedia/Routledge, 1988), p. 182.

10. Douglas Crimp, "Pictures," catalog essay (Committee for the Visual Arts, 1977), p. 3.

11. Richard Bolton, "Enlightened Self-Interest: The Avant-Garde in the '80s," *Afterimage* 16, no. 7 (Feb. 1989): 17.

12. Hal Foster, *Recordings: Art, Spectacle, Cultural Politics* (Port Townsend, WA: Bay Press, 1985), p. 170.

13. Stuart Hall, "The Emergence of Cultural Studies and the Crisis of the Humanities," *October* 53 (Summer 1990): 12.

14. Ibid., p. 15.

15. Subsequently other intellectuals as diverse as Tony Bennett, John Fiske, Hall, Dick Hebdige, Angela McRobbie, Colin Mercer, Meaghan Morris, and Paul Willis have analyzed the central role of culture in the formation of identity.

16. Judith Williamson, "Woman Is an Island: Femininity and Colonization," in *Studies in Entertainment: Critical Approaches to Mass Culture*, ed. Tania Modleski (Indianapolis: Indiana University Press, 1986), pp. 100-101.

17. Meaghan Morris, "Banality in Cultural Studies," *Block* 14 (1988): 15-26.

18. Paula A. Treichler, "Teaching Feminist Theory," in *Theory in the Classroom*, ed. Cary Nelson (Urbana and Chicago: University of Illinois Press, 1986), p. 57.

19. The lineage of "contemporary" feminist theory is generally traced to the 1960s and 1970s in writings of such thinkers as Nancy Chodorow, Dorothy Dinnerstein, Germaine Greer, Catherine A. MacKinnon, and Juliet Mitchell.

20. Due to the overlapping character of concerns among feminists and within feminism it is problematic to label practitioners by category. However, the following have made important contributions to discussions of language and the body: Hélène Cixous, Catherine

Clement, Teresa DeLauretis, Jane Gallop, Luce Irigary, Laura Mulvey, Kaja Silverman, Gayatri Chakvorty Spivak, and Monique Wittig.

21. Editorial, "The Biggest Secret of Race Relations: The New White Minority," *Ebony* (April 1989): 84.

22. Howardina Pindell, "Breaking the Silence, Part 2," *New Art Examiner* 18, no. 2 (November 1990): 18.

23. Hector St. John de Crevecoeur, as quoted in Constance Wolf, "The Multicultural Debate: Challenges of the 1990s," unpublished manuscript (1991).

24. See Catherine Lord, "Bleached, Straightened, and Fixed," *New Art Examiner* 18, no. 6 (February, 1991): 25-27.

25. Ibid., p. 27.

26. Stuart Hall, "New Ethnicities," ICA Document 7, *Black Film and British Cinema* (London: Institute for Contemporary Art, 1988).

27. Cornell West, "The New Cultural Politics of Difference," *October* 53 (Summer 1990): 105.

28. Chantal Mouffe, "Radical Democracy: Modern or Postmodern? in *Universal Abandon? The Politics of Postmodernism*, ed. Andrew Ross (Minneapolis: University of Minnesota Press, 1988), p. 42.

29. Lorraine Kenny, "Traveling Theory: An Interview with Kobena Mercer," *Afterimage* 18, no. 2 (Sept. 1990): 9.

30. Samuel P. Huntington, *The Crisis of Democracy: A Report on the Governability of Democracies to the Trilateral Commission* (New York: New York University Press, 1975).

31. Allan Bloom, *The Closing of the American Mind* (New York: Simon and Schuster, 1987), pp. 246–47.

32. Ibid., p. 247.

33. Antonio Gramsci, *Selections from the Prison Notebooks*, ed. and trans. Quintin Hoare and Geoffrey Nowell Smith (New York: International Publishers, 1972). Particularly in recent years the all-encompassing aspects of Gramscian principles have been overstated in pedagogical theory. Clearly the institutional matrix in which schools reside exerts an influence upon the individual that is partial, at best. However, as one of the last great totalizers, Gramsci provides an important means of bridging gaps among disparate fields.

34. Among numerous reader response theorists, see especially works by Jonathan Culler, Stanley Fish, Wolfgang Iser, and Jane Tompkins.

35. Dick Hebdige, *Subculture: The Meaning of Style* (New York: Methuen, 1979).

36. These contemporary practitioners of critical pedagogy include Stanley Aronowitz, Henry A. Giroux, Michelle Fine, Peter McLaren, and Roger Simon, among numerous others.

37. Stanley Aronowitz and Henry A. Giroux, *Education under Siege: The Conservative, Liberal and Radical Debate over Schooling* (South Hadley, MA: Bergin and Garvey, 1985).

38. Gayatri Chakravorty Spivak, *The Post-Colonial Critic: Interviews, Strategies, Dialogues*, ed. Sarah Harasym (New York: Routledge, Chapman, and Hall, 1990), p. 9.

2

Living in the Material World:
Institutions and Economies

How does one encourage a dynamic pedagogy that is linked to the production of culture, as well as its reception? Doing so requires new structures to alter the positions from which we send and receive messages. Texts would be little more than abstractions without enabling institutions for their delivery. In the realms of cultural pedagogy this material apparatus comprises the range of schools, universities, galleries, museums, funders, government agencies, corporations, and publishers that mediate the flow of textual material. But who has access to these institutions? In whose interests do they function? What effect do they have on the operation of a democratic society?

Answers lie in the way these institutions mediate debate in a free society. The framers of the Constitution believed that the ability of citizens to openly express their views insured that government would never become more powerful than the populace. Yet history has repeatedly revealed the ways that such high-minded principles are subverted by capitalism. The market's predisposition to private interest creates a paradox when entrusted with the public good. In the modern age of the commodity sign, speech cannot be free and for sale at the same time. Although conservatives would have us believe otherwise, a direct contradiction exists between the expectation that the marketplace will provide a diversity of cultural offerings and the reality that it treats cultural texts as goods to be bought and sold.[1]

Many bitter debates of public policy have been fought over such issues. As a result entities have been legislated to work between public and private interests: from government agencies to philanthropic foundations. Needless to say, the extent to which these bodies can mediate the profit motive are subject to political influence. Capitalism adapts to changing circumstances that challenges its hegemony, and culture provides one of the most insidious masks for this process. The cultural apparatus subtly shapes the public imagination and legitimates the agendas of the status quo by equating them with "universal" human values. Long ago Western society abandoned outright oppression. Instead it produces consent by forging identities, framing alternatives, and even determining the questions it can be asked. Just as culture provides a vehicle for these strategies, education acts as its enabling mechanism.

Exacerbating these political circumstances are symptoms of a growing fiscal crisis within the United States that threatens national security, and along with it the control of its current leadership. Due to such factors as the post–Viet Nam arms buildup, the space race, the savings and loan fiasco, the Persian Gulf War and the generalized sluggishness with which U.S. industry made the transition from heavy industry to high-tech manufacturing, the nation's ability to command markets and insure profits has declined. This has resulted in a broad range of conservative prescriptions for a more corporate approach to civic management. The reasoning has been that government works best when its components are subjected to competitive scrutiny. Philip Wexler has analyzed this pattern of institutional reorganization in recent decades. Employing "long-cycle" economic theories, Wexler has described the current crisis of accumulation as yet another periodic downturn resulting from the structural contradictions of capitalism.[2] Exacerbated by the material exigencies of declining industrial growth, heightened wage demands, increasing inflation, and unemployment, the ability of corporations and government to jointly mediate economic tensions has deteriorated.

Making matters worse in the 1960s and 1970s was the growing strength of organized labor. The resultant inability of industry to generate surplus value and to control workers led the U.S. capitalist class to develop new methods. These became manifest in the political movement that would emerge in the 1980s as Reaganism. However, as Wexler points out, the movement exceeds the simple demands of the Right, per se: "The social reorganization is corporatist. Corporatism surpassed the internal contradiction of conservativism by providing solidarity and integration through the organization of groups of market-commodity actors."[3] This corporatism articulates itself in two interrelated languages: one of the market; the other of morality. In the first instance, one finds an effort to promote the virtues of capitalism through an emphasis on economic expansionism, individualism, and consumer "freedom of choice" as an inalienable American liberty. The second, more moral, language, is the familiar call for cooperation, assimilation, loyalty, tradition, and "common culture." As recent circumstances have demonstrated, these premises are not so much advanced by the corporate or government sectors themselves as they are promoted by alliances between them: antiunion legislation, industry deregulation, government bail-outs of private financial institutions, grants to corporations. To implement these views the Reagan and Bush administrations have attempted to change the shape of government by introducing "private–sector initiatives" and "public/private partnerships." This has meant the wholesale transfer of many formerly publicly administered functions—from health care to education to culture—into the hands of corporate America.

THE PRIVATIZATION OF CULTURE

As social services have been reoriented along lines of profitability, the government's ability to correct economic inequities has declined. The growing privatization has exacerbated divisive hierarchies of work (professions) and study (disciplines) that stratify human activities in disproportion to their community function. This has excluded large segments of the population from social services and democratic decision-making, increasing the extent to which the United States is becoming a divided society. The explanation offered by a growing list of analysts is that the capitalist class is simply struggling to maintain its grip on a declining profit source, a situation that inevitably results in restructuring the accumulation process itself.

In both subtle and not-so-subtle ways the privatization of cultural philanthropy is part of this process. The Right is quick to decry the evils of big government and its associations with bureaucratic inefficiency and lack of competitive drive. It argues that government arts and humanities programs typically use the money of the common taxpayer to finance projects of specialized constituencies—when instead this should be left to "private" patronage. What this argument fails to acknowledge is the extent to which private donations are subsidized by the government in the form of forgone taxes.[4] The development of the private foundation as an institutional form can be dated to the 1916 reinstitution corporate income tax and the subsequent introduction of philanthropic tax incentives. The major difference between public and private charities is that the former operates under public scrutiny and that the latter does not. It is now a commonly known statistic, for example, that the obscenity controversies surrounding the National Endowment for the Arts were the result of problems associated with less than 30 of the 90,000 grants scrutinized by congressional staff. In contrast, the idiosyncratic giving of an entity like the John D. and Catherine T. MacArthur Foundation through its "genius" grant program continues to be both a public mystery—and, to a certain extent, a joke. Yet the uncollected taxes on the MacArthur Foundation's $2 billion nest egg approximate the total yearly budget of the NEA.

There is little subtlety in corporate philanthropy. In the business world charitable giving is increasingly becoming a part of business itself. Abandoning its former altruism, such giving is recognized as a means of winning new clients, rewarding personnel, getting publicity, and forging a positive public image. As stated by *Corporate Philanthropy Report* editor Craig Smith, the late 1980s demonstrated that "more companies refuse to make gifts at all unless they're convinced that doing so will benefit their bottom line."[5] As one consequence of this, Smith forecasted that "marketing dollars will be diverted increasingly from advertising to support non-profit cultural events."[6] These sentiments are shared by Sandra J. Ruch, manager of cultural programs and promotions for Mobil Oil's public affairs department: "All of the projects we sponsor must meet a corporate objective or a direct business need. We don't sponsor events just because they're cultural."[7]

Within education we see this in the growing trend toward corporatization in vouchers for private schools, in pressures for schools to compete for students, in performance evaluations of schools based solely on test scores, in new business relations with schools, and in curricula increasingly tailored for the needs of industrial management. A parallel situation has been facing the arts, as government philanthropy has steadily diminished and nonprofit cultural institutions have increasingly become obliged to imitate their profit-making counterparts. In real dollars, federal expenditures for cultural support have declined 27 percent since 1981.[8] As many experimental spaces have gone out of business or reduced their programs, others are now obliged to consider the star status of the artists they exhibit. Museums must cater to wealthy patrons, and the value of art itself is measured on the auction block.

At the same time, competition for patronage has considerably eroded cooperation among artists and their organizations. Gradually the movement toward privatization is returning art and culture to the domain of the market—and ultimately of the wealthy. Marx would label this an inevitable consequence of a system premised on profits rather than social utility. And indeed the logic of most conservative policymakers would confirm that analysis. As Vermont Republican Jim Jeffords crassly joked in a recent interview, "The arts are the soul of this country, and there is no better way to promote the country than to sell its soul."[9] Is it any wonder that in such an environment popular support for the arts has begun to dwindle?

PUBLIC PHILANTHROPY AND THE CIVIC TRUST

As a nation, the United States has remained a notoriously parsimonious arts supporter in the Western world. While our government commits less than one dollar per citizen toward arts support, countries like Canada and Great Britain spend many times as much. In 1989, France, with a population less than one-fourth that of the United States, spent $560 million on a music, theater, and dance program.[10] By comparison, the total budget of the NEA was less than $180 million that year. A historic impediment to domestic cultural support has been the ambivalence felt by Americans about the validity of their hybrid colonial culture. Among conservatives this impulse lingers in the xenophobic fear of foreign "others" who might dilute our common heritage. Throughout U.S. history, claims of a distinctly "American" voice were undermined by insecurities about the ultimate inferiority of U.S. art in comparison to that from Europe. Despite the intellectual nationalism of writers like Ralph Waldo Emerson ("Our day of dependence, our long apprenticeship to the learning of other lands, draws to a close"), a fundamental disbelief in frontier culture persisted throughout much of the nineteenth century.[11] These attitudes began to change after 1900 with the increased migration of European artists to the United States and the development of regional aesthetic styles.

With the collapse of Europe and the subsequent emergence of the United States as an international superpower following World War II, domestic cultural products came to be regarded as symbols of American might. During the cold war years Washington politicians and bureaucrats recognized the publicity value of domestic culture as evidence of the benefits of a free society. Modern art forms of minimalism and abstract expressionism were aggressively promoted throughout the world by the Rockefeller Foundation and the U.S. Information Agency, among other entities. In the 1960s' atmosphere of international competition with the Soviet Union (the nuclear arms buildup, the space race) and domestic government largess (CETA [Comprehensive Training and Employment Act], VISTA, HUD [Housing and Urban Development], Medicare), the National Endowments for the Arts and Humanities seemed logical expenditures. In creating the NEA and NEH in 1965, Congress made an explicit "Declaration of Purpose" stating that "the world leadership which has come to the United States cannot rest solely upon superior power, wealth, and technology, but must be solidly founded upon worldwide respect and admiration for the Nation's high qualities as a leader in the realm of ideas and the spirit."[12]

For many cultural activists the birth of the government-subsidized artists' space and media center movements provided the promise of an escape from corporate domination. During the 1970s the budget of the National Endowment for the Arts swelled from $8 million to $159 million, catalyzing comparable funding increases from many private foundations and state arts councils. This growth is largely attributable to the early efforts of founding NEA chairperson Nancy Hanks, who mobilized the political clout of large cultural institutions (along with their influential trustees and patrons) on the endowment's behalf. But although the lion's share of federal patronage was earmarked for the likes of Lincoln Center, a more radicalized movement began to quietly develop in its shadow.

Responding to the growing commodification of art, increasing numbers of artists were drawn to conceptual and performance genres. These practices focused attention on the ideas or processes of artistic production rather than the material objects so valorized by museums and commercial galleries. Artists were also getting more political. In an atmosphere of civil rights marches and antiwar rallies, comparable strikes, protests, and sit-ins were conducted against institutions like New York's Metropolitan Museum and the Museum of Modern Art. These institutions were criticized for disregarding the interests of living artists and excluding them from decision making. Thus a grassroots movement of "artists' spaces" was born.

In the analysis of Ruby Lerner, a consultant for the National Association of Artists' Organizations, this phenomenon occurred within a broader social movement "to break the tutelage of the larger bureaucratic institutions that dominated American political and economic life." More specifically, Lerner explains,

> the traditional not-for-profits were indeed perceived as presenting work that was "safe" artistically. Saleability was obviously the motivating force for the commercial sector. Artists' organizations were created by artists shut out of opportunities to exhibit or perform their own— perhaps more daring—work in existing venues, such as commercial galleries, museums and regional theaters. It was hoped that these new organizations would be non-elitist, attracting audiences diverse in color, ethnicity, and income. It was also hoped that these organizations would be able to build a broad base of community support, rather than relying on patronage of the wealthy few. In short, a new kind of organization was envisioned: one that would be more adventurous artistically and less bureaucratic organizationally, able to respond more directly to the changing needs of local artists.[13]

No one needs to be reminded what happened next. The perceived "conservative mandate" of the Reagan administration meant a philosophical reorientation toward traditional definitions of culture. Like the educational reformism championed by Bloom, Finn, Hirsch, and Ravitch, the cultural reform movement worked to suppress dissent with a systematic elimination of oppositional voice. Analyzing the endowments in the 1981 *Mandate for Leadership* transition document prepared by the Heritage Foundation, Michael S. Joyce wrote that the NEA had grown "more concerned with the politically calculated goals of social policy than with the arts it was created to support. To accomplish goals of social intervention and change . . . the Endowment . . . serve(s) audiences rather than art, vocal constituencies rather than individually motivated artistic impulses."[14] In a similar fashion, the report suggested that the NEH should stick to the ideologically "neutral" business of supporting "humanities, rather than social crusades, political action, or political education as demanded by narrowly partisan interests."[15] In the name of "depoliticizing" the nonprofit sector, the government restructured funding with a conservative vengeance— purportedly to increase the proportion of private philanthropy.

Yet the changes had very specific political and economic consequences. As Martha Rosler pointed out in a 1982 essay, rather than catalyzing private funding for avant-garde art, the move to reduce government cultural support had the opposite effect, as corporations perceived a signal to either reduce their contributions or to focus on more traditional cultural forms.[16] The result was a disproportionate reduction of support to community-based arts organizations, many of which served constituencies comprising people of color, sexual minorities, the elderly, or the infirm. (It is important to note that even in the best of times such groups have been a low priority at the NEA due to its mandate for serving "professional" artists.) Rosler correctly predicted an increasing bifurcation of the art system, mirroring the labor-market segmentation in the economy as a whole: "The lower end of the art system will continue to strangle, and the upper will swell and stretch as more of the money available from all sources will be concentrated in it. . . . Many small organizations, especially those serving ethnic communities, will close."[17] In the years since Rosler's article, her predictions have proved prophetic. Dozens of low-budget organizations have indeed gone out of business, while entities like museums and symphonies with conservative appeal have continued to prosper. With an emphasis on more traditional or historic programs, these mainstream institutions are less likely to present programs that might offend audiences. They are therefore more attractive to both governmental and corporate funders.

These dynamics were exacerbated throughout the 1980s by periodic assaults from conservative extremists angered by the progressive character of some NEA-sponsored projects. Those attacks hit home in the censorship controversies of the early 1990s. Led by politicians such as North Carolina senator Jesse Helms and religious fundamentalist groups like the American Family Association, a movement emerged in 1989 to expose allegedly immoral and anti-American projects supported by tax dollars. The specific implications of these restrictive efforts will be taken up at length in the following chapter's discussion of texts. Despite the Right's failure in enacting its most extreme sanctions, the battle that ensued (and continues to ensue) on the floor of Congress and in the national news media exacted a heavy toll on the cultural funding apparatus. In addition to further alienating artists from the general public, endowment critics obtained a reallocation of 25 percent of NEA money for state and local distribution, thus damaging the prospects of many progressive groups in conservative regions. The preeminence of the presidentially appointed chair of the endowment over artists' juries was also reaffirmed, thus casting an additional conservative cloud over grant making.

Other, more subtle, changes have taken place elsewhere at the Endowment. Perhaps the most notable differences have appeared in the NEA's Artists in Education program, renamed near the close of the Reagan years the Arts in Education program. The name change was significant, for it signaled a structural shift long sought by conservative policymakers. The bulk of the $5.5-million Artists in Education budget had supported state and regionally administered artist-in-residence programs—primarily in school districts, a function that in many areas provided the only government funding individual artists could receive. Even more significantly, in states like California that have largely eliminated art from the K–12 curriculum, state-funded residencies enabled by NEA support represent the only contact young people have with working artists.

Since its inception in 1969, Artists in Education brought more than 40,000 professional artists to an audience of some 20 million school children. Under the revised plan, residencies compete with programs in curriculum development, teacher training, informational services, and testing. The shift to Arts in Education had been a priority for Frank Hodsoll ever since his 1981 appointment by Ronald Reagan. "Our emphasis has always been on artists and arts institutions," Hodsoll remarked at the time, explaining that "in this case, we're putting the emphasis on the kids."[18]

Such pronouncements were not made in a political vacuum. Although the NEA's previous evaluation of its residency program, contained in *The National Endowment for the Arts: Five Year Plan, 1986–1990*, indicated that it "has proven enormously popular" with artists, parents, and state agencies, advocates for educational constituencies argued that teaching was best done by those trained to do it.[19] Moreover, the growing popularity of artist-in-residence programs was seen as a potential threat to teachers' jobs. Writing in *Design for Arts Education*, David B. Pankratz stated that "Artists in Education is actually more a policy to provide employment for artists than an education policy."[20] Pankratz added that, although it was never the intention of such programs to replace teachers with artists, many schools were continuing their collaborations with artists after initial residencies. "This would seem to suggest a growing dependence on or orientation to outside resources is a more frequent consequence of Artists in Education than the development of sequential K–12 in-school programs."[21]

Despite such practical exigencies, it is also important to consider the threat artists sometimes represent to school districts. Increasingly under pressure to maintain order, enforce discipline, and produce quantifiable results, many administrators are less than enthusiastic about potentially disruptive or critical projects by artists from the "outside." One such artist-in-residence who has achieved considerable success despite the controversial character of her work is Branda Miller. During a residency at Boston's Madison High School, Miller organized a group that named itself the Teen Vision Posse to produce a tape addressing the issue of school dropouts. The resulting *Talkin' 'bout Droppin' Out* (1988) is a fast-paced montage of student life, with scenes staged in locations ranging from the classroom to the street to Burger King. Accompanied by a group voice-over, the multilayered narrative conveys the complexities of the problem.

> The bulk of kids who drop out have family problems. . . . You drop out because you weren't raised right. . . . I go there every day and I get an insult from a teacher because of something I don't understand. . . . I'm sick of this garbage. . . . I'm tired of them teaching only white history.

Though acknowledging student complicity in the dropout dilemma, the tape is largely critical of both the school and the society it serves. Moreover, its rough, hand-held camera technique and MTV-style editing hardly make the work look like conventional television. As compensation for this iconoclasm the piece closes with legitimizing sections of statistical data on dropouts and a brief epilogue by two young women producers. As one explains:

> Each of us are doing our own segment about why high school students are dropping out and the reasons why they're dropping out. It's a lot of hard work and we're doing it. It's a lot of hard work and we had to, like, you know, direct, shoot, edit, and write down the scripts and everything. We had to have the right lighting, the right props, and the right talent to put into different parts of our production.

Such rationales notwithstanding, most schools in the United States have little time, money, and patience for such experiments in activating student voices. The Reagan and Bush administrations have incrementally shifted the burden of school financing to the state and local level—and the resulting budget squeeze has encouraged a narrow back-to-basics pragmatism. Within this atmosphere of economic hardship, the former NEA Artists-in-Education program played an important role in leveraging local money for the arts and artists. Now matters have changed dramatically.

Initial funding for new components of Arts in Education were modest, with grants totaling $2.1 million beginning in its initial phases. However, in NEA terms these are hardly trifling sums; the total disbursed for all visual artists fellowships is typically less than $2.5 million. Some observers have questioned the logic of reducing already minimal NEA funding for artists in order to supplement the billions spent annually on elementary and secondary school education. In response, NEA officials stress the strategic importance of demonstrating the government's commitment to art education. A similar argument was made in assigning $1.9 million of NEA money, primarily from the NEA Media Arts Program budget, toward a children's arts television series cosponsored by the Getty Center. Other awards of up to $650,000 have been made through the NEA's Challenge Grant Program to such institutions as the Exploratorium in San Francisco and Boston's Cultural Education Collaborative. More modest projects have been initiated within the Design Arts, Folk Arts, Inter-Arts, Literature, Museum, and Opera-Musical Theater programs.

Given these proclivities, it should come as no surprise that the NEA continues to promise a more educational orientation, and in its 1992–93 guidelines education is listed as a "chairman's priority." As these plans progress it is important to keep in mind that in directing the arts and humanities along a more pedagogical course, conservative bureaucrats have seized the political high ground. Intellectuals on the Left need to rethink their positions as scholars and artists in order to regain lost territory. This will necessarily involve removing the humanities and arts from the narrow confines of the academy and bringing them into such public arenas as the elementary and secondary classroom. Accomplishing this will require changes from both within and without the school. It will take the willingness of teachers to form alliances with parents, students, and each other to build meaningful coalitions for change. It will also involve reaching outside the bounds of education as traditionally defined to bring new faces into the classroom and to take learning into the community.

ACROSS THE GREAT DIVIDE: ARTISTS AND EDUCATORS

Given these circumstances it is indeed ironic that the initiative for cultural educational incentives has come from conservatives. The Right has recognized the tactical importance of schooling as an instrument for instilling discipline and canonical values. As a consequence, even the federal government has seen the need for elementary and secondary school programs to help students grapple with a world in which the image has become the final form of commodity reification. However, in adopting this program of educational innovation, the Right has applied its own vocabulary. The Reagan/Bush government unapologetically framed issues of critical viewing in free-market terminology, as evidenced in the claim that "understanding of the media arts could affect the Neilsen and Arbitron ratings which dictate the broadcast agenda."[22] Although this crude populism satisfies Republican sensibilities, it does little to disrupt patterns of passive reception. Viewers are given the illusion of choosing from a prescribed range of goods—from soap operas to presidents—with freedom defined as the ability to turn off the set.

Why, then, have radical cultural workers failed to take the initiative in struggles over culture and pedagogy? How has the Left's vocabulary been so easily appropriated? In part this is a function of the Left's tendency to deliver populist messages through elitist forms and speaking positions. One might expect that activist artists would be flocking to the classroom, where art can be most effective in revealing corporatist manipulations. But despite the pedagogical implications of their practice, cultural workers have been both ineffective and underutilized in the classroom. Part of the blame for this must fall on artists themselves, for as a group they prefer making films, paintings, or musical compositions over teaching about them. The assumption has been that status quo representations are most effectively subverted by alternatives to them. These attitudes have held sway even in difficult economic times.

At the same time, the educational establishment has concentrated little on working artists, in part because teachers rarely engage in such practical work themselves. The situation is exacerbated by the low status of art within most universities, coupled with a reactionary elitism that, until quite recently, precluded examination of such anomalous activities as media, popular culture, or crafts. Serious examinations of these latter discourses are virtually nonexistent in elementary and secondary schools, where students encounter the powerful mechanisms of socialization that will follow them the rest of their lives. Clearly changes will need to be made if we are to lay the groundwork for a society of cultural democracy. Without a pedagogical imperative, the broader mission of the Left stands in jeopardy.

A number of factors have conspired to divert artists and writers from their functions as teachers. One is the profound reverence for individual authorship that motivates a preoccupation with production, particularly regarding the "alternative" text. Indeed, cultural work is typically identified via an eschewal of bureaucratic affiliation, a characteristic nowhere made more apparent than in debates over government patronage. Groups like the Association for Independent Video and Filmmakers and the National Coalition of Independent Public Broadcasting Producers have encouraged the Corporation for Public Broadcasting to adopt a definition of an independent as one "who is in complete control of the content and budget of a production."[23] Through funding structures that make fellowship awards the top priority, foundations and government agencies often emphasize the work of "individual artists" and discourage collaboration. The rhetoric of those financial discussions intensified during the Reagan/Bush years, as philanthropy has continued to dwindle. The resulting capital squeeze on cultural enterprises drove attention back to artists and products. Competition in the granting arena replaced competition in the market.

The fetishization of self-expression has been further exacerbated by the identification of cultural production as a high art activity. Art is thought to be something best suited for gallery walls or specialized publications. Because this art is in the gallery we come to believe that it cannot be anywhere else. After all, that is where one gets this very special kind of experience, an experience that one obtains by escaping from one's daily routines. Why? Because ordinary people and their activities are deemed to be lacking in any potential for enlightenment, transcendence, or cultivated pleasure.

An entire institutional mechanism has grown up to support this view—from galleries, museums, and alternative spaces to art schools and professional guilds like the College Art Association and the Society for Cinema Studies. All of these institutions promote a disdain for everyday culture—a position validated and supported by government subsidy programs. This is one of the real reasons that conservative reactionaries were able to gain so much ground in the NEA censorship debates. More people thought that Andres Serrano and Karen Finley were arrogant snobs than ever believed they were immoral. At the height of the controversy, a survey conducted by People for the American Way found that 93 percent of the population opposed arts censorship, but most didn't care enough to do anything.[24]

This isn't simply an inside-the-art-world/outside-the-art-world issue. It is also a dynamic that affects cultural workers everywhere. Through this cult of expertise the market enforces divisive hierarchies that allow a handful of cultural producers to dominate distribution, publication, and exhibition, thus denying access to others. These competitive values encourage artists and writers to fight each other for audiences, while promoting a top-down view of culture in which stars dictate to nonstars and academic power accumulates in the hands of a few.

BACK TO SCHOOL

The dilemma of cultural pedagogy also has roots in the educational realm. The current situation can be traced to a number of general causes, not the least of which were the well-meaning efforts of progressive educational reformers several decades ago. The United States has always regarded education as a great social leveler, providing all citizens access to the American Dream. In the 1960s era of desegregation, urban renewal, and other liberal initiatives, standard pedagogies and tests were recognized as culturally biased. Theories of "educational formalism" were introduced into many schools as a means of deemphasizing differences of race, gender, and class. Based primarily on the philosophies of John Dewey, these approaches stressed student experience over rote mastery of detail. Regrettably, the programs also often entailed a degree of anti-intellectualism.

With the economic downturns of the 1970s and 1980s came sweeping indictments of such approaches. Supply-side analysts blamed schools for the nation's inability to compete in world markets while, ironically, arguing for reductions in federal education spending. This resulted in intensified ideological intervention through curriculum changes and corporate management techniques. A renewed emphasis was placed on course content—specifically content that would reinforce conservative subjectivity. As Lynne V. Cheney argued, the biggest "culprit is 'process'—the belief that we can teach our children how to think without troubling them to learn anything worth thinking about."[25]

The conservative reform movement of the last decade has resulted in broad cutbacks in many elementary and secondary school offerings that were not deemed necessary to the preparation of workers. At the same time, initiatives like the recently unveiled "America 2000" plan have encouraged schools to adopt the methods and ideologies of business interests. Beyond the elimination of so-called "soft" courses like social studies, this has led to the curtailment of arts and music courses in some states. When the arts have been maintained it has been within the context of either a quantified or traditionalist curriculum, as in the case of the Getty Foundation's discipline-based approach.

The pressures of a quantifiable curriculum have an equally negative effect on educational workers. Considerable recent criticism has been focused on teachers, a group already subjected to public criticism, low pay, and difficult working conditions. Rather than seeking solutions in federal budget revisions, schooling is regarded as a local concern, for which conservative reformers offer rigidly prescribed formulas. Such educational reforms reduce teachers to low-level functionaries who implement the will of state-appointed experts. Someone else decides what is worth teaching and how it will be taught, thus shifting the locus of power, not merely from students, but from teachers as well.

As a professional community teachers find themselves confined by the limitations of a system geared toward quantification, regimentation, routinization, and discipline. Progressive action of any kind is frustrated by the demands of a lockstep bureaucracy that increasingly regulates curricula and diminishes the potential for individual action. As the Rockefeller Foundation's Constance Wolf asserts,

> One could easily get the impression that public schools across the country are a hotbed of activity for teaching a "new" history or that classrooms have become a political battleground for confronting such diverse issues as racism, national identity, cultural literacy, and language. But this is far from reality. Public school classrooms (K–12)—urban and rural—continue to conduct business as usual: exhausted, understimulated faculty with limited resources try to bring life and add fresh perspectives to outdated textbook accounts of history, social studies, literature, and the arts to reach students who are bored and disengaged. With fifty minute periods, constant disruptions on the school intercom system, state and locally mandated standardized tests, inadequate in-service programs for teachers, and an intrenched bureaucracy that has yet to embrace change, schools are not poised to transform and infuse their classrooms with new models of curriculum and instruction. Education for students continues to consist of little more than rote learning and filling in bubbles on standardized tests.[26]

These difficulties are structurally reinforced by the local character of primary and secondary education in the United States, an arrangement that relegates responsibility for school life to the vagaries of individual districts. This lack of a broader exchange results in decentralized and often inequitable distribution not only of resources, but also of approaches to schooling. On a micropolitical level this decentralization is further exacerbated by the individualized practice of teaching itself in which teachers work in isolation from each other.

Teachers in virtually all formal settings are limited by the bureaucratic controls of increased standardization, performance rating, and advancement regimens. Although college and university instructors encounter some of the same restrictions as their colleagues in grade school and high school, they generally suffer less curricular scrutiny and are more able to implement change. If they teach art or writing, they are also more likely to have contact with other practitioners. Unfortunately these instructors are bound by a greater emphasis on vocational preparation, for either the commercial sector, the art world, or the academy itself. In addition, this system has its own set of debilitating rules and an ever-decreasing set of professional rewards. Photographer and critic Allan Sekula discusses these aspects of university art teaching with appropriately corporate metaphors:

> If school is a factory, art departments are industrial parks in which the creative spirit, like cosmetic shrubbery or Muzak, still "lives." Photographic education is largely directed at people who will become

detail workers in one sense or another . . . Most of us who teach, or make art, or go to school with a desire to do these things, are forced to accept that a winner's game requires losers.[27]

This stratification applies to the university itself, as reflected in the critiques of college education by Russell Jacoby, Page Smith, and Charles Sykes, among others.[28] Of primary concern is the extent to which higher education and its work have become commodified. As Smith explains, the system pits student against "student through the grading system, and faculty member against faculty member for promotion and other academic favors."[29] In Jacoby's account, this results from a glutted academic marketplace now in the process of contraction. The post–World War II GI Bill and baby boom opened the university as never before to job-hungry intellectuals who hitherto had struggled as intellectual outsiders. Once inside the academy, these people quickly advanced through tenure regimens, slamming the doors behind them. Today they comprise a class of elder professors, deans, and department chairs who command exorbitant salaries, do little scholarly work, and exploit their younger counterparts. Consequently most teaching in colleges is done by underpaid and overworked instructors who are bitter about their jobs, insecure about their futures, and under intense economic pressure to produce research.

Considering the important role of education in the public mind, one would imagine that artists would be welcomed into the schoolroom, particularly in an age in which other vocational opportunities and sources of support are on the decline. Unfortunately, just as these options might become more utilized, conservative pressure is closing them off. Within the conservative educational reform movement, the overwhelming argument is that instructors need to be more strictly trained. It recommends teacher certification examinations reflecting the new emphasis on art history—while minimizing process-oriented skills.

THE FINE ART OF BUSINESS

In recent decades critiques of the art world have often focused on the way its institutional forms perpetuate commodity relations either directly (by enhancing the market value of art objects) or indirectly (by endorsing the cultural representations of capitalism). By extension, museums, galleries, publications, and artists' organizations further contribute to forms of oppression (racism, sexism, homophobia) that accompany the bifurcation of culture into high and low registers. More pessimistic commentators go so far as to suggest that as part of the hegemonic social order, even the most radicalized artistic practices are ultimately neutralized by virtue of their inclusion within this system.

It does not take much insight to recognize that art has become big business and that as a consequence big business has fallen in love with art. During the 1980s the art market repeatedly outperformed the stock exchange, the bond market, and even real estate, with a tenfold increase in paintings selling for over $1 million. Although sales of works by well-known artists have garnered the most publicity (like the sale of Van Gogh's *Irises* for $53.9 million), it is now not unusual for paintings and mixed media works by younger, up-and-coming figures like Julian Schnabel, David Salle, and Jennifer Bartlett to sell for $100,000 or more. Although such meteoric price increases have been a boon to collectors and investors, they have created a nightmare for museums who have been priced out of the acquisitions market. This in turn has obliged museums to court wealthier patrons, to align themselves even more closely with corporate funders, and to subscribe even more heavily to marketing schemes for "blockbuster" shows, gift-shop promotions, splashy fundraising parties, and public relations consultants. Increasingly museums are becoming nonprofit theme parks, with the same emphasis on income as their corporate sponsors.

The commercial value of art works is largely a matter of the imagination, a commodification bestowed through the collaborations of exhibitors, curators, collectors, critics, and artists themselves (although they hardly share equally in the benefits of these efforts). Lacking significant intrinsic value, the worth of cultural products is largely constructed by the marketplace. This value is itself conferred through a range of abstractions, often mystically described in terms of (depending on one's social orientation) beauty, taste, elegance, innovation, or radicalism. As Richard Bolton has pointed out, the aura of artistic investment has in recent years become of great benefit to the modern corporation that can invest in art to enhance its image of sophistication, to appear to be a public benefactor, or to realize profits from market speculation.

> Why should we worry about this? The reasons offered by corporations for their support are diverse, but all add up to the same result—a public realm brought under corporate control. Conservativism has extensively restructured cultural production. The corporation that performs as a good citizen doesn't really donate its capital, it invests it, developing a corporate culture and extending business's reach into all walks of life. The role of the corporate citizen as a shadow government is strengthened. Citizens become accustomed to official art.[30]

For Bolton, the most sinister consequence of this corporate "enlightened self-interest" has been the enhanced capability of the corporation to appropriate even the most radical practice into its publicity mechanism. Yesterday's subversives have become today's hottest advertising icons, as Philip Glass touts Cutty Sark scotch and Keith Haring sells Absolut vodka. "Capitalism constantly evolves, and critical approaches to it must be constantly reconsidered," Bolton concludes. "As these artists are elevated to fame, it is the system that proves to be the master at appropriation and interruption, stealing back from these artists all they have stolen."[31]

Ironically it primarily has been such conservative institutions that have seized upon the concept of education and not their progressive counterparts. In the cash-driven context of the museum, education is typically regarded more as a form of public relations than as a means of enlightenment. Just as museums deliver art to audiences, they also deliver audiences to sponsors. Corporate funders in particular weigh the visibility of philanthropy as an important consideration. Consequently there is little a museum will not do to get people to come inside.

Polite terms like "community outreach" and "audience development" mask the underlying concern for attendance figures. What it really boils down to is the use of marketing to bring otherwise disinterested (or powerless) groups like children or the elderly through the gate. More often than not, these uninitiated audiences are then fed an interpretive tour by a museum employee or docent— an exercise that unambiguously confers value to the work on display and, by extension, to the experience of being in the museum. Suitably indoctrinated, the visitors presumably become return customers.

This concept of developing new museum clients through education departments was articulated in the 1972 publication of the American Association of Museums (AAM) entitled *Museums: Their New Audiences*. The book identified an institutional "crisis" resulting from changing demographics and the inability of museums to maintain audiences. It stated that "the museum as an institution is a city institution," adding that "the city in America has changed profoundly over the last generation."[32] The suburban flight of whites from many metropolitan areas during the 1960s and 1970s had left museums without a constituency. Indeed, this recognition of the growing irrelevance of European culture to urban communities of color spurred many museums to develop education programs— hitherto thought to be mere frills.

But beyond this, education was increasingly seen as a new market for cultural institutions whose sources of financial sustenance were dwindling. Arts organizations and museums were believed to be ideally suited to offer specialized education that schools could not. The 1984 AAM publication *Museums for a New Century* put the case simply, explaining that "education is regarded as one of many commodities competing for the consumer dollar. Educational establishments are increasingly asked to deliver custom-tailored products on demands. They are asked to be accountable and to revise programs to meet the needs of customers."[33] In many respects this has proved to be the case. For example in California, a state that cut art programs from its public school budgets, community museums function as contract service providers. Children now far outnumber adults as museum goers in California, as they do throughout the nation. According to the AAM, students visit the average museum twice as often as adults.

Ironically then, adults are seen as an untapped resource. Again the AAM on this issue: "Adult education is the fastest-growing type of education today, and education is the most common adult discretionary time activity outside the home."[34] As a consequence, museum education programs often hire advertising and marketing companies for assistance. This applies to elite institutions such as the New York Museum of Modern Art as well as more prosaic organizations like the Henry Ford Museum. In the words of Ford Museum director Donald Adams, "We're in competition with every other leisure activity. Our market is the same people who go to theme parks, buy VCRs, attend movies, and spend weekends gardening at home."[35]

Such pedagogical pandering has itself become the object of art work as practiced by New York performance artist Andrea Fraser. In the last several years Fraser has developed a variety of parodic gallery talks and "art appreciation" lectures. Posing as docent Jane Castelton, Fraser conducted a tour of the New Museum in which she explained the "New Museum started its Docent Program because, well, ah, to tell you the truth, because all museums have one. It's one of those things that make a museum a museum."[36] Mimicking a convention typically employed to valorize and objectify the works in a museum, Fraser turns the device back on itself to foreground the institutional apparatus: "Over here, conveniently located in the bookstore/gift shop behind this panel is the control board for the Museum's security system. Of course all museums have security systems—owning and exhibiting art, like all valuable property, is a responsibility, and the Museum's first responsibility is to protect the culture it fosters."[37] Through this ironic double articulation Fraser both describes the museum's putative purpose and critiques its underlying function, specifically, as noted by Craig Owens, "its avowed purpose of protecting cultural artifacts in the name of the public."[38] Through repeated references to the institution's building, staff, marketing, sales, fundraising and trustees, Fraser brings to light the sociopolitical matrix in which cultural experience is constructed.

Fraser's work provides an appropriate point on which to close this chapter on the material apparatus. Throughout this book I have sought to make connections among disparate fields of discourse and between discourses and the practical events they affect. Fraser's practice combines art and pedagogy in a manner that focuses attention on their lived implications. In demonstrating relationships of aesthetics and production, she offers an important "lesson" about looking critically at the subtexts that underlie institutions and events. This is a lesson in taking ideological readings of a world built to conceal such workings.

NOTES

1. Sut Jhally, "The Political Economy of Culture," in *Cultural Politics in Contemporary America*, ed. Ian Angus and Sut Jhally (New York: Routledge, 1989), p. 66.

2. Philip Wexler, *Social Analysis of Education: After the New Sociology* (New York: Routledge, 1987), p. 61.

3. Ibid., p. 62.

4. See Dick Netzer, *The Subsidized Muse: Public Support for the Arts in the United States* (New York: Cambridge University Press, 1978), p. 6.

5. Craig Smith, "Are Corporations Less Charitable?" *New York Times*, Feb. 21, 1988, sec. 3, p. 2.

6. Ibid., p. 2.

7. Sandra Ruch, as quoted in Carol Squiers, "Wheel of Fortune: Corporate America Speaks Its Mind about Funding the Arts," *American Photographer*, October 1987, p. 16.

8. William H. Honan, "Arts Dollars: Pinched as Never Before," *New York Times*, May 28, 1989, sec. 2, p. 1.

9. Ibid.

10. Robert Hughes, "Whose Art Is It Anyway?" *Time*, June 4, 1990, p. 46.

11. Ralph Waldo Emerson, "The American Scholar" (1837), in *Selected Essays, Lectures and Poems of Ralph Waldo Emerson*, ed. R. E. Spiller (New York: Simon and Schuster, 1965), p. 63.

12. Congressional "Declaration of Purpose," as cited in The Independent Commission, "A Report to Congress on the National Endowment for the Arts," *Journal of Arts Management and Law* 20, no. 3 (Fall 1990): 21.

13. Ruby Lerner, *Comprehensive Organizational Assistance for Artists' Organizations* (Washington, DC: National Association of Artists' Organizations, 1988).

14. Michael S. Joyce, "The National Endowments for the Humanities and the Arts," in *Mandate for Leadership*, ed. Charles L. Heatherly (Washington, DC: Heritage Foundation, 1981), pp. 1040–41.

15. Ibid., p. 1041.

16. Martha Rosler, "Theses on Defunding," *Afterimage* 11, nos. 1–2 (Summer 1982): 6–7.

17. Ibid., p. 7.

18. Frank Hodsoll, as quoted in Grace Glueck, "Arts Endowment Begins Broad School Program," *New York Times*, May 19, 1986, sec. C, p. 14.

19. National Endowment for the Arts, *The National Endowment for the Arts: Five Year Plan, 1986–1990* (Washington, DC: National Endowment for the Arts, 1986), p. 33.

20. David B. Pankratz, "Aesthetic Welfare, Government, and Educational Policy," *Design for Arts Education*, July/August 1986, p. 18.

21. Ibid., p. 19.

22. National Endowment for the Arts, *Toward Civilization: A Report on Arts Education* (Washington, DC: U.S. Government Printing Office, 1988), p. 18.

23. Letter dated Sept. 7, 1983, from Lawrence Sapadin, executive director of the Association of Independent Video and Filmmakers, to Sharon Rockefeller, chair of the Corporation for Public Broadcasting.

24. *The American Public's Perspective on Federal Support for the Arts, and the Controversy over Funding for the National Endowment for the Arts* (Washington, DC: People for the American Way, 1990).

25. Lynne V. Cheney, *American Memory: A Report on the Humanities in the Nation's Schools* (Washington, DC: National Endowment for the Humanities), p. 5.

26. Constance Wolf, "The Multi-cultural Debate: Challenges of the 1990s," *exposure* 28, nos. 1/2 (1991): 43.

27. Allan Sekula, *Photography against the Grain: Essays and Photo Works, 1973–1983* (Halifax: Nova Scotia College of Art and Design, 1984), p. 223.

28. See Russell Jacoby, *The Last American Intellectuals: American Culture in the Age of Academe* (New York: Basic Books, 1987); Page Smith, *Killing the Spirit: Higher Education in America* (New York: Viking 1990); and Charles Sykes, *Profscam: Professors and the Demise of Higher Education* (New York: St. Martin's Press, 1988).

29. Smith, "Are Corporations Less Charitable?" p. 13.

30. Richard Bolton, "Enlightened Self-Interest: The Avant-Garde in the '80s," *Afterimage* 16, no. 7 (February 1989): 12–18.

31. Ibid., p. 17.

32. American Association of Museums, *Museums: Their New Audiences* (Washington, DC: AAM, 1972), p. 12.

33. American Association of Museums, *Museums for a New Century* (Washington, DC: AAM, 1984), p. 25.

34. Ibid.

35. Donald Adams, as quoted in Roberta Silverstein, *Adult Education in the Museum: A Comparative Study* (unpublished manuscript, San Francisco, CA, 1986).

36. Andrea Fraser, as quoted in Craig Owens, "The Yen for Art," in *Discussions in Contemporary Culture: Number One*, ed. Hal Foster (New York: DIA Art Foundation, 1988), p. 18. For an annotated transcript of one of these presentations, see Andrea Fraser, "Museum Highlights: A Gallery Talk," *October* 57 (Summer 1991): 103–22.

37. Owens, "The Yen for Art," p. 18.

38. Ibid., p. 20.

3

Is There a Class in This Text? Writers, Readers, and the Contest of Meaning

Recently, the most widely publicized debates within culture and education have been waged over texts. The emotionalism that surrounds particular books, movies, and the broader "social texts" they represent stems from their role as junction points between individuals and institutions, readers and writers, teachers and students. It is through such narratives that these parties negotiate their relationships. But beyond the struggles that accompany daily uses of texts, antagonists on both the Left and the Right have recognized their capacity to assume a symbolic meaning in the public mind. This is a function of the way signs become unhinged from their referents in the age of the simulacrum.

The resulting slipperiness of meaning has been exploited by various groups—as in debates during the last decade over schoolbooks and arts funding. By focusing on particular stories or pictures as ideological emblems, public figures have used these discourses for political gain. It is worth remembering that recent debates over artistic censorship were not driven by popular outrage or scholarly concern but by religious extremists and headline-hungry politicians. Even though the potential has always existed for partisan misreadings of cultural signs, until the late 1980s the political incentive (and strategic wherewithal) was insufficient to elevate the practice above name-calling. It took the catalyzing influence of forces outside the art world to capitalize on the avant-garde's civic alienation and to cast cultural workers as the terror of the heartland.[1]

Initially this chapter will focus on texts as they have become reified as figures for external political and educational issues. I will review some major debates over canons and curricula in an effort to describe the textual terrain as conventionally written. Discussion will then turn to such broader texts as citizenship, patriotism, and the "good life" as they are inscribed within popular entertainment, advertising, and social rituals. By necessity these considerations will address issues of reading and response. Considerable emphasis will also be placed on the role of electronic media in the textual environment. The chapter will conclude with thoughts on ways to reach beyond the mere reception of texts to more actively produce culture in everyday life (or to recognize the ways this is already occurring). The discussion will draw a continuum from the notion of subversive reading to one of cultural "writing."

To readers within the field of education many of these issues will have a familiar ring, because teachers, parents, and school administrators have long recognized the strategic importance of texts in shaping identities and forging values. To readers in the cultural realm, these controversies may still seem rather new. Both debates have roots in "functionalist" views of social reproduction, which have dominated educational policy for much of the past century. In such thinking learning is regarded as a process of adaptation to a stable array of social mandates. Personal agency inevitably succumbs to the will of existing institutions and behavioral norms, as difference is assimilated into the common culture. Implicit in this view is a faith in traditional texts as keys to this culture— a belief in narratives that exist as timeless knowledge outside the flow of history. To facilitate this abstract functioning of the text, it becomes standardized into the forms that remove it from everyday application. By elevating textual use to the status of ritual, it is imbued with a quasi-religious aura.

The result is a regressive system of discursive positions. By staging the argument within this functionalist framework, relationships are reinforced in which professionals always speak for nonprofessionals and the value of daily experience is inherently devalued. This establishes a hierarchy that identifies writers, teachers, artists, and scientists as "experts" to whom "ordinary" people must always look for knowledge, insight, or inspiration. Intellectual products pass from institutionally certified senders to commonplace receivers in a manner that translates very well into the economic metaphors of modern capitalism. Culture is viewed as the reified product of "genius" production. Rather than a dialogic process that develops among people, knowledge becomes a static currency that can be accumulated and exchanged.

This view of knowledge fails to acknowledge that stories and images change when viewed by different people, at different places, and at different historical moments. It cannot recognize that reception is an inherent part of the process and that signification is therefore always local and contextual. Nor does it ac-knowledge the reciprocal character of speech acts, the realization that know-ledge is partly produced in the act of interpretation, and that this production needs to be encouraged and expanded. What this view of culture does is to support existing power structures and forms of authority by discouraging inquiry, criticism, or change. For obvious reasons, it is a program that conservatives have found very attractive inasmuch as it reinforces many of their values. However, until recently the Right took a passive position in enforcing such beliefs. Like

money, culture was viewed as a trickle-down affair that passed from the highest
social registers downward—never the other way around.

LITERACY OR LITERACIES?

"Give them books, give them wings," is the slogan Barbara Bush uses in her
campaign against illiteracy.[2] Bush, whose platitudinous approach to education
has gained considerable publicity, is specifically concerned with the failure of
nonreading parents to convey a proper interest in literature and culture to their
children. Like a growing list of conservative ideologues, she prescribes a method
of social reproduction in which parents concentrate on exposing their kids to the
"best" of American thinking. "We pass along our good traits as well as our bad
ones," Bush recently said.[3]

Unfortunately the question of cultural literacy is hardly that simple, for de-
terminations of *what* should be read and by *whom* are bitterly disputed. As
producers of cultural works, artists and writers have an obvious stake in these
debates, especially considering the frequency with which cultural workers enter
the teaching profession themselves. To the extent that literacy determines one's
role in society, one's relationship with language(s) can function as both social
empowerment and ideological oppression.

But exactly what is behind all the recent fuss about reading? In many ways
the issue really is not about illiteracy but about good old-fashioned social
control. Although no one disputes the importance of communication skills,
most Bush administration literacy incentives cast negative implications on
the nation's disadvantaged. For this reason we should question the attitudes
of public policymakers who directly attribute social dilemmas to a lack of
English competence. Although conservatives readily draw connections between
illiteracy, unemployment, poor health, welfare dependency, and mental illness,
the notion that illiteracy might result from economic inequities (rather than
cause them) is rarely considered. Consequently most government programs have
difficulty attracting students.

A major factor in this dilemma is the low regard students hold for education
in general. Recent statistics indicate that more than 4.3 million young people
drop out of school each year, and that in major metropolitan areas like Los
Angeles, Chicago and New York the numbers can exceed 30 percent of those
enrolled.[4] After years of negative experience with the system, youngsters come to
view academic achievement and compliance with school regulations as socially
repugnant. Students see schools as oppressive institutions that promise little in
terms of genuine reward. One of the main planks of the Bush literacy program
is its focus on "proper" literature. Yet many students (regardless of race, gender,
or class) find the works of Poe, Wordsworth, and Longfellow irrelevant. Young
people are alienated by the disparity between the type of literacies sanctioned
in school and the literacies they practice in their daily lives. Missing in most
school curricula are notions of *active* writing, whereby individuals tell their

own stories or explore community concerns. Experiences of popular culture or personal history are rarely given credence. Instead normative standards of achievement are set forth, against which any inability to conform is equated with poor performance. This creates a chain of failure that brings students to blame themselves rather than question the system. The result is a situation in which students know full well that schools are racist, sexist, and generally unfair, yet they nevertheless fault their own lack of discipline, intelligence, or will. As a result students are forever left with confused impressions of school failure.

These issues are increasingly the subject of both political debate and cultural expression. In recent years, artist Clarissa Sligh has circulated a series of interactive exhibits entitled "Reading Dick and Jane with Me." The works incorporate texts and images from the familiar children's reader, which are collaged with additional material provided by Sligh. *See Me Jump* (1990) shows conventional Dick and Jane characters adjacent to a typeset text that reads "See me jump Who can jump What can I do See me jump Who can jump. . . . " Behind Dick and Jane are three black children and the handwritten statement, "Our parents want us to read this stuff we heard our teacher say we're not smart enough." This visual dialogue is then framed with dark blue drawing paper on which viewers are encouraged to write their own responses. Implicit is the invitation by Sligh to "talk back" to texts, authority, and official pedagogy. When displayed in Northfield, Minnesota, the piece collected the following responses:

Reminds me of my old home.

Don't take away my creativity before my childhood.

You might be able to learn vicariously, but you can't live that way.

You are smarter than they are.

Issues of linguistic interpellation are not simply problems of contemporary urban America. They symptomize a consolidation of authority that has characterized the Enlightenment ethos. An expansionist dream of global control is still the hallmark of much Western foreign policy. The privileging of specific literacy forms for purposes of social domination has been experienced by three-quarters of the world's population. As explained by Bill Ashcroft, Gareth Griffiths, and Helen Tiffin, the colonial practices of nations like the United States, Great Britain, and France often have been profoundly bound to issues of language and literacy. These writers date the very development of "English" as a discrete academic discipline to the vast expansion of colonial empires that occurred in the nineteenth century.

It can be argued that the study of English and the growth of Empire proceeded from a single ideological climate and that the development of the one is intrinsically bound up with the development of the other, both at the level of simple utility (as propaganda for instance) and at the unconscious level, where it leads to the naturalizing of constructed values (e.g. civilization, humanity, etc.) which, conversely, established "savagery," "native," "primitive," as their antitheses and as the object of a reforming zeal.[5]

Language is qualified according to the norms of the colonizer, as are the canons of writing to be studied, the academic standards to be accepted, and even the development of subsequent "native" literature. Language becomes a medium through which hegemony is reproduced because it has the ability to define standards of quality, aesthetic merit, truth, and ultimately, reality itself. In more subtle terms, "writing" is deployed to maintain Western distinctions between oral and written culture, between "civilized" and "primitive" peoples.

At home this program operates as well, but with more subtlety. Certainly recent debates over literacy and textbooks reveal the agendas of those promoting normative standards of cultural worth. The form this now takes is the familiar assimilationist strategy. In California, a state famous for its multiracial composition, a powerful group of educational traditionalists with links in the Reagan and Bush administrations has promoted the blend of pluralism and nationalism underlying California's recently revised history curriculum. Influenced by consultants like Diane Ravitch, these conservatives have successfully deployed the argument of a "common culture" forged by different ethnic groups who "competed, fought, suffered, but ultimately learned to live together in peace and even achieved a sense of common nationhood."[6]

Responding to the prescriptions issuing from conservative think tanks and from government itself have been a plethora of progressive groups who point to the unfulfilled promises of the assimilationist program. From the numerous critiques of discipline-based art education (DBAE) to publications like *Graywolf Annual*'s "Multicultural Literacy: The Opening of the American Mind," the indignation of those who would be suppressed by the "new traditionalists" has found expression.[7] These advocates of pluralism argue that a healthy democracy encourages a diversity of voices, something that the assimilationist program covertly functions to suppress. Such issues become particularly important in school, where young people acquire not only knowledge, but also attitudes about personal identity, group process, and citizenship.

Within mainstream education, localized pockets of resistance to cultural homogenization are slowly becoming more visible. Urban communities in which people of color hold a majority are recognizing the influence they command— or should command. This has resulted in increasing calls for textbook revision or for the creation of new texts. Along the way young people and adults are developing methods for expressing their frustrations with standard learning materials. At Jefferson High School in Los Angeles, a class project organized by Humanitas Program instructor Gina Lamb produced its own video narrative about the absence of certain stories in California history books. The 11-minute tape entitled *Textbook Mystery: Oral History* (1990) uses a dramatized classroom setting as a point of departure for a series of revisionist inquiries by student historians.

The scene opens with a racially mixed class receiving new schoolbooks under the supervision of a dowdy white instructor. As the books are piled on students' desks, the teacher begins to drone in incomprehensible gibberish about the Constitution (apparently accomplished by reading an actual text backwards). One by one the students drift into daydreams, leaving the domains of "official" history and entering worlds of their own heritage. With the platitudes of the Constitution ringing in the background we hear a Japanese mother telling of her family's incarceration in a World War II internment camp, an elderly couple recounting their jailing during the 1950s for espousing socialist views, and a Sioux elder describing the suppression of tribal rituals: "They took away our religion, then they gave it back to us in 1932. Not very long ago. Now they're taking it away again. Peyote, they say it's a hallucinogen. Eagle feathers, they say we can't use them. . . . I don't know what they're so afraid of."

As a narrative, *Textbook Mystery: Oral History* explicates the problem of the "monoculture" and begins to offer a remedy by very directly addressing the place of such curricula in students' lives. As a classroom exercise, the tape allows young people to begin the important process of educational critique. Even more significantly, the work demonstrates the potential of productive learning. Rather than passively receiving information, students actively construct knowledge by bringing their own cultures, histories, and desires to the pedagogical "event." In this scheme education is seen, not as the simple transfer of instructional units, but as a complicated set of transactions filtered through an environment of competing interests and subjectivities. Knowledge is *made* through the critical examination and testing of ideas.

THE PUBLISHED WORD

As debates rage over canons and curricula, those on the Left need to be aware of the formidable forces confronting them. The sustenance of academic and political conservatism lies in the consolidated economic strength supporting it. No amount of theorizing by itself will place an alternative textbook on a store shelf or an independent video on television. Those institutions are firmly under the thumb of a corporate power structure that functions strictly in its own interest. Utopian speculations of the 1960s promised to replace alienating written texts with a humanizing electronic network. But such aspirations of technological determinism could not forecast that the mere exchange of medium would not disentangle the message from the capitalist order.[8]

This effect of economic reproduction across a range of productive fields was documented by Ben J. Bagdikian in his often quoted study of the early 1980s, *The Media Monopoly*. Bagdikian described the nearly complete control of U.S. publishing, moviemaking, and broadcast media by a handful of multinational conglomerates. Less than 20 companies (Westinghouse, Gulf + Western, Time, ABC,

CBS, McGraw-Hill, The New York Times, and Harcourt Brace Jovanovich, among others) control all leading television networks, 70 percent of the major book publishers, 45 percent of the dominant magazine companies, 75 percent of the leading movie companies, and 70 percent of the major radio networks. As Bagdikian explains,

> this is more than an industrial statistic. It goes to the heart of American democracy. As the world becomes more volatile, as changes accelerate and create new problems that demand new solutions, there is an urgent need for broader and more diverse sources of public information. But the reverse is happening.
>
> Today there is hardly an American industry that does not own a major media outlet, or a major media outlet grown so large that it does not own a firm in a major industry. These media report the news of industries in which they either are owners or share directors and policies.[9]

The school textbook industry is a subsidiary of this system. With 90 percent of titles produced by the top 20 educational publishers, the top four publishers—Prentice-Hall, McGraw-Hill, CBS Publishing, and Scott Foresman—control 40 percent of all sales. One might think that with such large market shares, the producing companies might command a modicum of autonomy. But as Michael W. Apple explains, the costs of large-scale production for massive educational markets creates a tendency instead to appeal to the lowest common denominator. Because costs for introductory college texts can run as high as $250,000, publishers are extremely cautious about what they choose to print.[10] The editorial process is akin to that of a Hollywood film, with an endless cast of professional editors, executive consultants, and marketing analysts joining to orchestrate the "managed" text.

Given that the commercial success of these books often hinges on bulk purchasing, their contents are often geared to the largest customers—the handful of states in the southern tier and the western Sun Belt that approves books on a statewide basis.

> The simple fact of getting one's volume on such a list can make all the difference for a text's profitability. Thus, for instance, sales to California or Texas can account for over 20% of the total sales of any particular book—a considerable percentage in the highly competitive world of elementary and secondary school book production. Because of this, the writing, editing, promotion, and general orientation and strategy of such production is quite often aimed toward guaranteeing a place on the list of state approved material.[11]

Because of this the political and ideological climate of such states often tempers the content of curricular materials offered to the rest of the nation.

Needless to say, texts are but a component of any pedagogical transaction. Freethinking teachers have long devised ways to circumvent even the most oppressive schoolbooks—as have students. But textbooks constitute a considerable measure of the basic material with which all teachers have to work, and their role in the classroom is increasing. As the conservative reform movement has intensified demands for a quantifiable "basic" curriculum, teachers have come to rely more on prepackaged materials that help them "teach to the test." As a tightening economy has given teachers larger classes, less time, and fewer resources, the practical appeal of text-driven teaching is likewise enhanced. Within the United States, resistance to mandated texts continues to be primarily a local matter. Yet even these decisions are frustrated in the 22 states that select books for local use. Obviously in such an atmosphere many districts have little latitude in supplementing book purchases.

Matters were somewhat different two decades ago, particularly in Great Britain, where community publishing of textbooks enjoyed a brief renaissance under the government of Harold Wilson's Labour party. Numerous experiments were conducted during the 1970s with books for school and adult education programs. Underlying what became known as the Worker Writer and Community Publisher's movement was the belief that consumers of "official" culture could benefit from exercising their own potentials to discuss, criticize, and participate in public discourse. Often working together, schools and bookstores would produce texts by communities typically excluded from publishing—working people, the elderly, people of color. These were usually inexpensive works, printed with mimeo, xerox, or small-scale lithographic processes in quantities of 25 to 1,000.

A subset of this movement devoted itself more explicitly to student writing. In suggesting that young people might have something valuable to say to adults (and to each other), these works dramatically reversed conventional teaching dialectics. And occasionally they were remarkably popular, as evidenced by a poetry book by Vivian Usherwood, a young black writer from a "remedial" class, which sold over 10,000 copies. The pedagogical value of such activities are well articulated by Keith Kimberley:

> Students are encouraged to see themselves as able to act upon the world through their writing. In this characterization, emphasis lies with the school student, both as writer and reader, having "textual power." This is the power as reader to defamiliarize and interrogate and as writer to inform, excite, entertain, challenge and persuade. It is the power to understand the contexts in which published writing is produced and the audiences for whom you as school student may wish to write.[12]

On one hand, this puts young people in positions of expertise as "authors," as individuals actively seeking to know and articulate. On the other, it interrogates the myth of the author as a distant and abstract seer. Simply put, authoring becomes deconstructed as "a process by which the individual gives expression to content which has not previously been 'abstracted and formulated by others.' "[13]

MISUNDERSTANDING MEDIA

Television entered the pedagogical picture in the decade following the Second World War. As the first wave of the baby boom hit the classroom in the 1950s, video was instantly seized upon as a means of increasing teacher productivity. By simply eliminating the need for duplicate presentations, video was credited with reductions in labor of up to 70 percent.[14] It was also recognized as a powerful tool for observation and evaluation.[15] Concurrent advances in computer and telecommunications industries prompted more elaborate speculation. While in residence at New York's Fordham University during the late 1960s, Marshall McLuhan attracted a quasi-religious following based on his vision of a telecommunications network designed on biological (and therefore "natural") principles that would undermine all hierarchical structures. At the core of McLuhan's program lay a concept of media as "information without content" that defined political turmoil as the result of failed communication rather than ideological confrontation.[16]

This pop-philosophy approach to new technology fit perfectly into 1960s educational reformism. In an atmosphere of desegregation, urban renewal, and other liberal initiatives, efforts were made to eliminate the biases inherent in standard pedagogies. As a means of deemphasizing differences of race, gender, and class, theories of educational formalism were introduced into many schools to stress the structure of learning over culturally specific content. As John Culkin put it in 1970, "one doesn't have to know all about a subject, but one should know what a subject is all about."[17] Educators saw photographic media as tools for directly engaging student experience. They developed concepts of "visual literacy" to compete with what some viewed as oppressive print-oriented paradigms.[18] In the introduction to their 1971 book *Need Johnny Read?* Linda Burnett and Frederick Goldman explained that many students "demonstrate a lack of proficiency and lack of interest in reading and writing. Can we really expect proficiency when interest is absent? To what purpose do we force students through traditional subjects in traditional curricula?"[19] Within this movement, many teachers adapted photography and video equipment to their purposes.

With the economic downturns of the 1980s and the ascendancy of the Reagan government came sweeping indictments of liberal programs. Supply-side analysts blamed schools for the nation's inability to compete in world markets, while ironically arguing for reductions in federal education and cultural budgets. Because they often required expensive equipment, media programs were terminated in the name of cost reduction, as renewed emphasis was placed on a "back to basics" curriculum. This did not mean that television disappeared from the classroom, only that its more complicated, hands-on, applications were replaced by simple viewing.

The reemergence of the television as teacher in the 1980s paralleled distinct shifts in production and distribution. These were outgrowths of large-scale changes in the film and television industry brought about by the emergence of affordable consumer video cassette equipment. For the viewer, home recording and tape rental allowed hitherto unknown control over what was watched. The same was true in the classroom. For the instructional media industry, the costly process of copying 16mm films was quickly supplanted by inexpensive high-speed video duplication. The entire concept of educational media products began to change, as films could be mass produced (in effect "published") like books. Market expansion in this type of video was exponential. So profound was the technological change that 16mm processing labs from coast to coast went out of business overnight. This created severe difficulties for artists who preferred the visual qualities of film. As a consequence, a new type of highly specialized processing lab emerged to fill these needs, as 16mm viewing became an "aesthetic" issue and thus the province of the museum.

In many respects, the real beneficiaries of this video proliferation are viewers, along with the profiteering business interests who serve them. Beyond making available a wide variety of materials—from Hollywood movies to aerobics tapes—the VCR revolution has afforded viewers an unprecedented degree of autonomy. With the options of time shifting, editing, and even producing videotapes, the average television user has become significantly more involved in TV culture. The creative potentials of orchestrating video within family life, building tape collections, documenting important programs or personal activities are all active gestures of cultural production. They are practices that artists and teachers can encourage as means of promoting citizen agency and voice.

There is also a negative side to the VCR boom, particularly in the classroom. Beyond obvious arguments that pit time efficiency against human interaction lie the more subtle issues of subjective address. The vast majority of educational films position students in submissive roles, as passive receivers of information, while at the same time validating an intellectual process based on stereotyping. This approach is typified in the flood of slickly produced and moralistic videos for the school market from such entities as the Children's Defense Fund, the Center for Humanities, and Guidance Associates, among others. These latter organizations offer an enormous range (the current Guidance Associates catalog lists over 500 filmstrips, slide series, and tapes) on topics from drug abuse to "values clarification," all stressing a prescriptive and conservative ideology.

A common topic is youth sexuality. Lorraine Kenny has detailed the efforts of educational media producers to construct a normative subjectivity for young women based on fear and coercion.[20] In one of the most insidious examples, the Children's Defense Fund evokes the dual specters of teen pregnancy and HIV contagion as consequences of sexual transgression. In such materials both adolescent sexuality and homosexuality are equated (metaphorically or literally) with illness, humiliation, crime, poverty, or death—as in this excerpt from a Children's Defense Fund report: "Teen pregnancy affects everybody's family, community, neighborhood, and region. Like the prospect of nuclear war, illegal drugs, and Acquired Immune Deficiency Syndrome (AIDS) and other sexually transmitte: diseases, teen pregnancy is becoming an equal opportunity threat."[21] As Kenny asserts, "given that AIDS and teen pregnancy are seen to result from amoral sexual practices, i.e. homosexuality and sex between 'children,' in both cases legally unmarried partners, it is perhaps not surprising that public response to each issue falls within a similar domain."[22] Both are referenced in terms of "epidemics" or "crises" that threaten personal well-being and the social totality. Clearly, such media materials do more than simply teach students about the consequences of unprotected sex. They constitute elements of a broader mechanism of social control in which young people are socialized into specific belief systems and institutionalized behaviors. In the 1980s the use of such instructional aids increased dramatically, as video was seized upon as a means to increase teacher productivity. Witness the phenomenon of Channel One. Since going on line in 1990, the Whittle Communication Corporation's Channel One has been piping its MTV style blend of news programming and commercials for corn chips and acne medicine into 8,600 secondary schools. In exchange for up to $50,000 in free video equipment, schools agree to present the 15-minute programs to their students. As explained by company president Chris Whittle, normally "you can't make people who don't watch television watch television."[23] In school you can.

In recent years a number of grass-roots groups have worked to produce alternative teaching aids. Countering the influx of conservative industrial material are such classroom programming services as the Media Network (New York, NY) and the Video Data Bank (Chicago, IL), the role model project organized by Women Make Movies (New York, NY), the media for the handicapped project of Film in the Cities (St. Paul, MN), and the juvenile court school program of the Masada Community Day Center (Los Angeles, CA)—to name but a few. The Media Network's *Images of Color* directory and the Video Data Bank's "What Does She Want?" series take different approaches to placing noncommercial work in an educational marketplace overwhelmed by corporate production. *Images of Color* is a published reference guide of productions and distributors from and for the Asian, black, Latino, and Native American communities. Films and tapes by makers like Ayoka Chenzira, Lourdes Portillo, and Luis Valdez are listed according to such categories as civil rights, health, housing, immigration, and work. "What Does She Want?" is a series of feminist video works assembled into packages addressing themes of history, the family, and media representation.[24]

A recent pilot program organized by Women Make Movies brought filmmakers Christine Choy, Jacqueline Shearer, Sharon Sopher, and Peggy Stern into contact with students at Manhattan's Muse School. Muse is part of the Pompeii Youth Program, an off-site education service of the New York City Board of Education, which works with long-term truants and dropouts. The project sought to foster a nonsexist media curriculum by introducing participants to both filmmakers and their films. By doing so, it furnished positive role models of women, including those engaged in nontraditional occupations and from different racial and ethnic backgrounds. As the screening series progressed, Women Make Movies instructors overcame the resistance with which students often greet liberal pedagogy. Project coordinator Margaret Cooper explained, for example, that in the prescreening discussion of Sopher's *Witness to Apartheid* (1986), the class doubted the ability of a white filmmaker to adequately analyze South African race relations.[25] Yet after seeing the film and discussing the issues with Sopher, the group was sufficiently moved to draft a series of letters to President Reagan. Obviously these latter programs brush against the grain of both conservative ideology and bureaucratic organization—and as such they are anomalies. At the same time such programs provide models through which the promise of progressive pedagogy is kept alive.

Clearly, the importance of audiovisual materials will continue to grow in school, in the workplace, and at home with the proliferation of videocassette equipment, added cable channels, home shopping networks, computer information services, telecommunications linkups, and interactive texts and games. We should not delude ourselves that these new technologies by themselves have the capability of changing social relationships or economic structures. As quickly as a new gimmick is developed, Madison Avenue finds a way to turn a profit from it. Yet these new tools offer potential for innovative use and subversion, for the establishment of new forms of alliance, and for the creation of new strains of cultural production.

AUDIENCE AND RECEPTION

Much of the above discussion has stressed the autonomy of texts and the struggles being fought to replace regressive narratives with progressive ones. However, one also needs to consider the role of the audience and the independence with which viewers can interpret particular television shows or advertisements. Within debates for the preservation of diverse heritage it is important to stress that culture is not only something fashioned by famous people of the past. It is also "ordinary."[26] Culture is a sociological substance produced every day by each of us. As explained by Howard Becker, our cultural negotiations with people and objects are constantly changing.

Even in the simplest societies, no two people learn quite the same cultural material; the chance encounters of daily life provide sufficient variation to ensure that. No set of cultural understandings, then, provides a perfectly applicable solution to any problem people have to solve in the course of their day, and they must therefore remake those solutions, adapt their understandings to the new situation in the light of what is different about it. Even the most conscious and determined effort to keep things as they are would necessarily involve strenuous efforts to remake and reinforce understandings so as to keep them intact in

the face of what was changing. . . . So culture is always being made,
changing more or less, acting as a point of reference for people engaged
in interaction.[27]

This is especially true with texts, and it is what makes a static view of cultural
value problematic. Our narrative relationships are constantly in flux—both those
we find in books and the diverse narratives we encounter in such items as movies,
television, clothing, appliances, food, and housing. Our understandings of many
of these texts are, as Becker stated, always partial and incomplete, always in
need of some revision to adapt them to change and circumstance. As people
continue to adjust and adapt our interpretations, they are making the meaning
that is culture.

. Because so much of subjectivity is shaped through the media, the effects
of communications industries have become the object of intense intellectual
scrutiny. In part an outgrowth of cultural studies, the new media studies
movement (as opposed to its older "market research" counterpart) is an amalgam
of reader response and resistance theories. While acknowledging the persuasive
properties of images, practitioners of the new "media literacy" movement assert
that viewers use media in exceedingly individualized ways. Moreover, because
moviegoers and television watchers can recognize the artifice of representation
they need not always be fooled by it. They can recognize what Roland Barthes
termed the "mythic" textual power used by advertisers and politicians:

> [It] abolishes the complexity of human acts, it gives them the sim-
> plicity of essences, it does away with all dialectics, with any going
> back beyond what is immediately visible, it organizes a world which
> is without contradictions because it is without depth, a world wide
> open and wallowing in the evident, it establishes a blissful clarity:
> things appear to mean something by themselves.[28]

The media literacy movement holds significance for cultural workers in the
ways it seeks to connect theory and practice—often by attempting to literally
explain (or demonstrate) complex theories to young people. By doing this it
diplomatically reconciles opposing concepts of the viewing subject. Media
literacy refuses to blame media, as postmodernism does, for warping our
collective psyche, but refrains from letting the world of imagery completely
off the hook. While explicating the constructed character of representation,
important acknowledgments of human agency are also made.

On a basic level, the movement argues that our abilities to resist media can
be improved with study and that these skills can be taught to children regardless
of age or grade level. One can teach kids to use the media for their own ends
by actively interpreting how it functions and by choosing how to read it. Put
another way, the movement proposes to begin identifying strategies for contextual
reading, thereby suggesting changes to the "institutional structures" that condition

spoken and interpretive norms.[29] This is done by encouraging children to look beyond specific texts by asking critical questions like "Who is communicating and why?" "How is it produced?" "Who receives it and what sense do they make of it?" A characteristic exercise might ask kids to explain what TV programs they like and dislike. In the course of the discussion the class quickly divides into groups of Voltrons, Noozles, and Smurfs. What becomes apparent is the relatively simple, yet important, notion that media texts are not uniformly received. By examining their own preferences children come to recognize that mass media do not define a unified mass audience, but a heterogenous universe of spectator groups. From this a discussion can evolve on the ways advertisers and media producers tailor their programming based on media use.

In a class conducted by the San Francisco–based group Strategies for Media Literacy, students compare pictures of their own families with ones they find on TV.[30] By making visual comparisons between the Huxtables, the Keatons, and themselves, kids are asked to ponder "which is real?" Of course the answer is none, because depictions—private and public—are fictional. Through this exercise youngsters begin to learn not only how they are indoctrinated by the forces of corporate mythmaking, but also the ways they have internalized received narratives of family. By drawing attention to their own attitudinal biases and stereotypes the lesson underscores the relationship of self to image. In doing so it introduces young children to a set of concepts about the ideological unconscious that many adults have trouble grasping. Because youngsters occupy an early stage of ego development, they can face this notion of an unstable self without the anxieties of their older counterparts.[31] Young children have not developed the same investment in personal identity as teenagers have.

On the other hand, older students can accommodate a broader range of topics— from discipline-oriented inquiry and values education to cross-media studies and critical thinking. Through technical, linguistic, and sociological discussions one can convey the ways corporate interests construct reality through media, as well as the audience's role in creating these meanings. Although the United States has been slow to address these issues, our neighbors to the north have not. This is partly a function of the extent to which Canada is inundated by U.S. media and commerce. The Canadian Ministry of Education workbook *The Media Literacy Resource Guide* characterizes reception in the following manner:

> Basic to an understanding of media is an awareness of how people interact with media texts. When we look at a media text, each of us finds meaning through a wide variety of factors: personal needs and anxieties, the pleasures and troubles of the day, racial and sexual attitudes, family and cultural background. All of these have a bearing on how we process information. For example, the way in which two students respond to a television situation comedy (sitcom) depends on what each brings to the text. In short, each of us finds or "negotiates" meaning in different ways.[32]

Media Literacy's approach is typified in its chapter on photography. The section opens with a formal analysis of photographic framing, focus, lighting, and depth of field—and then moves to more contextual issues of sequencing, collage, page design, and captioning. Classroom activities link personal, public, theoretical, and practical concerns, with exercises that include the use of a pinhole camera, a discussion of family snapshot rituals, an analysis of magazine design, and a critique of a local gallery exhibition. Photography is shown to be not merely a "medium," but a set of social transactions.

In practice such lessons can often be quite explicit in discussing the ideological implications of commercial (and noncommercial) media practices, even going so far as to point out the ways that Hollywood obscures its ideological messages to hide its political intent. Cultural workers can use media to describe the way values are conveyed both directly in the specific contents of works and indirectly through the "structured absences" that systematically exclude certain viewpoints.

Unfortunately such activism hardly characterizes media literacy as practiced within most of today's schools. In large part this political ambivalence is attributable to the relative intransigence of North American educational markets and to the low status of media studies within school districts. In such a conservative environment would-be media educators can hardly afford to do much boat rocking. As a discourse largely devoted to popular culture, media studies is often dismissed by school officials as an educational frill. Such courses are vehemently opposed by conservative "back to basics" advocates, who claim that they undermine traditional culture and values. (The difficulty, of course, is that the popular appeal of mass cultural texts comes largely from their antieducational character.) Also, it hardly goes unnoticed that media courses are by definition student-centered and subversive in their critiques of capitalism and patriarchy. The result is a form of institutional control that limits the extent to which criticism can be raised or even discussed.

GOVERNMENT AND CULTURAL EDUCATION

Judging from their sudden notoriety one might think the National Endowments for the Arts and Humanities were recent inventions—or recent political discoveries. Yet to diehard conservatives the endowments have long been objects of terrific scorn. This is in part due to conservative suspicions about leftist ideology lingering in the practices of these agencies. On another level such views stem from legislative pressures to maintain pragmatic rationales for cultural spending, ones that would translate (at least theoretically) into economic gains for the nation: a more perceptive citizen, a more productive worker, a more discriminating consumer. These attitudes provide an important context within which to discuss the more widely publicized controversies of recent years over obscenity. Indeed, setting the stage for these attacks was a decade of behind-the-scenes legislative maneuvering. For the most part such efforts became manifest in criticisms of particular projects that appeared shocking or odd when decontextualized. Not surprisingly, such assaults have come from conservative members of Congress, a group that has historically opposed the idea of government support for culture.

With the ascent of the Reagan government came an intensification of conservative rhetoric, as evidenced in a 1982 issue of the Heritage Foundation's *Policy Review*. An article entitled "The National Endowment for Pornography" cited what it deemed "the gross vulgarity, obscenity, viciousness, fierce antireligious sentiments, contempt for democracy, and sheer perversity of writings by recipients of awards from the NEA literature program, and the "cronyism which helps to select the recipients of subsidies."[33] The article then isolated purportedly salacious or anti-American passages from poems by such writers as Diane DiPrima, Amira Bakara, Allen Ginsberg, Ann Waldman, and Peter Orlovsky. Occasionally these charges made their way into more widely read publications like the *Reader's Digest*. One of the more amusing (or disturbing) chapters in this saga came in the form of a savagely xenophobic 1982 article entitled "While You're Up, Get Me a Grant." It opened with the following:

> Interested in "The Romantic Poetry of the Young Karl Marx"? Or "The Folk Rituals of Birth, Marriage, and Death Among Urban Polish-Americans"? Or "The Contributions of the Gay Experience to American Visual Arts"? You should be. Your tax dollars are paying for these—and hundreds of other dubious projects funded by the National Endowment for the Humanities.[34]

With its three-part anticommunist, antiethnic, and antigay platform, the article typifies the ridicule the National Endowment for the Humanities (NEH) suffered for its "dubious" excesses under Carter-appointed chair Joseph Duffey. Essays like this one were but the public face of the program of change to follow. Within the humanities and arts endowments subtle and not-so-subtle efforts were underway by Reagan appointees William Bennett and Frank Hodsoll to sabotage selected proposals. Behind the closed doors of endowment review processes, it was not unusual for politically troublesome projects to receive excessive scrutiny and rejection on technical grounds. Applications that satisfied procedural guidelines might be subjected to repeated reviews by different readers until rejected. Ultimately, because the chairs of the endowments hold the final authority on grant awards (panels function purely as advisory bodies) both Bennett and Hodsoll would also personally veto grants.

Such institutional erosions were symptoms of a broader cultural backlash against liberal advances of the 1960s and 1970s. During those decades the alternative arts movement had grown from a handful of grassroots groups into a network of hundreds of artists' spaces, media centers, performance collectives, and avant-garde musical ensembles that, despite their marginality, symbolically challenged the primacy of the museum and the symphony. At the same time, the popularity of such polemic works as Allan Bloom's *The Closing of the American*

Mind and E. D. Hirsch, Jr.'s, *Cultural Literacy: What Every American Needs to Know* reflected a broad-based recognition of shortcomings in the nation's schools.[35] Unfortunately this also betrayed the public's willingness to accept one-dimensional solutions for complex social problems.

Such attitudes of government policymakers toward cultural texts are well documented in two highly partisan congressional reports drafted late in the Reagan presidency. These analyses of the endowments provided blueprints for the shake-ups that occurred at the end of the 1980s. The NEH's *American Memory: A Report on the Humanities in America's Schools* and its companion volume *Toward Civilization: A Report on Arts Education* from the NEA were prepared to influence congressional reauthorization hearings for the NEH and NEA.[36] Due to the infrequency with which such analyses are conducted (the last federal arts education study was prepared in 1884), they may have a lasting influence on the direction the endowments take.[37]

The reports fall within the larger movement of reactionary conservatism that has characterized the Reagan/Bush governments. Not surprisingly, both works paint dismal pictures of domestic cultural pedagogy, and both prescribe the same simple remedies: a return to traditional values, a standardized curriculum, and strict testing. In this way these reports functioned as blueprints of the cultural groundswell that caught the Left by surprise in 1990. They retain significance because the Right's campaign over texts continues to proceed with similar successes. In what follows I will place these two documents in the context of a range of reformist literature, much of it focusing either on the endowments (as instruments of textual production) and the nation's schools (as sites of textual delivery). I will analyze these works in considerable detail as key indicators of the Right's program—and ultimately of that program's failure to adequately account for the breadth of cultural production rising around it.

In the closing chapter of *American Memory*, then–National Endowment for the Humanities chair Lynne V. Cheney evokes a scene from *Life on the Mississippi*. Mr. Bixby advises the young Sam Clemens, "My boy, you've got to know the shape of the river perfectly. It's all there is to steer by on a very dark night. Everything else is blotted out and gone."[38] For Cheney, the river is a profound metaphor for humanities education, in that it represents the wisdom of received ideas—as she says, a guide for avoiding "the shoals and sandbars on which other civilizations have run aground."[39] In many ways the river story provides an apt figure for the conservative cultural agenda, as well. It is a tale of the way older men pass the reins of culture to their surrogate sons. It is also a vision of a slavishly repeated routine.

American Memory draws heavily on another government study, the 1983 report to then–secretary of education T. H. Bell entitled *A Nation at Risk: The Imperative for Educational Reform*.[40] Although less than informative about the actual causes of the nation's educational ills, *A Nation at Risk* remains remarkably instructive in terms of the ways conservative bureaucrats conceive of knowledge as human capital. In this scheme aggregate test scores become indicators of national wealth and grade point averages the credentials for career entry. Competition and individual achievement are stressed over community values. But more is at stake than the simple commodification of learning. *American Memory* is very direct in this regard:

> World competition is not just about dollars but about ideas. Our students need to know what these ideas are, need to understand our democratic institutions, to know their origins in Western thought, to be familiar with how and why other cultures have evolved differently from our own. They need to read great works of literature, thus confronting questions of good and evil, freedom and responsibility, that have determined the character of people and nations.[41]

There is a whole skein of claims here. Most can be summarized in terms of what Allan Bloom has derisively termed "cultural relativism"—the belief that ethnic and national differences are neutral in value. Like Bloom, Cheney attempts the tricky logical maneuver of establishing a cultural hierarchy for a nation that is itself a hybrid of cultures. Both writers see themselves on a quest for a purely "American" scholarship, but unlike Bloom, Cheney is careful to avoid racial slurs. Only through inference does the reader apprehend which "people and nations" are preferable. Of the dozens of "great thinkers" cited in *American Memory*, more than 85 percent are men from Britain or the United States (and 95 percent of them are dead). The civic rationale is one of majority rule—that a nation defined by cultural multiplicity needs to arrive at a single standard. Otherwise, one runs the risk of incoherence, or what E. D. Hirsch, Jr., has termed the "Babel" effect of ruined communication.[42] This was exactly the sort of thinking that troubled Alexis de Tocqueville when he wrote his 1835 critique of U.S. politics, *Democracy in America*. While acknowledging that one social power may inevitably dominate others, de Tocqueville was concerned about an apparatus that permitted what he termed "the tyranny of the majority." Such a system generates "a power which is physical and moral at the same time; it acts upon the will as well as upon the actions of men, and it represents not only all contest, but all controversy. I know of no country in which there is so little true independence of mind and freedom of discussion as in America."[43] The result, de Tocqueville noted, is a privileging of English-speaking culture over all others.

Beyond its obvious deleterious effects on excluded groups, the trouble with this narrow view is that even its proponents cannot agree about the best of what has been thought or said. Even in the staid pages of the *New York Times*, a recent article reported that "the idea of a literature as a fixed and immutable canon—the Great Books, five-foot shelf—is a historical illusion."[44] In the 1990s, academics of all disciplines and ideologies seem to be challenging the primacy of the Euro-American standard, just as they are disputing traditional definitions of what constitutes literature in the first place. For Roland Barthes, the challenge of education lies in pointing out what falls outside traditional formulations.

"Teaching should be directed toward exploding the literary text as much as possible. The pedagogical problem would be to shake up the notion of the literary text and to make adolescents understand that there is text everywhere," Barthes said.[45]

Other attitudinal changes can be attributed to shifts in the composition of the academic community itself. With the influx of women and people of color has come a reconsideration of such noncanonical forms as storytelling, personal history, and folk traditions. At the same time, the conceptualization of a static canon is being assaulted by those who stress the way meanings change over time. "Literary history (and with that, the historicity of literature) is a fiction," writes Annette Kolodny, explaining that the past is always filtered by the perspectives of a dynamic present.[46] Add to that the influence of competitive ideologies and the faddish nature of the canon becomes even more apparent.

But rather than acknowledging these issues, the conservative government insists on living in the past—manifest in a final desperate effort to enforce the Reagan agenda. This is evident in the continuum of budget reductions, strategic firings, internal restructuring, and smear campaigns that have been deployed (often covertly) against the agencies for the past decade.[47] Following the 1981 replacement of Joseph Duffy with William J. Bennett as NEH chair, the endowment immediately redrew its funding priorities. During the first two years of Bennett's term, progressive projects approved by peer review panels were often vetoed by Bennett and his staff, as grants to women dropped by 37 percent and awards to labor decreased by 100 percent.[48] Ironically this was done in the name of depoliticizing a funding process that was supposedly pandering to specialized constituencies.

"Feminists," "environmentalists," "ethnic minorities"—these constituencies are blamed in *American Memory* for cluttering curricula with their concerns. Of course, what some critics view as clutter, others see as healthy pluralism. Issues of cultural difference are typically explored in social studies classes, and it is just such programs that are anathema to *American Memory*. Cheney delights in deriding courses like "human relations," "values clarification," "communications," and "career planning," claiming that such offerings cheapen schooling by emphasizing the here and now. "We would wish for our children that their decisions are informed, not by the wisdom of the moment, but by the wisdom of the ages," Cheney writes.[49] The impulse is to keep education safely sequestered within the classroom. All references to students' own lives are discouraged.

The biggest problem with this approach lies in the sense of detachment it fosters. Henry A. Giroux and Peter McLaren have discussed how a closed and quantified curriculum discourages student involvement with material. This in turn lessens sensibilities of inquiry and criticality, which can have a long-term effect on attitudes toward civic responsibility. "Within this discourse, democracy loses its dynamic character and is reduced to a set of inherited principles and institutional arrangements that teach students how to adapt rather than to question the basic precepts of society."[50]

Similarly problematic attitudes circulate throughout *Toward Civilization*. "America's cultural literacy is at stake," announced Hodsoll upon the release of the report.[51] "We have found the arts to be in triple jeopardy: they are not viewed as serious; knowledge itself is not viewed as a prime educational objective; and those who determine school curricula do not agree on what art education is."[52] For remedies Hodsoll offers a parallel program of historical study and course standardization, but with a few added twists.

Toward Civilization borrows liberally from ideas developed by the J. Paul Getty Center for Education in the Arts in *Beyond Creating: The Place for Art in America's Schools*, the 1985 book that introduced the concept of discipline-based art education (DBAE).[53] Since its inception in the late 1980s, DBAE has provoked significant controversy in both art and education circles. The stated aim of DBAE is to secure academic credibility for the arts within the nation's schools by attaching art to four fundamental "disciplines:" art production, art history, art criticism, and aesthetics. As explained by Eliot Eisner, DBAE "ought to engage youngsters in the making of art, it ought to help them learn how to see visual qualities in both art and the environment, it ought to help them understand something about the relationship of art to culture over time, and it ought to engage them in conversations about the nature of art itself."[54]

These objectives have been implemented through a variety of strategies to quantify and measure the curriculum that, along with DBAE's emphasis on art as a "cognitive" endeavor, have made progressive educators quite nervous. Indeed, most of the debates over DBAE have resulted from fears that the program would somehow deaden the creative impulses of young people or that DBAE would enforce a particular brand of culture. However, as Eisner is quick to point out, DBAE was originally designed more as a structural model than a content-specific prescription.

Nevertheless, the problem that most DBAE advocates fail to adequately acknowledge is the extent to which the program is influenced by the politics of the curricular environments in which it is deployed. As in the case of *Toward Civilization*, the ideas of DBAE come wrapped in issues of cultural elitism, ethnocentrism, and testability. Perhaps most disturbingly, the plans inherently devalue the everyday cultural production of young people by limiting notions of creativity to the sphere of "art."[55] Within this scheme, the worlds of work and leisure are discredited as inherently artless, as are other areas of academic inquiry. There can be no joy or spiritual fulfillment in such areas as science, mechanics, or sports. This program becomes particularly disturbing when endorsed in a government publication.

At the same time, both the Getty and the NEA plans emphasize the production of audiences over the production of objects, a position consonant with the Reagan administration's repeated efforts to dismantle programs of federal support to artists. Throughout the 1980s, government advisors led by NEA council member Samuel Lipman urged the agency to leave the fortunes of painters to the laws of supply and demand. It is worth noting that *Toward Civilization* identifies only two of its 29 advisory-committee members as practicing artists. Like the group that brainstormed in preparation of *American Memory*, the NEA contingent was composed of a distinguished-sounding assortment of academic deans, college presidents, and school administrators.

Like the Getty report, *Toward Civilization* asserts that artistic study should entail more than mere practice for it to have scholastic merit. The study recommends sequential K-12 art instruction within the broader contexts of criticism and history. Most educators recognize the importance of critical viewing skills, because, after all, an informed citizenry needs to be able to decode the manipulative language of advertising and news (not to mention political campaigning). Hodsoll echoes the free-market appeal of this when he writes that art education can provide consumers "with the tools to make better choices and even to influence the marketplace of products and ideas."[56] The report goes even further in suggesting a heightened emphasis on media studies.

Unfortunately, these admirable goals eventually conflict with the report's overriding concern for high culture. *Toward Civilization* took its second cue from former secretary Bennett's *James Madison High School: A Curriculum for American Students*, a work that is not afraid to name names like Chaucer, Shakespeare, and Donne. To "put flesh on the bones" of his basic curriculum, Bennett recommends the following mandatory art course: "An analytic study of representative masterpieces from key periods in the history of Western Art, including classical Greece and Rome, Gothic architecture, the Renaissance, and the Baroque, Neoclassic, Romantic, Realist, Impressionist, Postimpressionist, and Modern periods."[57] Although *James Madison High School* received considerable criticism for its Anglo-European solipsism, the NEA embraced the book on the basis of the above citation. In one chapter Bennett acknowledges that "pluralism has always posed formidable challenges in our schools," yet, in the final analysis, he clings to the imperative of cultural absolutism.[58] "Responding to the needs and differences of individual students is a necessary but not necessarily sufficient mission for American education," Bennett writes, adding, "We've documented the remarkable academic success of poor, disadvantaged, and minority children who, when given the chance at solid education, take it— and learn. The fact is that though there may now be too many schools that fail to teach well, there is rarely anything "unteachable" about most of our students."[59]

Statistically speaking, the "solid education" articulated in *Toward Civilization* means 88 percent male, 96 percent white, and 99 percent U.S. or European. Advocates of this standardized curriculum argue that in addition to making the arts more academically viable, the program will provide more equity. Such mandatory art history courses would extend culture beyond the domain of the privileged. Of course, this also means force-feeding privileged-class values to everyone. It erroneously assumes that the same materials, pedagogies, and methods of evaluation are appropriate for all students, regardless of their varying interests, histories, languages, and skills.

As evidence of the national decline in cultural literacy, *Toward Civilization* points out (without apparent irony) that "less than half of 17-year-old high school students could identify Rembrandt's *Night Watch* as the work in comparison to three ordinary works."[60] To obviate such occurrences, the report suggests uniform standards for art appreciation. The rationale comes from the U.S. Department of Education publication *The Nation's Report Card*, prepared for Secretary Bennett—a document in which the redesign of standardized tests is recommended as a means of curriculum manipulation. "What is assessed tends to become what the community values," the report states.[61] But what community is this? The NEA program's emphasis on historical masterworks discourages students from seeing themselves in artworks or artworks in themselves. For this reason it is constantly fighting an uphill battle of imposing a world view that seems dated and irrelevant. Such a program will be forever looking for explanations of why it is "unteachable."

CENSORSHIP AND FREE SPEECH

Just as one's ability to read texts has a political value, so does the ability to produce them—in both a figurative and literal sense. Whether discussing culture generated in the act of interpretation, or culture negotiated in daily events, or the stories and images made as cultural objects, it is important to recognize that these are not artifacts that come from elsewhere. Culture is something that citizens shape just as it shapes them.

Regrettably the subject/object relationships that divide society into amateur and professionals, teachers and students, artists and audiences, "stars" and "ordinary" folks mitigate against this nonhierarchical form of culture. As a result it also often interferes with clear understandings of political circumstances. Recent controversies over artistic censorship are an excellent example of this phenomenon. Of course, the overt repression of intellectuals and journalists generally associated with censorship has largely disappeared in Western democracies. Besides its association with fascism and communism, such regulation of communication is extremely difficult to enforce in an age of cellular phones, desktop publishing, and junk FAX. Moreover, the continuing renewal of our free-market economy requires the illusion of unmediated free choice—in both the grocery store and the voting booth. Even the forms of publicly sanctioned censorship that we permit for the maintenance of social compacts—copyright and libel laws, for instance—are never acknowledged as such. Conservatives never use the word censorship, but prefer instead such terms as "public accountability" or "standards of decency."

Hence, in weighing in against the NEA during the 1990 congressional debate, editorial writers at the *Washington Times* hyperbolized issues of spending:

> If artists are going to pig out at the public trough, they have to expect
> that tax payers who pick up the tab for their swill might want to keep

an eye on what artists give in return. If it's as offensive as what Mr. Mapplethorpe and Mr. Serrano excrete . . . people who appreciate real beauty are entitled to flush the products of their imaginations down the nearest drainpipe.[62]

This recoding of censorship has diverted attention from its commonplace forms. The Right's all-American "democratic" fantasy has blinded much of the public to institutional censorship (which is practiced by bosses, teachers, and curators), economic censorship (which determines what gets made and who can afford to have it); domestic censorship (which stifles communication in the home); and discriminatory censorship (which denies voice to particular groups). These dynamics favor certain people and ideas over others by determining not merely what can be said to whom, but also what kind of questions can be asked and through what structures discourse can evolve. As a result, those traditionally excluded from the mainstream art world—women, minorities, lesbians and gay men—become further marginalized by campaigns that seek expressive freedom only to sustain business as usual. The racial implications of this are well characterized by Howardina Pindell:

> In the reams of articles, books, editorials, and programs I have studied concerning censorship in the visual arts, there is a glaring omission from the discourse: examination of the ongoing practice of censoring out artists of color except for the occasional, reluctantly included tokens. This seems to demonstrate a wariness and fear of uncovering and exposing something secret, a shunned topic—namely racism, as it reproduces and maintains itself as a potent force in the art world. When the topic has been introduced, it has been dismissed and labelled as potentially disruptive, accused of causing harm to the overall discussion of the issue of censoring by diverting attention to something considered divisive.[63]

Because this type of textual repression is so widespread, leftist cultural workers can no longer restrict their strategies to arguments for free speech. Avant-gardists often rationalize flamboyant or oppositional acts as part of their right to free expression. Artists create dramatic works or make brave speeches—to each other—as though these acts might actually dismantle the powerful social structures that hold censorship in place. If as much time were spent on congressional letter-writing campaigns and public outreach as is spent on kneejerk iconoclasm, the arts community might be able to garner the popular support it seeks.

All too often artists and writers conflate censorship with a romantic attachment to artistic genius, stylistic originality, and the sanctity of individual voice. These are, coincidentally, the same qualities by which the market enforces divisive hierarchies that allow a handful of cultural producers to dominate distribution, publication, and exhibition, thus denying access to others. These competitive values encourage artists and writers to fight each other for grants and audiences, while promoting a top-down view of culture in which well-educated artists from privileged families produce high culture for an equally well-educated and privileged audience. Everyone else is excluded.

Ironically, by fetishizing and objectifying famous incidents of censorship, cultural workers are often contributing to the problem. Although celebrity confrontations hold genuine value as symbols of collective determination, and need to be fought fiercely, one should bear in mind that they are rarely fought on behalf of ordinary people. For this reason one should be extremely cautious about one's position within the discourse of censorship. By focusing exclusively on punitive actions like those meted out to Andres Serrano, Mel Chin, Holly Hughes, and Karen Finley, activists become tricked into a one-dimensional argument the terms of which have been framed by their opponents. Thus artists permit themselves to debate issues of expression in arguments debased to the level of pornography and blasphemy. By entering this discourse they validate the legitimacy of the conservative frame, if not the claims it makes.

As recent circumstances have demonstrated, the effects of censorship do not stop with a specific act, but rather create a chain reaction of secondary repressions and resistances. The polarizing effect of these reactions has the unfortunate consequence of amplifying oppositions between contesting interests, generally to the benefit of the more powerful party. In reaction to the labeling of art as porn, artists make porn and label it art. Those excluded from a major exhibition organize a *refusés* exhibit that denies access to those in the major show. As important as it is to react in this way, cultural workers need to formulate alternative strategies. Otherwise they will be promoting a victim mentality in which they are perpetually cast as disenfranchised and subordinate.

Throughout history artists have used their work to give form to the ineffable, to speak of ideas and emotions otherwise difficult to articulate. In this spirit, cultural producers can continue to make the invisible visible by conceiving ways to expose hidden mechanisms of censorship, to see beneath the veil of corporate image production and government propaganda. This is a mission of critical pedagogy, a job of questioning the social arrangements we find ourselves a part of. As we encourage one another in such patterns of resistance, we begin to cultivate collective participation in government, a counter-hegemonic imaginary of genuine democracy in which all groups truly are free to speak.

Obviously it will take more than the recognition of repression to bring this about. Cultural activists will need to devise strategies to organize and build coalitions. On a discursive level this may involve establishing institutions and publications for the construction of a new political subject. On a textual level this will mean reclaiming the many symbols that have been falsely claimed by the Right. If deconstruction has demonstrated anything, it is that the meanings of cultural signs are variable, contingent on context and interpretation. Why has the Right been permitted to define the meaning of such concepts as the family, religion, and the flag—indeed of the human body? As Andres Serrano said, "I thought the symbol of the crucifix belonged to everyone, but it seems that some people think they own it."[64]

Cultural workers must answer this censorship of meaning by recognizing that censorship inheres in our everyday language. The task then is more than a simple response to a set of actions as defined within the agenda of the Right. It involves a reclamation of the vocabulary through which our struggle is expressed. It means redefining the iconography of freedom and oppression. It means forging alliances by expressing the message in a clear and accessible fashion. For if the Left can build a broad-based social movement from our common estrangement from power, it can banish censorship from its midst and dispel the internalized oppression that it carries inside itself. This is done through groups and actions like Paper Tiger Television, Take Back the Night, Greenpeace, Art Against Apartheid, the NAMES project—acts of active cultural writing. Such work gives people a tool far more powerful than a useful lesson for a particular book or film. It says that they have the authority (if they so choose) to challenge even the most regressive texts, to construct new meanings from such texts, to make their own texts from the ruins of old ones.

Such subversive writing provides the strategic underpinning for the collaborations of Tim Rollins + KOS (Kids of Survival). Rollins, a cofounder of New York's Collaborative Projects collective and former special education teacher at Bronx Intermediate School 52, works with 12-to-18-year-olds in KOS through an organization he developed called the Art and Knowledge Workshop. The paintings that Rollins + KOS produce often pivot on a heretic interpretation of a canonical literary work. Books like Herman Melville's *Moby Dick* or Nathaniel Hawthorne's *Scarlet Letter* are disassembled, and their pages are rearranged in grids and then marked upon by the group.

In *The Scarlet Letter* (1987–88), 220 pages of the book are affixed to a 9-by-12-foot canvas, over which eight individually styled versions of the letter *A* have been inscribed. The piece came about through a discussion relating *The Scarlet Letter*'s themes of social stigmatization to the exclusion felt by KOS students from mainstream white culture. In the manner of Hester Prynne, the book's protagonist, KOS collaborators fashioned personalized letters to project their own identities upon the text. As Rollins explained the process, "the pages became a kind of curtain of history upon which we re-wrote and re-read literature with our imaginary."[65]

In this instance students took what might otherwise be simply another culturally alien text of traditional literature and appropriated elements that could be recoded in terms appropriate to their own lives. Of course, this sort of double reading of dominant cultural texts is nothing new to people traditionally excluded from them. Those who find themselves outside the realm of conventional white heterosexual discourse have frequently found ways of subversively reinscribing themselves in such texts though means of displacement. What makes Rollins's practice radical is the foregrounding of the process. In this way Rollins and his student collaborators produce cultural artifacts that critique their surrounding ideologies by drawing attention to them.

On an even broader level it remains of crucial importance to introduce into the classroom voices and texts traditionally excluded. This means reconsidering the body of material previously excluded from "legitimate" academic discourse. These range from the specific subcultural articulations often regarded as too eccentric for inclusion in the common culture to mass media products generally thought of as simple or superficial. In either case, of course, these "illegitimate" narrative forms bear important affinities to students' lived experiences. This is not to suggest that these new discourses should be entered into the curriculum without critical analysis. But it does mean integrating them on an equal footing with canonical texts, and so admitting a variety of voices.

An example of this type of classroom practice is found in the video programs conducted by Rise and Shine Productions, a five-year-old collective that contracts for special services with Manhattan-area school districts. *Canciones del General* (1989) was produced by Dominican students in an 11th-grade English-as-a-second-language class at Manhattan's Martin Luther King High School. The tape presents the history of U.S. commercial and military involvement in Central America, including the role of the United States in supporting the country's dictator Rafael Leonidas Trujillo, who ruthlessly governed the Dominican Republic until the early 1960s. In recounting events of the last 25 years, students assembled archival film footage and audio recordings of the era.

Not only does the tape deal with a topic of cultural interest to class members but it incorporates the personal testimony of friends and relatives who survived the period. For some it provides an opportunity to personally revise "official" historical narratives. As one parent explains in the tape, "You have to understand that there are many myths about Trujillo. If you see a soldier go from lieutenant to general it usually takes his whole life. Trujillo in ten years goes from a second lieutenant to a brigadier general. In the 1930s Trujillo declared elections and, of course, you know who became president—by millions of votes." By focusing on familiar cultural experiences, *Canciones del General* draws upon the students' own literacies to encourage the study of English. Class members practice reading and writing skills while learning that their own perceptions are legitimate objects of articulation and study. Not only do such exercises admit alternative readings of history to those addressed in schoolbooks, but in this case the narrative of colonization and decolonization holds particular relevance as a lesson about collective resistance to government oppression.

Such exercises make the classroom a political microcosm in which student subjectivity is temporarily altered to open a fissure in the otherwise seamless environment of hegemonic interpellation. By encouraging young people to criticize normative narratives and write their own texts, we take the first step in integrating such practices into their social habits. These exercises can begin the process of reversing alienation and ambivalence, not only toward books and media, but to the entire range of received subjectivity that young people (and all of us) confront. Cultural pedagogy therefore is but a figure for the broader world text. Through one, young people can gain access to the other.

Ultimately our task lies in demonstrating that culture and pedagogy are but two sides of the same coin. This is education as the production of values and identities, rather than as the passive receipt of knowledge. It is a view of learning that is integrally linked to "writing" of cultural meaning. It is a celebration of the human capacity for inventing the continual recreation of society.

NOTES

1. See Paul Mattick, Jr., "Art and the State: The NEA Debate in Perspective," *Nation* 251, no. 10 (Oct. 1, 1990): 354.

2. Barbara Bush, as quoted in Eden Ross Lipson, "Reading Along with Barbara Bush: The Endings Are Mostly Happy," *New York Times Book Review*, May 21, 1989, p. 36.

3. Ibid., p. 36.

4. Branda Miller, *Talkin 'Bout Droppin' Out* (Boston: Boston School District, 1988, videotape).

5. Bill Ashcroft, Gareth Griffiths, and Helen Tiffin, eds., *The Empire Writes Back: Theory and Practice in Post-Colonial Literatures* (New York: Routledge, 1989), p. 3.

6. Diane Ravitch as quoted in Dexter Waugh, "History Textbook Feud Splits on Racial Lines," *San Francisco Examiner*, Aug. 30, 1990, p. A-10.

7. In their introduction to "Multicultural Literacy," Rick Simonson and Scott Walker put the cultural program of the Right in an international context: "The twentieth century revolution in communications, the rise and pervasiveness of mass media, and dramatic changes in the world economy have led to a softening of political and cultural boundaries. As the world is 'made smaller' and culture becomes more uniform (imperialism taking on cultural as well as political forms), we are simultaneously brought closer together and suffer the destruction of individual languages, imagination, and cultural meaning. As we learn more about ecology and of ways to preserve nature, we should also learn the great value of diversity and seek to preserve a diverse cultural heritage." See Rick Simonson and Scott Walker, "Multicultural Literacy: The Opening of the American Mind," *Graywolf Annual* 5 (1988): xi.

8. This error of technological determinism is most eloquently made in the much celebrated essay by Walter Benjamin, "The Work of Art in the Age of Mechanical Reproduction," in *Illuminations*, trans. Harry Zohn (New York: Schocken Books, 1969), pp. 217–51.

9. Ben J. Bagdikian, *The Media Monopoly*, 3d ed. (Boston: Beacon Press, 1990), p. 4.

10. Michael W. Apple, *Teachers and Texts: A Political Economy of Class and Gender Relations in Education* (New York: Routledge, 1989).

11. Ibid., p. 98.

12. Keith Kimberley, "Community Publishing," in *Language, Authority, and Criticism: Readings on the School Textbook*, ed. Suzanne de Castell, Allan Luke, and Carmen Luke (London: Falmer Press, 1989), p. 192.

13. Pam Gilbert, "Student Text as Pedagogical Text," in *Language, Authority, and Criticism*, ed. Castell, Luke, and Luke, p. 196.

14. Robert M. Diamond, "Single Room Television," in *A Guide to Instructional Media*, ed. Robert M. Diamond (New York: McGraw-Hill, 1964), p. 3.

15. John M. Hofstrand, "Television and Classroom Observation," in *A Guide to Instructional Media*, ed. Diamond, p. 149.

16. Marshall McLuhan, *Understanding Media: Extensions of Man* (New York: McGraw-Hill, 1964), p. 23.

17. John M. Culkin, "Films Deliver," in *Films Deliver*, ed. John M. Culkin and Anthony Schillaci (New York: Citation Press, 1970), p. 28.

18. The terms "visual literacy" and "media literacy" have been employed in a variety of differing contexts during the past two decades. The formalist media literacy of the 1970s should not be confused with the critical media literacy movement of the 1980s and 1990s.

19. Linda R. Burnett and Frederick Goldman, *Need Johnny Read? Practical Methods to Enrich Humanities Courses Using Films and Film Studies* (Dayton, OH: Pflaum, 1971), p. xv.

20. Lorraine Kenny, "The Birds and the Bees: Teen Pregnancy and the Media," *Afterimage* 16, no. 1 (Summer 1988): 6–8. More general issues of student interpellation through educational media are systematically addressed in Elizabeth Ellsworth, "Educational Media, Ideology, and the Presentation of Knowledge through Popular Cultural Forms," in *Popular Culture, Schooling and Everyday Life*, ed. Henry A. Giroux and Roger Simon (New York: Bergin and Garvey, 1989), pp. 47–90.

21. Kenny, "The Birds and the Bees," p. 6.

22. Ibid.

23. N. R. Kleinfield, "What Is Chris Whittle Teaching Our Children?" *New York Times Magazine*, May 19, 1991, p. 79.

24. See Nadine McGann, "Consuming Passions: Feminist Video and the Home Market," *Afterimage* 16, no. 1 (Summer 1988): 14–16.

25. Margaret Cooper, "Final Report and Documentation: Arts in Education Project" (unpublished manuscript, Women Make Movies, 1987).

26. This banality of culture is taken up at length in the often quoted Raymond Williams essay, "Culture Is Ordinary," in his *Resources of Hope* (London: Verso, 1989).

27. Howard S. Becker, *Doing Things Together* (Evanston, IL: Northwestern University Press, 1986), p. 19.

28. Roland Barthes, *Mythologies*, trans. Annette Lavers (New York: Hill and Wang, 1972), p. 143.

29. Stanley Fish, *Is There a Text in This Class? The Authority of Interpretive Communities* (Cambridge: Harvard University Press, 1980).

30. Donna Lloyd-Kolkin and Kathleen Tyner, *Media and You: An Elementary Media Literacy Curriculum* (San Francisco: Strategies of Media Literacy, 1991).

31. The problems of explaining the received character of identity to teenagers is taken up in Judith Williamson's "How Does Girl Number Twenty Understand Ideology?" *Screen Education* 40 (Autumn/Winter 1981/82): 80–87.

32. Ontario Ministry of Education, *Media Literacy Resource Guide* (Toronto: Ontario Ministry of Education, 1989).

33. Dinesh D'Sousa, "The National Endowment for Pornography," *Policy Review*, no. 20 (Spring 1982): 147.

34. Joseph A. Harriss, "While You're Up, Get Me A Grant," *Reader's Digest*, June 1981, p. 169.

35. Allan Bloom, *The Closing of the American Mind* (New York: Simon and Schuster, 1987); and E. D. Hirsch, Jr., *Cultural Literacy: What Every American Needs to Know* (Boston: Houghton Mifflin, 1987).

36. Lynne V. Cheney, *American Memory: A Report on the Humanities in the Nation's Schools* (Washington, DC: National Endowment for the Humanities, 1988); and National Endowment for the Arts, (NEA), *Toward Civilization: A Report on Arts Education* (Washington, DC: NEA, 1988).

37. I. E. Clarke, *Art and Industry, Instruction in Drawing Applied to Industrial and Fine Arts* (Washington, DC: U.S. Government Printing Office, 1884).

38. Cheney, *American Memory*, p. 27.

39. Ibid.

40. National Commission on Excellence in Education, *A Nation at Risk: The Imperative for Educational Reform* (Washington, DC: U.S. Government Printing Office, 1983).

41. Cheney, *American Memory*, p. 10.

42. Hirsch, *Cultural Literacy*, p. 2.

43. Alexis De Tocqueville, *Democracy in America* (1835; reprint, New York: Schocken Books, 1961), pp. 309–10.

44. James Atlas, "The Battle of the Books," *New York Times Magazine*, June 5, 1988, p. 26.

45. Roland Barthes, *The Grain of the Voice: Interviews 1962–1980*, trans. Linda Coverdale (New York: Hill and Wang, 1985), p. 149.

46. Annette Kolodny, "Dancing through the Mine Field: Some Observations on the Theory, Practice, and Politics of a Feminist Literary Criticism," *Feminist Review* 6 (Spring 1980): 1–25.

47. Carole S. Vance, "Reagan's Revenge: Restructuring the NEA," *Art in America*, Nov. 1990, pp. 49–55.

48. John S. Friedman and Eric Nadler, "Hard Right Rudder at the NEH," *Nation*, April 14, 1984, p. 448.

49. Cheney, *American Memory*, p. 27.

50. Henry A. Giroux and Peter McLaren, "Teacher Education and the Politics of Engagement: A Case for Democratic Schooling," *Harvard Education Review* 56, no. 3 (August 1986): 220–21.

51. Press release issued in 1988 by the National Endowment for the Arts announcing the publication of *Toward Civilization*.

52. NEA, *Toward Civilization*, p. 19.

53. See Getty Center for Education in the Arts, *Beyond Creating: The Place for Art in America's Schools* (Los Angeles: Getty Center for Education in the Arts, 1985); and Elliot W. Eisner, *The Role of Discipline-Based Art Education in America's Schools* (Los Angeles: Getty Center for Education in the Arts, 1987).

54. Elliot W. Eisner "Discipline-Based Art Education: Conceptions and Misconceptions," *Educational Theory* 40, no. 4 (Fall 1990): 424.

55. Donald Arnstine, "Art, Aesthetics, and the Pitfalls of Discipline-Based Art Education," *Educational Theory* 40, no. 4 (Fall 1990): 412–22.

56. NEA, *Toward Civilization*, p. 18.

57. William J. Bennett, *James Madison High School: A Curriculum for American Students* (Washington: U.S. Dept. of Education, 1988).

58. Ibid., p. 5.

59. Ibid., pp. 5–6.

60. NEA, *Toward Civilization*, p. 125.

61. U.S. Department of Education, *The Nation's Report Card* (Washington, DC: U.S. Government Printing Office, 1987), p. 45.

62. As cited in Richard Bolton, "The Cultural Contradictions of Conservativism," *New Art Examiner* 17, no. 10 (June 1990): 26.

63. Howardina Pindell, "Breaking the Silence," *New Art Examiner* 18, no. 2 (November 1990): 18.

64. Andres Serrano, as quoted in David Levi Strauss, "Chains of Silver (Art and Censorship, 1989)," *San Francisco Arts Commission Publication* 7 (1989).

65. Francine A. Koslow, "Tim Rollins + KOS: The Art of Survival," *Print Collector's Newsletter* 19, no. 4 (Sept.–Oct. 1988): 140.

4

Community and Agency:
The Ties That Bind

Texts and institutions are manifestations of the social arrangements created by communities. To understand the workings of schools, museums, governments, and legislatures it is useful to examine the groupings of people that call these entities into being. This chapter will consider ways communities develop, function, and define themselves—in both positive and negative ways. Discussion will cover entities of transmission (artists, writers, teachers) and reception (audiences, students) and the ways these bodies interact. It will also address our consumer society and the way community identifications are influenced by commodities and the mass media. In today's world we are increasingly linked to each other by patterns of consumption and desire. Clearly these relationships are strongly affected by the subject/object relations discussed earlier, which often stress such factors as professional certification or age—factors that are additionally complicated by sexual and racial bias. The emphasis of this chapter will lie in explicating these relationships, critiquing their implications, and discussing some of the means cultural workers have developed to implement progressive reform within them.

To do this one must first determine exactly who is the public for the new pedagogical cultural worker. Does such a singularly defined audience even exist? Or is this group an amalgam of the many art world constituencies, educational consumers, academic onlookers, teachers, students, and parents who make up the cultural universe? How does one situate one's practice in relation to such a complex constellation of interests? These issues of community and constituency are central to an expanded view of pedagogical culture, for texts and institutions can only function within groupings of people.

But what defines these groupings? In one way or another all civic compacts are defined in relationships between individual and community. Through such arrangements personal interests are balanced with a concern for the common good. Within the United States this relationship of individual to community has evolved in a particularly schizophrenic manner, as notions of success, accumulation, and liberty are conflated with themes of patriotism, philanthropy, and social justice. Indeed, it is argued that in the twentieth century, and particularly within the last decade, there has been a precipitous erosion of communal spirit. The rise of corporate capitalism has equated wealth with virtue in a "trickle-down" vision of civic responsibility. Ronald Reagan's exhortation "Are you better off than you were four years ago?" smacks of self-absorption. Everywhere one is surrounded by institutions that encourage citizens to assume roles of selfish individualism—from television programs valorizing wealth and success to religious tracts promising personal salvation.[1] With a rhetoric of anticommunism, the Right has equated humanitarian concern with liberal weakness. The collapse of economies in Eastern Europe is characterized as a triumph for the American system, a mechanism promising all citizens the opportunity to rise above their neighbors.

How then do alliances form among people? The relationship of individual to community is one of sameness and difference, for communities are identified by both what groups have in common and what sets them apart from other entities. This applies to constituencies defined in gemeinschaft/gesellschaft terms or by functionalist/structuralist analyses.[2] The partial, overlapping, and indeterminate character of certain communities is also important to consider in relation to intersections of race, age, sexual orientation, class position, nationality, occupation, geography, and so on. Just as an individual can belong to many different communities simultaneously and to various degrees, it is equally important to avoid generalizing about communities that have dramatic internal subdivisions. There are no single definitions for feminists, rappers, religious fundamentalists, business executives, or hospital patients—only singular *representations* of these groups.

Because communities tend to function in their own interests they can both bring people together and hold them apart. Affirmative action policies, hiring quotas, and "minority" scholarship programs constitute efforts to change the inequitable patterns of community organization sustained by what Martin Luther King termed "the white power structure." These are exactly the programs that the Right so vigilantly seeks to dismantle in the name of a purportedly "colorless" society. Not so coincidentally, such conservatively scorned programs as the civil rights movement, the peace movement, the women's movement, and the trade union movement all represent collective efforts to undermine the grip of competitive individualism.

Within the conservative ethos community differences are often seen as obstacles to be suppressed in favor of the common culture. So-called special interests are measured against the standard of the social "mainstream." But what are the epistemological grounds on which such notions are constructed? Although the imaginary mainstream purportedly includes a majority of people, it excludes everyone. Rather than functioning as a marker of the civil middle ground, it works as a mechanism for naturalizing social hierarchies. When stripped of its mystifying pretensions, the mainstream can be seen as an abstract representation that at best describes a rather small minority of people. By virtue of this fictional mainstream a diminutive "Eurocracy" has created an illusion of centrality. This illusion is held in place by material relations, to be sure, but also by the acquiescence of those it excludes. Such political ambivalence is largely premised on silence. Instead of encouraging citizen participation and criticism, the concept of the mainstream would suppress all opposition. By ignoring the repressive elements of social conformity, the Right has promoted the idea as a necessity for civic coherence. In this way the xenophobic "cultural literacy" movement is perversely equated with democratic consensus.[3]

During the 1980s, the arts and humanities came under increasing pressure to adopt uniform standards of academic worth. Perhaps the most telling marker of this phenomenon in the art world was the 1982 inauguration by publisher Samuel Lipman and *New York Times* art critic Hilton Kramer of a periodical dedicated to the neoconservative cultural movement. At the time, Kramer wrote that "it is time to apply a new criterion to the discussion of our cultural life— a criterion of truth. This is by no means an easy task. It is in the very nature of democracy, with its multiplicity of interests and tastes, for the task to be difficult."[4] More recently these debates have taken a vicious turn, as the Right has seized the offensive.[5] No longer content to play the role of the defender of conservative values, the Right has moved to eliminate dissenting opinion. It is perhaps a measure of the success of culturally diverse groups, that the forces of hegemony have felt so threatened.

Despite these advances one should recognize that the reified substance called art is produced and consumed by a rather small minority. According to a statistical survey sponsored by the federal government, the audience for visual arts organizations is but 2 to 5 percent of the population in any given locality—a constituency primarily defined as educated, affluent, and white.[6] Is it any wonder then that in the Reagan administration Heritage Foundation transition document, Michael S. Joyce could write that the nation "must finally acknowledge that the enduring audience for art is largely self-selecting, a relatively small public marked by a willingness to make sacrifices of other pleasures for the sake of artistic expression."[7]

Central to the conservative ethos of common culture is an insistence on the fundamental correctness of current social arrangements. This is a political imaginary that represses a recognition of the inequities resulting from an unregulated market economy. In a solipsistic denial of difference it clings to an illusion of social equality and sameness. For obvious reasons, the conservative will to ideological homogeneity has been frustrated by the separateness of diverse constituencies. Individual communities are not simple constructions but formulations of multiple subjectivities that combine and contradict each other. At the same time, no community is a homogeneous entity, but a complex of the many identities of occupation, age, ethnicity, geography, sexual orientation, and gender that it encompasses. Of equal importance is historical location, for group behavior also shifts over time and in different circumstances. This dynamic quality of community ideology is important to bear in mind, for it affords localized resistance to authoritarian interpellation.

But opposition alone is not enough, for all too often dissenting groups frame their arguments in the one-dimensional paradigm of ideological reproduction. As a result, their struggles are structured by the language of their oppressors. Counterpractice is conceived only in relation to the prevailing social order. Locked in the reactionary and often a historical logic of critique, cultural workers fail to formulate a plan of positive action. Worst of all, resistances are generally fragmented according to single issues or particular groups.

Cultural workers need to address the issue of community in two ways: first, by promoting views of community that celebrate difference; second, by critiquing the mechanisms that would elide these differences. This constitutes the distinction between the radical democracy of the Left and the conformist democracy of the Right. To achieve this radical vision, a unified counterpractice is needed that reaches beyond the androcentric realm of binary power relationships. This will entail both theoretical and practical reformulations of the roles of cultural producers and consumers. Pedagogical cultural workers must address the difficult task of developing coalitions in an era in which the Left has become particularly suspicious of normative ethics and universalizing agendas. Doing this will require a recognition of the inherently pedagogical character of cultural work. Activist artists and teachers have a vital role to play in opening a public space where the lessons of participatory democracy can be relearned and its history reexamined. Without such a program of organized citizen empowerment, progressive culture condemns itself to an endless repetition of divisive conflict.

Achieving this level of community activism will mean activating mechanisms of personal agency that encourage people to act politically. This is what tells people that their actions have an impact in the face of governments and corporate bureaucracies. But to accomplish this task one must first examine in more detail the structures that hold such apathy and indifference to political involvement in place. Generally speaking, perhaps the three most damaging impediments to radical democracy are objectification, rationalization, and commodification.[8]

Objectification can be described as the process through which people come to be seen as passive and manipulable objects, rather than active and autonomous subjects. Objectification perpetuates a fatalism that tells people they can do little to alter the course of history of their own lives. This ideology of passive spectatorship is deployed in many forms, including the mass media. Movies, television, magazines, and newspapers suggest that the production of ideas and images is something that is always done by someone else. This message is perhaps most powerfully transmitted through traditional educational practices that stress a distant, immovable body of official knowledge that can only be verified and delivered by a certified teacher. It is the regressive embodiment of the Hegelian master/servant dialectic.

Rationalization is the process often associated with modernism, structuralism, and functionalism that imposes bureaucratic regulation, surveillance, and measurement to human activity for the purpose of increasing efficiency. In this scheme, people submit to a larger structure in the presumed interest of the common good. What often gets lost in the process is any sense of accountability or any ability of the individual or group to challenge the common order. Beyond being told that they cannot make a difference, this thinking implicitly tells citizens that they should not rock the boat, cause trouble, upset the system. It suggests that disagreement is a function of individual anomaly, maladjustment, perversion, inadequacy, lack of will, or genetic defect.

Commodification foregrounds valuation and exchange as elements of objectification and rationalization. It encourages acquisition and consumption as means of personal satisfaction, while on a structural level promoting hierarchies of production and distribution. On a broader scale commodification frustrates community ethos by encouraging competitive acquisition. Debilitating fictions of "making it" and "the good life" are defined in terms of solitary consumption rather than civic concern.

THE ACADEMY

As its own very complicated community, the academy encompasses numerous competing interests and subject positions. The more reified of these are separated from other social functioning by a complex mechanism that defines "disciplines" in the arts and humanities. The modern academy determines the content and form of scholarship and, as a consequence, the structure of its constituencies. Its dual effect is to fragment knowledge while distancing it from practical circumstances. This has obvious implications for the notion of community, for it drains the aesthetic of any practical dimension. In strictly materialist terms, the community an artist addresses is fundamentally a clientele that uses (or purchases) professional expertise. Edward Said has pointed out that as this role is accepted by artists, what they do can become neutralized and nonpolitical. This creates an ethic of specialization that encourages practitioners to minimize the content of their work and increase the "composite wall of guild consciousness, social authority and exclusionary discipline around themselves. Opponents are therefore not people in disagreement with the constituency but people to be kept out, non-experts and non-specialists, for the most part."[9] This exclusion extends to amateurs, students, eccentric practitioners, and anyone without some form of institutional validation.

Meanwhile a similar ranking and sorting function is carried out inside the university. As in other jobs, academics are under pressure to perform and produce. But the university has developed its own peculiar strains of vocational reward and punishment. Exacerbated by the tenure system, higher education has evolved into a mechanism that pits faculty member against faculty member for promotion and other academic favors and promotes an academic marketplace in which senior professors exploit their younger counterparts. Yet, all of these people—from the old fogies to the young Turks—are obliged to sustain a separatist view of knowledge for purposes of self-preservation.

Given the limited number of other options and the professional currency afforded by such arrangements, the vast majority of cultural producers are obliged to enter this arena of certification. Eventually their very careers come to depend on the maintenance of the guild.[10] Obviously, the situation is bound to provoke an identity crisis for individuals at odds with the system. This is the dilemma of progressive culture under capitalism. The most immediate and familiar (some might also argue safe) place to confront these issues is within one's own backyard. Thus for many activists the suggestion of social reform is pitched directly to their own constituency by addressing the "politics of representation." Common to much of this work is the view of art as the cultural arm of a larger apparatus that conveys human relations through distortions. The collector, curator, critic, and professor conspire (often inadvertently) to create false value by rendering art a mythic commodity.

Unfortunately, as important as it is to struggle within the political contexts one knows best, one can easily become deceived about the overall effectiveness of local action. This has become nowhere more apparent than in the arts community's response to recent censorship controversies. Instead of seizing upon these circumstances as opportunities for public education and outreach, many cultural groups have retreated to a domain of self-righteous elitism. Rather than carefully examining the *causes* of public indignation over sexually or religiously difficult works, most cultural workers have clung to a dogged free speech argument.

The simple truth is that most avant-garde expression does indeed ignore the concerns of working people, older people, people of color, people with little education. The ire of southern religious fundamentalists has provoked a vicious backlash among many artists. When Karen Finley wants to evoke a persona of stupidity in her performances, she adopts an Alabama drawl. This does little to integrate art and life, or to promote genuine solidarity between artists and their citizen patrons. Instead it perpetuates an atmosphere of alienation in which art is seen as something that is useless to average people, or as a substance they cannot judge. Interviewed after the famous trial over the Robert Mapplethorpe exhibition at Cincinnati's Contemporary Arts Center, most jurors said they were convinced to acquit the curator by the expert testimony of scholars and critics.[11]

Although this phenomenon worked to the advantage of defense attorneys in Cincinnati, its broader ramifications resulted in permanent damage to the funding structure of the academic arts community. Rev. Donald Wildmon, the religious extremist whose two-million-member American Family Association successfully mounted a national boycott of Martin Scorsese's *The Last Temptation of Christ*, was largely responsible for initiating the 1990 congressional debate over funding for the National Endowment for the Arts. The efforts of Wildmon and others eventually led to a restructuring of the endowment to lessen the role of artists in conferring grants. During the controversies he wrote the following tirade:

> The response (of the NEA) . . . has been that "artists" such as Mapple-thorpe and Serrano are an elite group of people, superior in talent to the working masses, who deserve to be supported by . . . tax dollars . . . imposed on the working people of America. . . . We ask that the Senate stop all funding to the National Endowment for the Arts, or provide equal funding for all other groups of artists—carpenters, brick masons, truck drivers, sales clerks, etc.[12]

Rather than dismissing such statements as rabid extremism, cultural workers need to examine the source of their popular appeal. Only in this way can credible counterarguments be staged. Remarks like Wildmon's can be profoundly misleading, inasmuch as conservatives have stridently opposed all such "entitlements" to the working class. While exalting the cause of the common citizen, conservatives have led campaigns for freezing the minimum wage, breaking unions, and curtailing educational spending, job training, and health care.[13] At the same time, the Right has fought to uphold elite canons of masterworks and standards of aesthetic "quality" (within its own definition of such terms).

In education this system of certification has historically been very strict, purportedly to protect parents and children from the malpractice of the uncre-dentialed. In practical terms, such professional training functions to regulate teachers and adapt them to bureaucratic demands. They become acclimated to core curricula, testing methods, and advancement regimens. It is also worth acknowledging that as a microcosm for a society that places little value on teaching as a profession, the academy views education departments as one of the lowest disciplinary arenas.

ART WORLDS

Rather than a singular entity, the art world is both a constellation of diverse groups (viewers, curators, critics, patrons, gallerists, publicists, administrators, government bureaucrats) and the labyrinthine relationships among them.[14] At the putative center of this universe stand artists, the mythically valorized and materially pauperized assembly-line producers in the aesthetic economy. Of the 1.6 million individuals who identify themselves as practicing artists in the United States, 95 percent hold undergraduate degrees and 59 percent have graduate degrees—as art schools continue to crank out an average of 40,000 graduates per year.[15] Yet only a small percentage of these individuals actually support themselves from art-related work. For every David Salle or Jennifer Bartlett there are scores of younger and older artists who supplement their creative work by teaching or waiting on tables. In Massachusetts, the average artist earned $13,000 in 1989, of which $4,535 derived from artwork itself.[16] In fact, from 1970 to 1980, artists' earnings declined by 37 percent, as opposed to 8 percent for all other technical and professional workers.[17] Despite this discouraging atmosphere, the number of artists continues to grow.

Galleries, auction houses, and private dealers perform the merchandising function for collectors, patrons, and to a certain extent, museums—all of whom share a vested interest in maintaining the real or imagined value of artwork. Commercial galleries, particularly those in major cities like Los Angeles and New York, act purely as marketing sites; their nonprofit counterparts either play an auxiliary promotional role as the "farm league" for younger artists or take a more anticommodity stance. In the latter case, economic necessity demands attention to different forms of currency that help one attain grants, reviews, speaking engagements, jobs, seats on funding panels, residencies, or professional contacts.

Publications and criticism itself collude in this process. As described by Abigail Solomon-Godeau,

> the promotional aspect of most art criticism derives from the larger institutional and discursive structures of art. In this respect, the scholarly monograph, the temporary exhibition, the discipline of art history, and last but not least, the museum itself, are essentially celebratory entities. Further—and at the risk of stating the obvious—the institutions and discourses that collectively function to construct "art" are allied to the material determinations of the marketplace, which themselves establish and confirm the commodity status of the work of art.
>
> Within this system, the art critic normally functions as a kind of intermediary between the delirious pluralism of the marketplace and the sacralized judgment seat that is the museum.[18]

It is not that the cultural community lacks idealism, only that material realities complicate its high-minded motives. The declining economic atmosphere of the 1980s and 1990s has only exacerbated the dilemma. While monetary pressures have increased for all but the affluent, public support for alternative culture has dwindled. As a result, many socially conscious artists have had to reconsider their antimaterialist idealism and take a hard look at the bottom line. Financial necessity has encouraged a view of art as a consumable product rather than a community service, thus undermining broader notions of collectivity that once formed the bedrock of the alternative arts movement. The presumed need for disciplinary specialization and standards of "quality" has widened the gap between "fine" artists and their amateur or commonplace counterparts. This has increased the distance between the avant-garde and broader community art movements defined by such factors as language, occupation, geography, ethnicity, gender, or sexual orientation. It has divorced the making of art and the celebration of local culture from the daily experiences of most people.

In critiquing these mechanisms of commodification and cultural stratification, some artists have sought to reveal its methods of ideological reproduction. Rather than directly confronting the material practices of the art world, these practitioners have worked to undermine the system's repressive logic with strategies of quotation, pastiche, denial of authorship, and disunity of subjectivity. This has often involved fetishizing the very signifiers of taste and connoisseurship that lie on the surface of class-bound racism, misogyny, and greed. Regrettably the larger apparatus of capitalism has proved remarkably adept at coopting such aberrant behavior by blurring the ground between critiques and their referents. This is largely because much postmodern practice (even the "affirmative" variety) remains stalled in a dehistoricized textual critique. On both structural and economic levels, the work implicitly supports the system by speaking its language and replicating its rules. As a consequence, anticommodity works become best-sellers, and radical style is transformed into the latest consumer fashion.

Meeting this challenge head-on are a variety of groups like Feminists In eXile, the Guerrilla Girls, and the Mothers of Medusa. In recent years these collectives have mounted poster campaigns that contest the retrograde practices of art-world institutions. These anonymous entities, with chapters in many metropolitan centers, have eluded the political debilitation (or individual retribution) attached to the cult of the personality. Their strategy is to plaster messages on the unofficial spaces of walls and utility poles in neighborhoods surrounding galleries and artists' spaces. Typically, these works involve statistical information or polemical statements about those excluded from the job market, the museum, or the history book. For example, in 1987 the Guerrilla Girls' *Advantages of Being a Woman Artist* poster ironically listed the following benefits: "Working without the pressure of success. Not having to be in shows with men. . . . Not being stuck in a tenured job. Seeing your ideas live in the work of others. Having the opportunity to choose between your career and motherhood." Three years later the Guerrilla Girls responded to the censorship crisis with a poster directly addressing the exclusionary community of the mainstream art world. It read in part:

RELAX SENATOR HELMS, THE ART WORLD IS YOUR KIND OF PLACE!
—The number of blacks at an art opening is about the same as at one of your garden parties.
—Because aesthetic quality stands above all, there's never been a need for Affirmative Action in museums and galleries.
—Most art collectors, like most successful artists, are white males.
—Women have to earn their place: after all, they earn less than one third what male artists earn.

—The sexual imagery in most respected works of art is the expression of wholesome white males.

—Unsullied by government interference, art is one of the last unregulated markets. Why, there isn't even any self-regulation.

—The majority of exposed penises in major museums belong to the Baby Jesus.

In reaction to the oppressive relations of the mainstream art world, growing numbers of artists have moved outward in search of new audiences and less restrictive production contexts. Partly this results from an avant-gardist impulse to overcome the art/life dichotomy through instrumental change. In California, video artist Branda Miller produced *What's Up?* (1987), a 32-minute tape created in collaboration with nine teenagers from the Los Angeles County Court School. The project came about as part of the art curriculum organized by the Mark Taper Improvisational Theater Project for the Masada Placement Community Day Center, a juvenile transitional facility serving 88 white, African-American, and Latino young men. Miller was selected in part for her nontraditional production style, which emphasizes freewheeling camera work and disjunctive editing techniques. Participants planned, performed, and recorded personal anecdotes that the group later cut into a fast-paced MTV-style tape. Considerable emphasis lay in self-analysis during the production—something that many students viewed with skepticism. "I was kind of edgy at first," one participant observed, "if they can find one little thing they can pick out, they'll fuck with you here."[19] Miller has recounted the difficulty of functioning as an agent for empowerment within the confines of institutional correction. In this way Miller's circumstances epitomize the paradox of the alternative educator. On one hand, teachers want to encourage questioning of the status quo; yet at the same time they need to overcome the willful unknowing that impedes student development.

SCHOOLS

It is no secret that teachers are undervalued, overworked, and poorly paid—and that, as a result, the profession itself is in trouble. As fewer and fewer young people have ambitions to work in education, the quality of teachers has continued to decline. From 1970 to 1985 the number of the nation's $2.1 million elementary and secondary school teachers under 25 years of age dropped from 17 percent to less than 1 percent.[20] At the same time the aggregate SAT scores of first-year college students enrolled in education departments fell to 852—72 points below the national average. Women account for 70 percent of all of those who teach in K-12 programs. This disparity is most pronounced in the lower grades, where women outnumber men in elementary schools five to one. In secondary education the proportions are more or less equal. The vast majority of teachers are white (89%), married (74%), and significantly less happy with their jobs than other segments of the workforce. In a national survey in which 52 percent of respondents said they were "satisfied" with their jobs, 40 percent of teachers said they were satisfied. Among those who said they were "dissatisfied," teachers were 38 percent more likely to respond negatively than the national average.

These demographics are exacerbated in an atmosphere in which teachers are reduced to roles of low-level functionaries. Oppressive bureaucracies, teacher-proof curricula, and intransigent school boards have chipped away at the autonomy so important to positive attitudes toward work. This is particularly true for art instructors, who are increasingly faced with demands for quantified results. So what is a teacher to do? Like other cultural workers, activist educators in the arts suffer a lack of viable structures of mutual support. This is the reason radicalism is often localized within individual classrooms. Organizations like the National Art Education Association (NAEA) and the National Education Association (NEA) are unable to formulate coherent policies due to the size and complexity of their memberships. Although they appear to provide forums for divergent viewpoints at various national and regional meetings, their overarching function is the amelioration of interests into a generalized position of advocacy. They act as pseudo-coalitions that neutralize activism and difference. The College Art Association, the Society for Photographic Education, The University Film/Video Association, and other organizations for teachers in colleges and universities suffer many of the same shortcomings.

A classic example of this leveling approach can be found in *Focus on the Arts: Visual Arts*, a publication from the NEA and NAEA, which attempts the paradoxical task of reconciling liberal and conservative curricular theories. Author Don L. Brigham initially offers a critique of Discipline-Based Art Education, arguing that it "would unintentionally reduce or eliminate the essential quality of art while attempting to vivify, strengthen, and extend it in our schools."[21] As a remedy Brigham would reintroduce notions of experiment and play, but only in the context of a byzantine quantification procedure (i.e., a 20-point evaluation form scoring each student on the way he or she "detects and depicts an object's major gestalt form," "depicts analogous/metaphoric memory imagery," etc.).[22] He rationalizes this as an inevitable response to school board empiricism. As a result, students continue to be measured and ranked, while broader problems of art education go unchallenged. This contorted logic reflects an attempt to enact a progressive change without altering the limiting structure of bureaucratic "accountability." It is a classic example of the way teachers are obliged to respond to issues, areas of research, and academic practices in a manner that is predetermined by the dominant culture.

One of the ways that teachers can begin to combat such debilitating relations is by forming coalitions among themselves. Such issues of social concern define the overriding mission of Artists/Teachers Concerned, which formed in New York City in 1985 to explore the relationship of art and community through education. Currently comprising 100 members, the organization has received funding from the United Federation of Teachers as a subcommittee of the New

York City Art Teachers Association. So far the group has functioned largely as a local network for politically oriented art teachers, and indeed, it may well be the only art teachers group in the country devoted to cultural activism. With plans that include a traveling exhibition program, annual publications, and the sponsorship of workshops and seminars, Artist/Teachers Concerned is currently encouraging the establishment of chapters in other local communities.

One of Artists/Teachers Concerned's initial projects was an exhibition entitled "Out of the Classroom: Social Education through Art." Presented in a working-class Brooklyn neighborhood, the exhibition showcased the collaborative efforts of over 400 elementary and secondary school students. One might have expected this to produce a dismal display, and to be sure, the exhibition contained more than its share of heartbreaking imagery. But balancing stories of violence, drug addiction, and poverty were remarkable demonstrations of moral concern and involved citizenship. Almost without exception, the artwork focused on the lives of students themselves. As such the show stood as a counterpoint to the increasingly influential movement for "cultural literacy," which stresses emulation of European traditions and classical masterworks.

In *Protests of the Native* (1989), by Sam Binkley's class in Manhattan's West Side High School, a central image of a crown inscribed with the word "power" is connected to a coiling maze of handwritten texts. Emanating from all sides of the crown are anecdotes written by students about personally observed human rights violations. (As Binkley noted in the accompanying catalog, this is one of the "fundamental" impulses in the creation of activist art.) The statements often reflect the frustrating powerlessness felt by adolescents: "Father hits me, mother hits me, teachers yell at me. This makes me angry." In this way *Protests of the Native* provides a form of symbolic (and nondestructive) resistance to the institutions of control (the family, the school, the court) that intervene in students' lives. But the piece does more than illuminate solitary anger. By joining young people's experience through a common issue, the activity demonstrates that individual circumstances of abuse are part of a larger network of repression. Working together to articulate their feelings of victimization, students can understand that they are not alone.

Indeed, the importance of group process forms a central theme of the Artists/Teachers Concerned approach. One of the group's founders, Herb Perr, has noted the unfortunate tendency of traditional art education to foster student alienation through an undue emphasis on individuality and competition. Coupled with an often formulaic view of art as a commodity rather than a community service, art classes can dampen student creativity and discourage participation in school: "By rewarding only a few students we divide our youngsters into the active and the passive—the successes and the failures. In the final analysis the subject of art—which is meant to be a bridge, a form of communication—ends by creating in our young people a sense of skepticism, cynicism, and disinterest."[23] Teachers can counteract these tendencies by rendering the classroom a consensual environment. When youngsters receive collective authority for the execution of work, art class can become a laboratory for the practice of democratic decision making.

One finds a good example of this in the mural work done by Jorge Luis Cordero's class at Intermediate School 44. In creating *Through the Eyes of the Children* (1989), Cordero's students first studied ways that murals were used throughout history to illustrate community issues and to build solidarity. Working in small groups, the youngsters were permitted to pursue their own insights into such topics as homelessness, environmental pollution, media saturations, and New York politics. At the same time, the students were encouraged to utilize the common materials they find around themselves, rather than relying on expensive art supplies or complex imaging techniques. The result is an energetic collage of pretzel wrappers, foil, and magazine clippings exhorting viewers to resist consumer hype and to become more ecologically sensitive. As such it is a testament to the capabilities of these young people to call forth everyday icons in the service of their productive concerns. But even more importantly, the unmediated character of the piece stands as a validation of student perceptions rather than a reification of a teacher's prescriptions.

Meryl Meisler teaches collaboration on an even larger scale. Working in a dropout prevention program at Intermediate School 291, Meisler considers each of the 200 or so "drop-ins" to her classes as coauthors of the works produced. In the "Windows" series (1989), shown in the "Out of the Classroom" exhibition, each student contributed a narrative panel (in the form of a pinhole photograph, cliché verre print, or written story) to a gridded arrangement in a wooden window frame. The personal observations of events seen from the students' homes range from the banal ("From my window I see cars passing. I can also see the houses and people passing. I can see the light blue sky") to the grotesque ("It was a boy who had been shot. His name was Michael. Some boys shot him in the neck. He had blood coming down all over him and you could see his veins").

Clearly this is not the sort of work one finds in a typical New York City art room, where more often than not the pedagogical emphasis is on the replication of art-market formulas of acceptability. Joan Davidson's class at John Adams High School focused on money and school district politics by redesigning dollar bills. This required students to consider currency both as a signifier of value and as an object of exchange. Twelfth grader Christine Safina responded with an image critical of ineffectual liberalism. Replacing Washington's portrait with an enormous set of smiling teeth captioned *In Morton Downey We Trust*, Safina inscribed the bill with the statement "Put your money where your mouth is. Repair our school buildings."

Mario Asaro takes student responsibility a step further by asking classes at Junior High School III to critique the institution of school itself. This has the therapeutic effect of allowing students to evaluate and contribute to the pedagogical environment they are obliged to inhabit. In its initial stage the project took the form of a book entitled *Why We Do and Don't Learn* (1988). According to Asaro, "the book served as a vehicle for the students to make a critical statement about themselves and their school; afterwards it was important for them to realize that they had a responsibility to both."24

In this way, Asaro and other members of Artists/Teachers Concerned have been able to make use of relatively conventional materials and techniques to encourage student voice and to stimulate a scrutiny of daily life. This application of an emancipatory pedagogy that affirms indigenous subjectivity (along with the contradictions and contestations that go with it) is demonstrated in the work of these Brooklyn art teachers to lie within the reach of cultural workers in the most strictly budgeted and regulated environments. By encouraging young people to represent themselves, critique their environments, and begin to offer solutions to local problems, Artists/Teachers Concerned fosters an ethos of involvement in political life. This delicate process is a prerequisite to the existence of a democratic community.

One of the most important lessons of democratic citizenship lies in the translation of agency into action. This is the moment in which people recognize the moral imperative of breaking through isolation and hopelessness to begin the process of change. I stress the ethical character of this phenomena because the gains often accumulate slowly in the early stages of the process. The nonprofit Educational Video Center, a group of media producers and schoolteachers in New York City, works with high-school students to produce projects about themselves and their communities. Often these projects demonstrate not only the relationship of ideas to actions, but also the way school culture can reach into the community.

2371 Second Avenue: An East Harlem Story (1986) is an inspiring example of this work. The first-person narrative about housing in New York opens with contrasting views of city architecture, accompanied by the following voice-over:

> This is New York, one of the richest and most glamorous cities in the United States of America. It is a city of skyscrapers, expensive hotels, and high-priced condominiums. It is one of the most beautiful cities in the world—a playground for the rich and famous.
>
> But there is another side to New York, an ugly side, a side that is ignored by many. My name is Millie Reyez. I am a teenager and I was born and raised in East Harlem. I live in a building with broken windows, garbage, rats, and no hot water. This is a documentary I made with other teenagers about my family and neighbors about how we struggle to survive under these conditions.

What follows is a series of interviews with building occupants, conducted in their squalid apartments, which culminates in a collective attempt to confront their landlord. Reyez and other tenants go door to door collecting names on a petition that they try to deliver to the building's owner. However, they are unable to get an appointment with the landlord and are subsequently ejected from his office. The scene then changes to the office of the housing magazine *City Limits*, where the editor contextualizes the scenario as a regrettably commonplace occurrence in landlord/tenant disputes. The tape concludes with an interview with a particularly destitute family, whose members state that their devotion to each other gives them strength to continue their struggle.

In its unselfconscious and straightforward delivery, *2317 Second Avenue* makes an important statement about the use of media in the classroom. As described by Chris Bratton, who included the tape in the encyclopedic "Teaching TV" exhibition at New York's Artists' Space, "the tape tells us that the power to represent is tied to other forms of power, in this case giving the student and her neighbors both a means to speak and act."[25] This dramatic reversal of media's role, from an alienating and silencing force to a means toward collective voice and action, constitutes a strategic revelation for cultural pedagogy. It would seem to demonstrate that technology and media are not in themselves determinative of ideology (as is often thought). Such matters lie in the hands of those who use the media.

A TOWN MEETING

A central element in the integration of cultural education into community life is the establishment of alliances between cultural workers in various fields. This is not an easy task in an atmosphere of enforced disciplinary boundaries and professional certification. Nevertheless, we need to search for useful models in establishing such coalitions. Recently in New York City, the artists' collective Group Material brought together a range of cultural producers and school people in a project sponsored by the DIA Art Foundation entitled "Democracy: Education." Group Material (at the time comprising Doug Ashford, Julie Ault, Felix Gonzales Torres, and Rollins) initiated a series of exhibitions and school projects that marked a rather extraordinary moment of exchange between the avant-garde art world and the educational community.[26]

In many ways what transpired at those events reflected the potentials and difficulties facing the development of an integrated field of artists and educational cultural workers. For this reason I will discuss the events in some detail, in particular the town meeting that functioned as a centerpiece for the project. In the words of moderator Tim Rollins, the 200 artists, teachers, and critics who assembled at the event did not represent a typical local community, but rather a "community of interest." "We are about to engage in an act of political imagination," he said as the meeting came to order. These comments set the tone for an evening of heated debate over curricular issues in New York City schools and political issues in the art world. In terms of the former, a preoccupation with course content largely precluded discussion of pedagogical method, institutional politics, or models for change. What resulted as an often rambling list of complaints about former secretary of education William Bennett and the conservative canon. This occurred despite the best intentions of the meeting's organizers, who had structured the 90-minute event to follow a series of tightly scripted questions: "Who has the greatest access to organized forms of education? Who is denied access to these same institutions? How is democracy served by current educational policies?" After more than an hour of brooding over reading lists and conservative hegemony, Herb Perr countered that status quo pedagogy may ultimately bring about its own undoing. "How can white European education be superior if the world is coming to an end? How can it be superior when people don't help each other? How can it be superior when people cannot recognize their common purpose? Aren't these the goals of education?"

Rollins attempted to shift the conversation by pointing out that students themselves are almost never consulted on pedagogical decisions, a point underscored by the lack of young people in the audience. "The first question I ask at the beginning of each course is, 'What do you want to learn?' " Rollins said. Fortunately a range of student viewpoints was represented in the accompanying "Democracy: Education" installation that provided a backdrop for the meeting. Group Material had filled a nearby Wooster Street gallery space with 50 works of school-related art displayed in the random manner that has become the collective's trademark. The pieces were hung floor to ceiling on black-painted walls surrounding a mock classroom composed of two dozen formica school desks. The classroom setting lent a unifying ambience to works from such diverse makers as Faith Ringgold, Andy Warhol, Lorna Simpson, Jenny Holtzer, Reverend Howard Finster, and Rise and Shine Productions. In this way the Group Material approach leveled both the famous and the obscure to a common denominator.

The exhibition provided a number of well-conceived examples of student-teacher collaborations, the most graphic of which was the pair of six-foot question marks by Meisler and "the drop-ins." Like Meisler's "Windows" series, it emphasized the student point of view. *Question Marks* (1988) was a layered combination of school snapshots and hand-written comments through which young people commented upon their school, its effect on them, and their (sometimes destructive) responses to it. One area of the piece entailed a series of images showing bathroom vandalism and graffiti, along with an explanation that read, "Kids wreck the school to get back at teachers." This project was also notable in that it listed the names of student collaborators. For the most part, "Democracy: Education" credited students only as anonymous members of groups, their identities subsumed below those of their teachers. This raises the sticky question of the roles students play in these collaborations, particularly when the products are elevated to the level of an avant-garde exhibition. Are the students true partners or are they merely executing imposed plans?

All things considered, the positive aspects of the Group Material "Democracy: Education" project outweighed any points of ambiguity. The well-attended town meeting demonstrated that segments of the cultural community are finally recognizing the importance of schooling as a site of progressive activism. But such gatherings are all too rare. The task facing cultural workers in the school, the gallery, and the alternative space is to continue struggling to overcome the forces that would hold us apart. This entails a recognition that initial efforts like the Group Material project will always be fraught with difficulty, but that they must be attempted nevertheless.

BEYOND BORDERS

The labor movement has long recognized the importance of education both as a tool for membership development and as a way to improve the quality of workers' lives. Labor has also learned that in the technocratic era of multinational capitalism it must reach beyond traditional definitions of "workers' " issues. One of the most visible of these programs is the Bread and Roses Cultural Project of Local 1199 (the 100,000-member Drug, Hospital, and Health Care Employees Union). Bread and Roses uses artists and artwork to promote a broad range of issues of both direct and indirect relevance to working people. In 1986 the organization sponsored the nationally touring exhibition "Disarming Images: Art for Nuclear Disarmament"—paintings, prints, and photographs made to protest the arms race. In addition to providing a much-needed venue for political artists and a positive publicity vehicle for Local 1199, the show demonstrated the interrelationship of two movements often considered separate. By combining activism for both peace and labor, the exhibition exemplified the sort of coalition that progressives need to consider.

Recently Bread and Roses issued a videotape based on a musical review performed for health-care workers and patients in the New York City area. The script for *Take Care* (1989) evolved from workshops at which Local 1199 members discussed their lives and jobs. This material was then crafted into songs and sketches and performed during lunch breaks at hospitals and nursing homes. Like the "Disarming Images" project, *Take Care* is not directly an exercise in union advocacy. Rather than preaching the benefits of organizing, the tape presents a collage of overlapping concerns ranging from job burnout to AIDS education. As such it fashions an image of a complex subjectivity in which commitment to various social issues exists simultaneously. Without privileging any one position, *Take Care* says that one can be a leftist, a humanist, a feminist, a person of color, and a worker at the same time. This is the essence of coalition politics.

It should go without saying that the trade union movement lost considerable momentum during the Reagan/Bush years, as it was systematically assaulted by government and slandered in the press. Fortunately this is not a universal scenario, and in other countries support for workers' culture is more forthcoming. In Canada, activists Carole Conde and Karl Beveridge use photography and texts to connect various struggles—much in the fashion of Bread and Roses. In the preface to their book *First Contract: Women and the Fight to Unionize* (1986), Conde and Beveridge state, "Women, more than men, have been forced to confront the interconnection of work and life after work."[27] They explain that "to many women, the conditions of work and home are not that dissimilar. The move from a man's castle to a 'man's world' is not necessarily a liberating one." For over a decade, Conde and Beveridge have created works that challenge the way we view seemingly disparate elements in our lives: work/home, art/advertising, text/image. They have involved the community around them in an effort to overcome what they term the "barriers that increasingly separate and isolate us," while helping to define a new educational role for the artist.

First Contract was the culmination of a project originally produced in 1981 under the title "Standing Up." It contained a series of photographic vignettes developed in collaboration with Canadian women union members. Each section is devoted to an individual worker, demonstrating the interconnectedness of job, union, home, and family. The written segments are based on actual interviews, as are the accompanying photo montages. However, the latter are acted by stand-in models to protect participants from management reprisals.

Conde and Beveridge became involved with union education following active careers as artists in New York. There they developed a montage technique that has become their trademark. It first appeared in a 15-panel piece entitled *Wendy's Right* (1979), in which a series of color photographs with overprinted captions depicted the daily routine of a working-class family. The key element was the visual subtext that Conde and Beveridge created within each scene by inserting incongruous black-and-white images into portrait frames, TV screens, and windows. The black-and-white images brought to the home environment a constant reminder of what lay outside. In a statement accompanying a published version of the piece, the artists wrote, "Against the pluralistic aestheticization of political and social life, a political art attempts to re-establish a genuine culture that reflects the reality of the social life around it."[28]

First Contract extends these techniques and premises in a book that places the artwork within the context of union history. An eight-page statement by Conde and Beveridge explains the way the two introduced themselves "as artists" to union officials. "What do unions have to do with art?" the president of the local asked. The resulting project provides first-person accounts by three women involved in a fictional strike. Text and images are paired on facing pages. By telling the same story from three points of view, the work seeks to avoid the linear conclusiveness of traditional narrative formats.

The first story is that of Natalia, a married mother of three who works as an order picker in a food-processing plant. The narrative hinges on issues of time: Time to get up, to go to work, to pick up the baby-sitter. "There's no time for gardening when you're working," Natalia says. "There's no time for anything." Natalia's story is visualized in the events that occur around her kitchen table. In the first frame we see her drying dishes as a montage scene of the factory looms behind her. Piecework at home is rendered equivalent to piecework at

"Linda" from Carole Conde and Karl Beveridge, *First Contract: Women and the Fight to Unionize* (Toronto: Between the Lines Press, 1986). Used by permission.

the factory. Later, as Natalia discusses the strike, her children sit at the table packing their lunches. The bags they use are inscribed with the same "boycott" slogans as the strikers' placards seen in the window.

Natalia tells of the way the union used photographs to identify scabs and the way the company recorded strikers on videotape. This kind of self-reflexivity is a frequent element in Conde and Beveridge's work, with viewers constantly reminded of the many ways our lives are inundated by visual representations. Magazines, books, newspapers are frequent props in the montages. In the Natalia sequence, the passage of time is further underscored by a calendar hanging on the wall—the kind that businesses distribute as advertising. In each montage, the calendar carries a different black and white photograph of women at work in a nineteenth-century factory. The vintage appearance of the inserts calls attention to both the historical context of Natalia's struggle and the constructed quality of the montage itself. This points up the contrast between Conde and Beveridge's work and advertising, whose function it is to conceal such information, particularly in matters pertaining to its own methods of persuasion.

Many of the theoretical issues raised in the "Standing Up" portion of the book have been discussed by Canadian critic Martha Fleming.[29] Although Fleming praised the work for creating "a discourse of direct economic politics and a self-reflexive discourse of the ideology of representation in a way that would suggest the relations between the production and use of both," she also questioned its use of the family and its reliance on narrative conventions. For Fleming, the union women were bound by their home relationships and locked within the confines of the story line. Conde and Beveridge responded that the union—as an organization of women—provides a structure for the development of alternative relationships. Narratives, they stated, need not always replicate the same bourgeois ideologies as those of Hollywood.

Of course, such esoteric issues are mainly the concern of those fortunate enough to have studied them—in other words, the privileged beneficiaries of a higher education. The real strength of Conde and Beveridge's work lies in its ability to communicate on many levels without sacrificing its major premises. It can be read and appreciated by line workers, students, homemakers, organizers, and art critics alike.

In this way cultural production can begin to exceed its elitist roots and to function as a force to unite people rather than separate them. Instead of suggesting that art is produced by a few for a few, this practice offers points of entry for a wide variety of viewers. Such work represents a form of culture that is inclusive rather than exclusive. This carries significant implications for democratic cultural workers as the gesture becomes a figure for broader unifications. Yet, in creating this potential such popular texts do not present themselves as standards to which all must subscribe. They represent offerings for many to share. It is just this sort of material that is needed to establish alliances among disparate communities— a mode of cultural production that breaks down boundaries of economic class, aesthetic hierarchies, and professional disciplines. Through such activity one can begin to open the door to a new universe of group identifications and community forms that celebrate human diversity and creativity.

NEW COMMUNITY FORMS

Increasingly the very concept of community is changing. Historic markers of community such as class and geography are gradually being supplanted in an era of mass consumption and high-tech communication. To a certain extent communities are all held together by the various products they buy and see, as well as the desires these commodities create and satisfy. Although the majority of these new community groupings develop from patterns of consumption and use, others are more active in origin. From consumer rights groups to Star Trek fan clubs to antiwar lobbies to Arsenio Hall's "posse," new means for people to come together continually emerge and disappear. As described by Paul Willis, "collectivity may be working increasingly through 'subjective' factors—shared cultural interests and aspirations, shared interests in removing blocks to them, shared interests in increasing control over cultural materials and conditions—rather than through given 'objective' factors such as factory and neighborhood."[30]

Many of these new community forms derive from the ways groups interpret and utilize mass media texts. Yet, technology should not itself be confused as the means of these new associations. Technological advances are little more than conduits through which broader discourses of desire and power flow. As such they can be invested with progressive or regressive ideology. By now most people are aware of the velocity with which the confluence of computer and telecommunications technology is invading their lives in the forms of data storage and retrieval systems, automated calling devices and home shopping, travel and investment services. Although it is sometimes argued that the interactive character of these technologies is inherently liberating, the underlying logic of capital is always at work within them. The trade is simply in the new commodity form of information.

This is not to suggest that the McLuhanesque era of technological utopianism is entirely dead, however. In fact, it is alive and thriving in a service located in Sausalito, CA, known as The Well (Whole Earth 'Lectronic Link, operated by the *Whole Earth Review*). Along with a growing number of electronic information exchanges, The Well offers a remarkably nonhierarchical means for people to gather and make culture. Anyone with a standard home computer and modem has the capability to read The Well's central "conference" menu (The Well has over 3,800 subscribers). This listing indicates the access codes to hundreds of ongoing conversations carried on by groups ranging from a handful of participants to those containing hundreds of respondents. All are open, and one can start a new conference at any time—simply by posting a message, question, essay, or polemic.

These conference groupings, also known as "virtual communities," are quickly becoming a new means of meeting, associating, and exchanging massive quantities of information. With a modem one has the capability of traveling around the United States (and the world) in minutes, visiting libraries, study groups, gossip circles, and service centers. According to writer Gareth Branwyn:

> As a community, The Well may be virtual, but it also lives and breathes—people work there (it's a haven for writers, editors, and researchers), learn there (thousands of conversations cover every conceivable topic), socialize there (through electronic mail and a chat feature), provide and receive therapy (in numerous health and "true confession" conferences), and recreate (through games, role playing, and just plain goofing off). The Well is decentered and asynchronous: people participate when, where, and how they like.[31]

I mention The Well, not as the panacea for cultural objectification, but as an example of a living form of community that as recently as a decade ago existed only in speculative terms. Although it is important to be wary of their exploitative tendencies, one also needs to be responsive to the potentials for group identification that media and technology offer. These need not be only the sorts of associations aided by computers or video screens; they are also the ever-changing communities that we invent in the course of our daily interactions.

Since all such acts of reception and use are productive gestures, these new community affiliations represent their own form of culture. This is the sort of culture made by people every day. Artists and teachers need to recognize that culture is not only something that hangs in galleries, but a substance that inheres in the very fabric of life. Like talking, it lives in the ways people communicate to each other, in the objects they make, and the stories they tell. It permeates the rituals of meeting, listening, dancing, joke telling, playing sports, and making pictures. It lives in the sophisticated meanings that people generate from their work, their parenting, their cooking, their letters, their record collections, parties, cars, yards, gardens, hairstyles, photo albums, wall posters, sketchbooks, home videos, and so on. Most important, it inheres in the ways that people make choices, invent their lives, and adapt to difficult circumstances. In this latter sense culture is, as Willis has stated, the very stuff of survival.[32]

For the pedagogical cultural worker these new community forms present new challenges to enlarge definitions of what counts as knowledge and where it can be found. Rather than perpetuating forms of expression that tell people that everyday forms of culture lack value, one should try to find ways to develop these forms. Rather than worrying constantly about esoteric strains of formalism and postmodernism, it is important to recognize that culture is made by people everywhere rather than handed to them by someone else. This does not mean ignoring the very important objective ways that people form groups or discarding the classics of culture. But it does mean making these structures prove their continuing relevance in our lives. By doing this one accepts the task of critically evaluating the ongoing nature of social contracts. This means summoning the courage to admit that what one might have thought was perfect might not be so. From this one moves on to invent the future public sphere through new community forms and new discursive spaces.

NOTES

1. Jesse Goodman, "Education for Critical Democracy," *Journal of Education* 171, no. 2 (1989): 88–116.

2. See Michael Hecter, *Principles of Group Solidarity* (Los Angeles: University of California Press, 1987).

3. Allan Bloom, *The Closing of the American Mind* (New York: Simon and Schuster, 1987); E. D. Hirsch, Jr., *Cultural Literacy: What Every American Needs to Know* (New York: Random House, 1987); and William J. Bennett, *James Madison High School: A Curriculum for American Students* (Washington, D.C.: U.S. Department of Education, 1988).

4. Hilton Kramer, "A Note on the New Criterion," *New Criterion* 1, no. 1 (September 1982): 7.

5. Carole S. Vance, "The War on Culture," *Art in America*, Sept. 1989, pp. 39–45.

6. Ruby Lerner, *Comprehensive Organizational Assistance for Artists' Organizations* (Washington, D.C.: National Association of Artists' Organizations, 1988).

7. Michael S. Joyce, "The National Endowments for the Arts and Humanities," in *Mandate for Leadership*, ed. Charles L. Heatherly (Washington, D.C.: Heritage Foundation, 1981), p. 1056.

8. Cornell West, "The New Cultural Politics of Difference," *October* 53 (Summer 1990).

9. Edward Said, "Opponents, Audiences, Constituencies and Community," in *The Anti-Aesthetic*, ed. Hal Foster (Port Townsend, WA: Bay Press), p. 152.

10. In a similar vein, bell hooks has written of the ways the academy neutralizes difference by enforcing conformity to scholarly conventions of speech and action. These conventions are often elements of the very structures that enforce injustice and inequality. In the account of hooks:

> The academic setting, the academic discourse I work in, is not a known site for truthtelling. It is not a place where the oppressed gather to talk our way out of bondage, to write our way into freedom. . . . Trapped as we often are in a cultural context that defines freedom solely in terms of learning the oppressor's language (language as culture; learning to live the oppressor's culture, what Baba, my grandmother, what Native Americans before her called "learning the white man's ways"); assimilating however slowly into the dominant hegemony, into the mainstream. It has been extremely difficult to move beyond this shallow, empty version of what we can do, mere imitators of our oppressors, toward a liberatory vision—one that transforms our consciousness, our very being.

See bell hooks, *talking back: thinking feminist, thinking black* (Boston: South End Press, 1989), p. 29.

11. Margaret Spillane, "The Culture of Narcissism" *Nation* 251, no. 20 (Dec. 10, 1990): 738.

12. Rev. Donald Wildmon, as quoted in Richard Bolton, "The Cultural Contradictions of Conservatism," *New Art Examiner* 17, no. 10 (June 1990): 26.

13. Richard Bolton, "Enlightened Self-Interest: The Avant-garde in the '80s," *Afterimage* 16, no. 7 (February 1989): 12–18.

14. Martha Rosler, "Lookers, Buyers, and Makers: Thoughts on Audience," in *Art after Modernism: Rethinking Representation* ed. Brian Wallis (New York: New Museum of Contemporary Art, 1984), pp. 311–40.

15. John P. Robinson, "Assessing the Artists' Condition: Some Quantitative Issues," in *The Modern Muse: The Support and Condition of Artists*, ed. C. Richard Swaim (New York: American Council on the Arts, 1989), p. 37.

16. Richard Harvey Brown, "Art as Commodity," in *The Modern Muse*, ed. Swaim, p. 19.

17. Ibid.

18. Abigail Solomon-Godeau, "Living with Contradictions: Critical Practices in the Age of Supply-side Aesthetics," in *Universal Abandon? The Politics of Postmodernism*, ed. Andrew Ross (Minneapolis: University of Minnesota Press, 1989), p. 191.

19. Linda Frye Burnham, "Mending with Tape," *LA Weekly*, July 3–9, 1987, p. 29.

20. C. Emily Feistrizer, *The Condition of Teaching: A State by State Analysis* (Princeton, NJ: Princeton University Press, 1986).

21. Don L. Brigham, *Focus on the Arts: Visual Arts* (Washington, D.C.: National Education Association, 1989), p. 13. Discipline-based art education is an approach to teaching introduced by the Getty Center for Education in the Arts. It seeks to legitimize art within elementary and secondary curricula by stressing measurable methods of art appreciation and technical imitation. It was first outlined in *Beyond Creating: The Place for Art in America's Schools* (Los Angeles: Getty Center for Education in the Arts, 1985).

22. Brigham, *Focus on the Arts*, p. 13.

23. Herb Perr, *Making Art Together: Step-by-Step* (San Jose: Resource Publications, 1988).

24. Interview with author, Minor Injury Gallery, Brooklyn, New York, March, 1989.

25. Chris Bratton, "Teaching TV: Toward Media Literacy," gallery notes (New York: Artists Space, 1990), n.p.

26. The project and its proceedings were subsequently documented in the publication *Democracy*, ed. Brian Wallis (Port Townsend, WA: Bay Press and DIA Art Foundation, 1990). Contributors include Henry Louis Gates, Jr., Ira Shor, Catherine Lord, Yvonne Rainer, Stuart Ewen, bell hooks, and William Olander, among others.

27. All quotations in this section are from Carole Conde and Karl Beveridge, *First Contract: Women and the Right to Unionize* (Toronto: Between the Lines, 1986).

28. Carole Conde and Karl Beveridge, *Words and Images/Mots et Images* (Ottawa: Photo Gallery, 1980), p. 8.

29. Martha Fleming, "The Production of Meaning: An Interview with Carole Conde and Karl Beveridge," *Afterimage*, Nov. 1982, pp. 10–13.

30. Paul Willis, *Common Culture: Symbolic Work at Play in the Everyday Cultures of the Young* (San Francisco: Westview Press, 1990), p. 142.

31. Gareth Branwyn, "The Virtual Salon," *Artpaper* 10, no. 3 (November 1990): 9.

32. Willis, *Common Culture*, pp. 128–52.

5

New Discursive Spaces: Reinventing the Public Sphere

Conservatives are seeking to gain the upper hand in the cultural realm with the same tactics they used to win the White House. With a program of moral traditionalism, the Right has seized upon popular symbols to put the Left on the defensive. In recent years this has included an appropriation of the very vocabulary of "democracy," "empowerment," and "community" once thought to be the province of the Left. As a result progressives find themselves in a reactive position in which the very terms of their antagonisms seem to be defined by the other side. In a continual battle against this or that conservative motion to censor or defund, a positive agenda has become difficult to formulate. And without such positive articulation the Left dooms itself to a position of marginality. Ernesto Laclau and Chantal Mouffe argue that "if the demands of a subordinated group are presented purely as negative demands subversive of a certain order, without being linked to any viable project for the reconstruction of specific areas of society, their capacity to act hegemonically will be excluded from the outset."[1] Framed in this manner, the solipsistic nihilism of much avant-garde practice is both defensive and counterproductive. We need a positive plan.

Given this challenge, it is incumbent upon radical educators and artists to assist in reconstituting an arena for civic dialogue by validating the significance of a people's culture and recovering the public function of art. In doing so, cultural workers must recognize their roles in the development of civic consciousness. This means promoting notions of shared responsibility for community life, along with the belief that change is indeed possible. At the core of the issue lies political education. This is what convinces people that individual acts of citizenship (like voting) can make a difference—that they themselves can command the authority to make community decisions. These attitudes are suppressed by the concept of the mainstream. Instead, an illusion is promoted of an imaginary polis set apart from the actual community. It is a paradigm that consolidates power in a myth of uniform consent and control. The "silent majority" becomes George Bush's "thousand points of light." This fundamentally phallogocentric vision, which would define otherness in terms of lack or absence, encourages a binary consciousness that compresses all difference into a single category. It promotes a manageable resistance framed in the language of control. Indeed, the very conceptualization of resistance becomes defined within a logic of linear reproduction as identified by the dominant order. This dramatically limits the potential reach of radical activism. For this reason one must be extremely wary of the internalized assumptions, naturalized languages, and invisible power structures that define (and undermine) one's actions.

At the heart of the struggle must lie a message through which cultural activists can demonstrate the discontinuity between power and the face it projects. At the same time we must connect a pair of concepts that conservatism seems unable to reconcile: difference and egalitarianism. Accomplishing this on a popular level will mean reclaiming many icons and values that conservatives have appropriated. Why, for example, have the definitions of such concepts as patriotism and the family been conceded to the Right? Why have progressives acquiesced as the notion of "alternative education" has been equated with the corporate classroom? If deconstruction has demonstrated anything, it is that the meanings of cultural signs are unstable. After all, it was through the false recontextualization of Mapplethorpe and Serrano as negative symbols that the Right made its recent congressional gains.[2] Cultural activists can work to unmask the methods of conservative image manipulation, while at the same time forging a positive iconography. Because interpretation plays such an important role in the process, this is a profoundly educational task. What matters is the framework in which a particular idea is placed. Therefore contexts of transmission and reception become vital components in this struggle. Signification becomes a matter of political strategizing.

The task ahead involves more than simply seizing popular symbols. It proposes a political imaginary yet unrealized in our history. The common shortcoming of all hegemonic regimes (including utopian ones) is their implication of totalizing ideology or subjectivity. This problem becomes particularly evident within conventional liberalism. Although frequently presented as a pathway to emancipation, the liberal ethos perpetuates distinctions between historical subjects and objects: those who act and those who are acted upon. It seeks to make surface corrections to a structurally flawed system without interrogating its underlying economic inequities.[3] Regrettably, this is the pitfall of much avant-garde art practice. In contrast, a radical democracy defines itself on all levels in pluralistic terms. There is no single set of attitudes or social group to which all others must conform. Instead, the unifying ethos is one of decentered authority. This "cyborg politics," to use Donna Haraway's expression, admits the continuum between the ideal and the material, the mental and the physical, the organic and the mechanical.[4] Yet it resists the vacuous amoralities of relativism and pluralism. For obvious reasons, such a scheme seems dangerously unstable to many neoconservatives who warn of the "threat" of unbounded egalitarianism.

To put these theories into practice, activists need to develop the mutually supportive character of their struggles. This presents a challenge to the co-operative tolerances and communicative capacities of the interests involved. Groups defined by gender, sexuality, ethnicity, nationality, or occupation need to recognize their unique roles in the social totality. To encourage a degree of coalescence, boundaries (and the hierarchies often implied) that separate groups via such distinctions as amateur/professional or mass/elite must be softened. We should work toward a world view that is horizontal rather than vertical. The ethical dimensions of this struggle cannot be overstated. The concept of guaranteed equal rights carries enormous popular appeal, as revealed during 1988 in the advances of Jesse Jackson and the Rainbow Coalition. Its many shortcomings notwithstanding, the Jackson phenomenon demonstrated the willingness of large numbers of people with different interests to coalesce around the issue of their common estrangement from power. This was accomplished despite a biased and xenophobic press. At the same time, we have seen remarkable progress in recent years in the reforms of Eastern Europe. The popular revolutions in Poland, Rumania, Czechoslovakia, East Germany, and the Soviet Union have demonstrated the ability of ordinary people to topple massive bureaucracies without resorting to violence.

To achieve these goals we will need to design cultural spaces unfettered by the debilitating separation of theory from practice, the distance between academics and "the people." Both inside and outside the university boundaries have been drawn and antagonisms entrenched between those who analyze and those who make films, novels, or paintings. It is time to recognize the aesthetic dimensions of theory and the theoretical character of aesthetic production. In this spirit artists and teachers can help shape a discourse of solidarity by reaching beyond single causes or issues (important as they are). The task entails working to create spaces for activism on many levels. In addition to creating unifying texts, this means strategizing in legislative and institutional arenas. As Fred Glass recently wrote of labor media, "If 'Union Yes' shows up on your car radio, in your living room, on a billboard you pass, etc., then unionism can become a part of the background of our daily lives. Thus naturalized, the spots can disarm a direct message at your antiunion workplace that unions are hostile and Other."[5]

Specifically, cultural workers need to consider various coalition strategies that groups have used to motivate community activism. Such efforts can challenge the debilitating impediments to human agency of objectification, rationalization, and commodification discussed earlier. One might ask how cultural workers in the school or the gallery can create situations that encourage dialogue and response. What strategies best promote a questioning of rationalizing scientisms and corporate bureaucracies? How can teachers and artists suggest that people's actions can have an effect in changing these structures? How can one enhance the everyday production of culture?

The answers to many of these questions are not as distant as one might imagine. In some cases they lie in the great emancipatory struggles of the past— the civil rights, antiwar, labor, and women's movements. In other instances they exist in the heroic efforts of small groups and coalitions—community organizations, experimental schools, artists' organizations, and environmental collectives. Finally, and most importantly, they lie in the uncelebrated creativity emanating from the work and play of "ordinary" working people. Lower- and middle-class populations are increasingly victimized by the consolidation of wealth and power in the hands of corporate oligarchies. As such this majority of citizens represents a constituency that has a great deal to gain from a socialist future.[6] In this context, one must acknowledge the importance of the local and the marginal as sites of critique. Rather than seeking a global revolution, the Left might develop more modest strategies for linkages among sympathetic struggles. As bell hooks has argued, the "outside" is a space of radical possibility for all of us who find ourselves at odds with the status quo. In this sense marginality is not something "one wishes to lose, to give up, or surrender as part of moving into the center, but rather as a site one stays in, clings to even, because it nourishes one's capacity to resist. It offers the possibility of radical perspectives from which to see and create, to imagine alternatives, new worlds."[7] This is not an attitude through which to exchange one center for another. Rather, it seeks to abolish the concept altogether, replacing it with a constellation of competing/cooperating interests. Although it points to the utopian imaginary of numerous centers, the place to begin lies in realizing the mutual dependency of all progressive groups. This is not to say that one should ever generalize struggles into categories of equivalence. Nor should one homogenize disparate elements within an artificially unified movement. Social problems and the activism they inspire are always individualized by the historical moments, identities, and locations in which they reside. What works in Des Moines may very well not wash in San Francisco, Houston, or Miami.

Cultural workers can play an important role in demonstrating the interconnectedness of various struggles. The national political apparatus and the news media simplify social problems by representing them as isolated phenomena. In this way public attention is diverted from the actual causes of human misery and inequity. The drug dilemma has been characterized as a monolithic war, with seemingly no relationship to the forces of economic imperialism, racism, and structural poverty (not to mention the wholesale marketing of various forms of "legal" intoxication) that lie beneath it.

This chapter will present a series of strategies for developing an activist political imaginary and the new discursive spaces to encourage its growth. In doing so I hope to add some specificity to recent reassessments of the "public sphere" as a site (or arrangement of sites) of democratic debate. Rather than devices for the rationalization of liberal/bourgeois elitism, these new public spheres would provide openings for critique and analysis from voices silenced by mainstream discourse.[8] Throughout the discussion a heavy emphasis will be placed on issues of media and media critique. Without denying the radical potential of poetry, theater, sculpture, and easel painting, an extra degree of attention will be placed on the ubiquitous technologies of film, video, and photography. In a contemporary world saturated with images, it seems difficult to imagine a more strategic site of political activity. I will first discuss several interventionist strategies at the level of text, which begin to offer alternatives to the barrage of debilitating stereotypes and binarisms one typically encounters both in "high" and "low" culture. This will develop into an analysis of the function of form in mediating the delivery of such narratives. How does the address of a stage play allow different possibilities from that of a movie? How might radical changes to these forms alter the way they convey information? From this will come a review of strategies cultural workers are employing to encourage viewers and students to become more critical readers of texts.

Next will follow a series of organizational models, many of which already exist, that encourage egalitarian relationships within and between groups of cultural producers and audiences. From experiments in popular education to the efforts of alternative art spaces and media centers to initiatives within existing school and government structures, this section will catalog a range of institutional possibilities for the development of positive cultural forms. This will lead to a discussion of communities both as they currently exist and as they might evolve in a radical democracy. It will examine the incentives and impediments to the formation of coalitions. Attention will then shift from group to individual, to address ways that cultural workers can encourage agency, involvement, and cultural/political production. Discussion will focus on strategies employed to restore discursive dialogue, an awareness of community history, the connection between individual and collective voice, and, ultimately, the importance of critical literacy to democratic citizenship. In the manner developed throughout this book, emphasis will be placed on concrete examples both as models and metaphors for larger applications.

TEXTS

Narrative Authority

Debates in recent years over First Amendment constitutional rights have underscored the importance of free speech. Who has the authority to speak? Which stories can be told? Where and when? Fundamental to a discussion of new discursive spaces is the acknowledgment of the dysfunctional character of many existing narratives and speaking positions. Indeed, the Right has been extremely effective in silencing or neutralizing opposition. The former is accomplished in brute materialist terms through legislation that eliminates progressive programs, cancels research projects, and cuts off funding. Such actions are bureaucratically implemented through a language of rationalist "efficiency," "basic skills," and "standards of quality." The latter is effected through the recoding of such concepts as "multiculturalism" and "patriotism" as means of eliding difference and discouraging dissent.

In the public arena, the consolidation of textual authority in the mass media has greatly diminished access to diverse opinion. News broadcasts increasingly rely on government "spokespeople" or other institutionally certified experts for analysis of political debates or international conflicts, as evidenced in the near total manipulation of the coverage during Operation Desert Storm. Although such recent examples abound, one of my favorite illustrations of such propagandizing involved a domestic program of the 1980s. I am referring to the comical publicity campaign waged for a concept known as Star Wars. No, not the film fantasy of director George Lucas, but the political fantasy of Ronald Reagan. Inasmuch as both versions were popularized via the media, their differences became exceedingly difficult to discern. Interchangeable subject matter, terminology, and hardware blurred the line between science fiction and fact— and the Reagan administration took full advantage of it. Narrowing the gap between futuristic fantasies and world events permitted the reduction of complex international issues into a realm of simplistic figuration: Manichaean battles of light against darkness, tales of wilderness conquest and Manifest Destiny. Comparable narrative displacements were called into service to popularize the invasions of Panama, Grenada, and Kuwait.

The Star Wars mythology was powerful medicine, indeed, which President Reagan was able to translate into budgetary success. One might logically ask why the voting public was so willing to swallow so "unreal" an explanation for the expenditure of billions of dollars that might otherwise have served more humanistic purposes. In part the answer is attributable to the circumspect pathways that propaganda travels in Western society. As the sophistication of the film industry's illusionistic capabilities has pushed the public's fantasy quotient to all-time highs, the press increasingly encourages a language of euphemism and analogy—a distancing from the real. In this vocabulary, war is not fought, but "prosecuted," as citizen massacres are rendered invisible by terms like "collateral damage."

This tendency to reduce difficult issues to simplistic sound bites has contributed to a broad-based information gap between the populace and those who administrate its business. Most people perceive that the information they receive is partial and often partisan, but they resign themselves to existing media forms, nevertheless. As a first step in opening new areas of public discourse, artists can fashion representations that illustrate social and political conditions in their full contexts, difficult as that may be. In the 1960s the confluence of civil rights struggles, antiwar activism, and New Left activism—particularly among college students—created an atmosphere of profound resistance to ruling-class values and institutions. As Althusser and Marcuse were popularizing views of a radically destabilizing historical subject, young people on campuses were stirring up trouble. In some quarters it was assumed that the baby-boom generation would overtake the entire nation. This period produced a plethora of cultural works nurtured by the alternative arts organizations funded by such agencies as the NEA. The era marked the beginning of the movements in independent publishing, photography, performance, and media that produced groups with names like the Basement Workshop, Franklin Furnace, La Raza Graphics, Painted Bride, and Videofreex.

Unfortunately, while seeking to forge a new political imaginary, such efforts often alienated more people than they persuaded. Just as the Right suffers a tendency to oversimplify issues into convenient clichés, so many groups on the Left have romanticized dissent in equivalent terms. This position of pure radicalism fails to take into account the many factors of identity and interest that we all carry with us. As described by film historian Michael Renov, the activities of the subversive journalistic collective Newsreel in many ways typified this reactionary radical practice. Positioning itself against what it perceived as a bourgeois media machine, Newsreel provided documentation of Left activism (demonstrations, marches, and sit-ins) on film. Its grainy, hand-held films took viewers behind the lines of protests, into occupied school administration buildings, and face to face with sometimes brutal police. The works projected an anarchistic, anti-Hollywood, antihegemonic view of a turbulent time. In the context of this discussion of new discursive spaces, Newsreel is an instructive object of a counterpractice that offers an alternative narrative but ultimately fails to recognize the complex dialectic of political positioning. Although its productions were dramatic, more often than not they focused on visible symptoms rather than on the underlying causes of ideological reproduction.

This is not to say that Newsreel's efforts lacked impact. The bicoastal collective became a virtual bellwether of activist sensibilities in such works as *Columbia Revolt* and *Summer '68*. More than 50 prints of *Columbia Revolt #14* circulated to colleges and universities nationwide, often with quite dramatic consequences. The coverage reported by the publication *Rat* of a 1969 evening presentation of a Newsreel film at the State University of New York at Buffalo, read as follows:

> At the end of the film, with no discussion, five hundred members of the audience arose and made their way to the University ROTC building. They proceeded to smash windows, tear up furniture and destroy machines until the office was a total wreck; and then they burned the remaining paper and flammable parts of the structure to charcoal.[9]

Despite the apparent "success" of the screening, the result was hardly what one would call a productive application of political power. Although useful in promoting camaraderie and inspiring enthusiasm, much early work of groups like Newsreel amounted to little more than knee-jerk iconoclasm. Although a heterogeneous and historically productive movement, many elements of 1960s counterculture failed to account for the exceedingly complex ways that alliances are negotiated, as well as the often partial and contradictory construction of civic subjectivity on both the Left and the Right.

Although much current cultural work suffers similar reductionist tendencies, certain efforts have been made to examine political formations with more complexity. From a pedagogical perspective, leftist cultural producers need to create works that depart from divisive binarisms and one-dimensional analytical strategies. In his photographic installation *Geography Lesson: Canadian Notes* (1986–87), Allan Sekula approached a task no less daunting than a deconstruction of Canadian civic subjectivity. Comprising 79 wall-mounted photographs, arranged in grids, and an accompanying booklet-format text on a reading table, Sekula wove various narratives into his text, all of which were tied to the central metaphor of money. In *Geography Lesson*, currency is depicted as little more than a *representation* of value. Not unlike other cultural signifiers, its extrinsic worth is largely a factor of public imagination.

Most of the photographs were shot in two locations: the Canadian capital of Ottawa and the northern mining town of Sudbury. Incorporating views of urban and rural landscapes, Sekula juxtaposed the splendor of Canada's nationalistic centerpiece with its industrially ravaged backyard. Particular attention was given to architecture as a site of corporate power and as a means to demarcate public and private space. This was effected through the exceptional figure of the Bank of Canada Currency Museum located in downtown Ottawa. The edifice, plaza, and interior displays of this bizarre institution reinscribe Canadian history within a narrative of exchange objects—from wooden beads to dollar bills.

From the (literally) glittering glass and metal of the Currency Museum attention shifts to the gray land and sky of Sudbury, the mining community at whose entrance rises the statue of "Big Nickel"—a gigantic coin. Here Sekula photographed the mine, the local union, the nickel smelting plant, and the workers themselves, whose numbers have dwindled to a fraction of their strength a few decades ago.

These photographic narratives are paralleled by a written text whose tone can be concrete:

> Sudbury is barren because it has been defoliated by years of roasting nickel ore over open fires, a practice which destroyed the region's agricultural economy in the early years of this century. Now a giant smoke stack, the "tallest in the world," carries acrid smoke into the atmosphere.

Or poetic:

> The Bank of Canada whispers to the Canadian bourgeoisie in two voices.
> A nostalgic voice recalls the immensity of Canada's natural wealth.

The bourgeoisie hears the whisper absent-mindedly, it knows that this wealth may not even be Canadian. A second whisper is more insistent: "Invest abroad, trade freely, you citizens of the world." Working class Canadians are encouraged to hear only the first voice, to accept their relative comfort in the world of nations, this wealth that is theirs only in the imagination.

The resulting work suggests in very complex terms the way we arrive in our social circumstances, and our common tendency to limit our aspirations to the possibilities presented to us. Awareness of such factors is a prerequisite for meaningful change brought about by what Cornell West has termed "demystification." Such a practice offers critical perspectives that unravel the logic of the reigning order:

> Social structural analyses of empire, exterminism, class, race, gender, nature, age, sexual orientation, nation and region are the springboards— though not the landing grounds—for the most desirable forms of critical practice that take history (and herstory) seriously. Demystification tries to keep track of the complex dynamics of institutional and other related power structures in order to disclose options and alternatives for alternative praxis; it also attempts to grasp the way in which representational strategies are creative responses to novel circumstances and conditions. In this way, the central role of human agency (always enacted under circumstances not of one's choosing)—be it critic, artist or constituency and audience—is accented.[10]

Reading History against the Grain

In an era in which conservatives would promote monolithic views of human culture, a restoration of community history needs to be a central element of the Left's organizational agenda. Cultural workers can no longer stand by as isolated fragments of the past are wrenched from their contexts and mythologized in the service of ruling elites. Instead one must work to resuscitate narratives (or readings thereof) that celebrate emancipatory struggles and social justice. Artists and school people can motivate human agency by legitimizing the place for people's stories and voices. In this way activists can broaden discursive spheres narrowed by partisan interests, while attaching such radical texts to broader political movements. This work will not be easy, for it will involve reading history lessons as typically received against the grain. It will mean searching out the erased passages, the absent characters, and the suppressed stories that were removed because they were difficult or troublesome.

Beyond such revision, the task entails developing attitudes that question received truth and dominant speakers. Here education is seen, not as the simpler transfer of instructional units, but as a complicated set of transactions filtered through an environment of competing interests and subjectivities. Knowledge is made through the critical examination and testing of ideas. An excellent example of this is the documentary production of *The Road to Mississippi: Reclaiming Our History* (1990), created at the Schomburg Satellite Academy High School in Bronx, NY. Working with social studies teacher Pam Sporn, a group of "at-risk" students produced a counterstatement to the film *Mississippi Burning* (1988, by Alan Parker), which depicted the violent killing in 1964 of three young civil rights workers in the South. As one student explains off camera:

> The movie was accurate about the violence and racism at the time, but the way it portrayed the FBI as heroes and its degrading portrayal of blacks raised questions in our minds about reality and fiction. Another question which was unanswered was where was the civil rights movement which was very strong at the time. Those who don't know about the civil rights movement might think that what the movie represented was history.

Although research began in local New York libraries, the students eventually made a research trip to Mississippi (with support from the Educational Video Center and Schomburg High), where they interviewed coworkers and relatives of the deceased. The final tape combines a serious critique of the original film's omissions with a series of alternative accounts of what transpired. In discussing the project, Sporn emphasized the pedagogical importance of rewriting received narratives. (It is worth noting that her group calls itself the "Through Our Eyes Video and History Project.") As students begin to fashion their own historical texts they "become profoundly involved, motivated by a need to know the subject matter to make a credible statement."[11] The resulting work reflects such enthusiasm. In contrast to the nihilistic vision of *Mississippi Burning*, the student tape offers an account of a period of great solidarity among the participant groups (NAACP [National Association for the Advancement of Colored People], SNCC [Student Nonviolent Coordinating Committee], etc.) of Freedom Summer. Rather than pessimism and defeat in the deaths of James Cheney, Andrew Goodman, and Michael Schwerner, *The Road to Mississippi: Reclaiming Our History* offers a story of unity and hope.

As an exercise in dialogic empowerment, the reclamation of history can have a dramatic effect in generating community solidarity. By attaching itself to popular narratives, the Left can begin developing a much-needed textual strategy. Dick Hebdige calls this the "virtual power of metaphor"—the ability of symbols to trigger displacements that cross constituency boundaries. One of the most successful examples of positive coalition building around a cultural project is the ongoing Great Wall of Los Angeles mural initiated in 1976 by the Social and Public Art Resource Center (SPARC) in Venice, CA. The longest mural in the world, the 2,500-foot work covers one side of a U.S. Army Corps of Engineers flood control channel in the San Fernando Valley.

It depicts California's multiracial history and has involved the cooperation of government agencies, local businesses, trade unions, and community groups. Executed by artists and teenagers from different economic and ethnic groups, the project has also drawn upon the scholarly expertise of dozens of historians, anthropologists, and folklorists. As project co-organizer Judy Baca has pointed out, the scale of any mural, particularly this one, makes collaboration a necessity: "The Great Wall of Los Angeles is based on a different conception of what art is for. The mural is not just a big picture on a wall. The focus is on cooperation in the process underlying creation."[12]

Central to the wall's pedagogical effectiveness are the lessons it provides about the living history of the community. This is not to suggest that the imagery itself is a tableau of harmony. Many of the scenes show the darker moments of California's past, such as the incarceration of Japanese-Americans during World War II or the present-day flight of undocumented workers across the Mexican border. These are intermixed, however, with positive scenes of community. Such projects encourage citizens to look for strength in their own collective memory. According to Baca, "With what historians bring in we develop images to turn back to the public consciousness information that has been lost."[13]

Form and Structure

There is nothing new about the idea of using art or literature to change the way people think about their lives. Notions of cultural objects as educational inducements for social betterment have been with us since antiquity. But beyond matters of content lie the forms such messages take, for such forms mirror their enabling social relations. The development of the novel in the eighteenth century can be attributed to such factors as the expansion of a literate middle class, new technologies of publishing, and a growing preoccupation with individualized narratives. Similar analyses have been written about phenomena ranging from the comic book to the video game.

Artists and writers have frequently asked themselves whether such dynamics work in reverse. Can radical form provide the impetus for social revolution? Such radical formalist thinking achieved a remarkable sophistication between the first and second world wars in the work of the Russian avant-gardists and their Eastern European and German successors. In this school of thought, artworks were fashioned to intentionally draw attention to their means of production. Self-references to technical contrivances, optical systems, or artistic processes would be used to demystify the art object, undercutting its aura of fetishized value by "laying bare the apparatus."

More to the point, in the works of artists like Alexander Rodchenko, Dziga Vertov, Vladimir, Mayakovsky, and El Lissistzky lay a belief in the possibility of radical practice linked by necessity to the activation of a radicalized spectator.[14] Apprehension of the work required a new way of seeing, a new paradigm brought about through the experience of the cultural object. The point of all of this was that content alone was insufficient in the conception of a radical vision. New containers, new structures, were required for the new messages of political reorganization. Much of this type of modernist thinking has been rejected in recent years as naive or romantically utopian. Yet one need only examine the reified formats of television soap operas, sit-coms, indeed MTV, to confirm the determinative influence of form. Not only does the immediate instrumentality of form exert an influence (as in a 30-second spot), but it also creates a range of overdetermined viewer expectations.

Such relationships between subjects and objects have been the focus of photographer Connie Hatch, whose installations call attention to the oppressive logic of conventional signifying practices by creating new ways to engage spectators. Through an ongoing project entitled "After the Fact," Hatch addresses issues of history and memory. These temporal concerns have preoccupied photographers since the medium's inception. In the component of the series entitled *Some Women . . . Forced to Disappear* (1987), the faces of seven deceased or missing women are presented as 11-by-14-inch black-and-white positive transparencies. Reproduced from newspaper and magazine sources, the portraits of Ana Mendieta, Rosa Luxemburg, and other personalities are combined with several images of "not famous" women. Both are accompanied by brief biographical statements on nearby placards. By integrating representations of known and unknown figures in this way, the piece becomes a series of memorials to disparate individuals. Yet at the same time it raises questions about the discursive location of women in general. Who is admitted into the domain of public memory? Who is made to disappear and why?

In this and other works by Hatch, transparencies are lit to cast projections of portraits on an adjacent wall. As viewers pass the pictures they interrupt the light source, causing the shadow images to vanish. In *Cornered* (1989–90), viewers must enter a space demarcated by larger-than-lifesize transparencies of former San Francisco supervisor Harvey Milk and his murderer Dan White. Once inside this small "corner" one is able to see the ghostly projection of each man's face beside a printed text about the other. According to Hatch, the architecture of the piece is intended to subliminally evoke the sensation of a voting booth—a solitary place to make a judgment. Here one ponders the "objectivity" of photographs and words. By manipulating arrangements within the gallery Hatch does more than simply foreground the material apparatus of media for analytical purposes. In obliging viewers to physically participate in the work, she renders the experience a productive event, an analog to all acts of interpretation.

Reception and Strategy

The widespread English translation and dissemination of European linguistic theory in the 1970s helped the cultural community in the United States find

Installation view of Connie Hatch's series *Some Women . . . Forced to Disappear: A Display of Visual Inequity* (1989). Photograph by C. Leavitt. Used by permission.

Installation view of "Two Citizens" from Connie Hatch's series *Cornered* (1990). Photograph by Deborah Lohrke. Used by permission.

new understandings of textual functions: new understandings of the relativity of signification, the uncontainability of meaning, and the indictment of cultural reification—in effect, a reaffirmation of the Platonic notion that every image is little more than a copy of its idealized and nonexistent master. The radical implications of these ideas were manifold, throwing the art world into a turmoil from which it has still not recovered. Upsetting notions of inherent genius, originality, and high-cultural value, postmodernism produced a strain of artistic production that critiqued the very language upon which such notions were based.

Artworks by Sherrie Levine, Silvia Kolbowski, Laurie Simmons, James Welling, Sarah Charlesworth, Louise Lawler, Cindy Sherman, Richard Prince, and Vicky Alexander, among numerous others, *re*-presented photographs from a variety of art and mass media sources to focus attention on the way such images were conventionally deployed and consumed. These practices implicitly asked viewers to rethink the ways they interpreted the world around them.

Unfortunately, these postmodern theoretical premises were rarely understood beyond an academic elite (ironically, appropriation was often misconstrued as a valorization of its objects, rather than a critique). Worse still, although art-world postmodernism criticized mainstream galleries, museums, and patrons, it relied on them for its material sustenance and its means of reaching an audience. Ultimately postmodernism was accused of replicating the very commodity values it sought to critique by reinforcing the modes of address and subject positions it stood to oppose.

This raises the unpleasant question of whether genuine opposition is even possible within the art world. Might it be true, as Raymond Williams once stated, that nearly all efforts toward reform, "even when they take on manifestly alternative or oppositional forms, are in practice tied to the hegemonic: that the dominant culture, so to say, at once produces and limits its own forms of counter culture."[15] If every critical strategy is ultimately co-opted as a formal device or personal style, what can an artist do aside from abandoning the arts community altogether? Indeed, for many diehard poststructuralists, counterpractice is reduced to a series of negotiations within an institutional matrix from which there is no true escape.

Given the often paradoxical effects of critical practices, opinions vary about how to proceed with a program of political activism. This has resulted in the evolution of three distinct approaches to radical cultural production, which can be characterized as interventionist, deconstructionist, and tactical.

The interventionist approach places itself squarely in the realm of lived relations and material objects. Its practitioners are often critical of the narrative manipulation that typifies postmodernism. Interventionists argue that unless one addresses injustice in concrete terms, one is suggesting that social relations and politics exist only in the world of images. Without a material grounding, critique becomes little more than abstract philosophy that deludes its practitioners. The solution is an instrumental practice that provides unambiguous evidence and evokes response. The union photography of Fred Lonidier, the environmental theater of Greenpeace, and the anonymous postering of the Guerrilla Girls come to mind as examples of this type of work. Interventionist practice typically circumvents co-optation through such strategies as collective authorship, ephemeral form, or constant shifts of style.

The problem with the interventionist approach, as deconstructionists are quick to point out, is the fallacy of conceiving a separation of the material from the philosophical. This critique of interventionism argues that although considerable merit lies in the direct confrontation of social inequities, it is equally important to engage the discursive construction of power, racism, commodification, and so on. This is the frequently debated difference between the "representation of politics" (intervention) and the "politics of representation" (deconstruction). The deconstructionist approach also focuses attention on the distancing of art from life. This is accomplished by fetishizing the process and directing scrutiny to the institution of art itself. Thus, the issue lies both in making a polemic and in challenging its enabling circumstances. Victor Burgin has provided one of the best descriptions of a deconstructionist approach that pragmatically accepts its own limits.

> Quite simply, there is no "outside" to institutions in contemporary society; they fit together like the pieces of a jigsaw puzzle—to leave one institutional site is simply to enter another, which will have its own specific conditions and determinations. The artist who works for a trade union as an "artist" has . . . simply exchanged the problematic of one institution for that of another; in so doing he or she risks abandoning a struggle to which they could bring some experience or expertise, for one to which they are novices. Moreover, more fundamentally, they remain firmly inside the dominant discourses. The major weakness of the "art outside the institution" position is the completely empiricist and untheorized concept of "institution" with which it operates.[16]

Although this position makes an admirable attempt to come to grips with the paradoxes of radical practice under capitalism, it nevertheless has been broadly criticized for the way it conveniently allows academics and theorists to disengage from struggles other than their own. Rather than directly engaging the forces of oppression, Burgin's postmodern activism relegates political fisticuffs to the seminar room and the aesthetic text.

The tactical approach selectively appropriates interventionist and deconstructionist elements. That is, it maintains the specific grounding that highly instrumental practice can provide, yet also stays attentive to the broader discursive configurations at work within and across institutional spaces. In this guerrilla role one chooses one's battles according to their potential effectiveness rather than their political correctness. Put another way, one evaluates the extent to which discursive parameters can be mediated. Some can be subverted, others will subvert you.

Situated Practice

The classroom is a good case in point. The relatively controlled setting of school offers an opportunity for activist artists quite unlike that of the gallery. Issues of bureaucratic surveillance and institutional gatekeeping notwithstanding, schools provide audiences in stable reception contexts, where the majority of students are hungry for material that breaks the boredom of conventional curricula. This creates a receptive atmosphere for the sort of situated activism practiced by Steve Papson in his video *Appropriation of Culture: The IBM Tramp* (1985). The tape is a sociological study exploring the way advertisers use historical figures or events to sell products.

By analyzing six IBM commercials and comparing them to the original Chaplin films, Papson demonstrates IBM's repeated use of certain technical devices to develop a common theme. Action was filmed at slower-than-normal speeds and then projected more quickly to resemble the screening of silent films; gels and various wiping techniques further add to the commercials' "antiqued" ambiance. The scenario generally opens with Chaplin's character frantically trying to manage a business growing out of control. In one commercial a factory assembly line goes haywire until restored to harmonious movement by a computer. From that point on workers smoothly perform their jobs on roller skates and eventually gather around Chaplin to celebrate their high production. A happy boss bestows honors on the leading supervisor and a truckload of merchandise disappears over the horizon. The ubiquitous male narrator tells us:

> In this rapidly changing world even the brightest and best manager may need more than a loyal staff to run a smooth operation. For when headquarters calls and pressure builds it becomes harder to keep things rolling without running into mix-ups, losing control of the operation, and falling behind. For rapid improvement a manager could use a tool for modern times, the IBM personal computer—for smoother scheduling, better planning, and greater productivity. It can help a manager excel and become a big wheel in the company.

The commercial recreates scenes from Chaplin's *Modern Times* (1936), a film, as Papson points out, with a radically different message: "For Chaplin, the industry upon which the livelihood of the workers depends is controlled by a privileged few. The choice is between hunger and mechanized labor." In the original version, the worker is constantly harangued by the assembly-line boss. Many of the film's comic effects derive from the film's mechanization of the Tramp's gestures, which results from his long hours on the line. When the Tramp appears on roller skates it is in a moment of escape from work. The factory workers gather around Chaplin to strike and riot against the company rather than to offer toasts to it. The truck that drives away is a police van that carries arrested protestors. As Papson comments, "It is the function of computer marketing to select signs and to recontextualize them in a way that the social dislocations that this new technological object may cause disappear from view. . . . The Tramp who represents human rebellion, who draws the line for humanity, won't be dehumanized any further, becomes IBM's yes man."

Papson's analysis suggests the need for consumer capitalism to manufacture consent for its action and desire for its products. In this light, the identity of the Tramp becomes even more insidious than that of "IBM's yes man." The system requires symbols of a depressed working class that can be upgraded by acquiring accoutrements of the good life. It is necessary for certain segments of society to be kept on the bottom in order to maintain an atmosphere of unappeasable desire. Meanwhile, a myth is promoted that promises prosperity and happiness to those who work hard—and in this case, to those who use the IBM PC.

It bears reiterating that this is not an "art" video per se, at least not in the sense of an object for gallery display. The tape is clearly geared for classroom audiences. Interspersed throughout *Appropriation of Culture* are intertitles that carry quotations from various theorists: Roland Barthes, Jean Baudrillard, Guy Debord, Henri Lefebvre, and others. Accompanying the piece is a printed version of many of the statements used. Yet, as pedantic as this sounds, the hard copy actually helps one follow the piece from point to point. The IBM campaign becomes a textbook example of myth wrenched from history (Barthes), transformed into simulacral mutation (Baudrillard) or grotesque spectacle (Debord) to support the bureaucracy of controlled consumption (Lefebvre).

It is largely the tape's educational character that helps *Appropriation of Culture* hold up so well in comparison with other works that analyze or deconstruct the idiom of TV commercials. Although it lacks the rapid cutting of Dara Birnbaum's "Pop-pop Video" tapes, the goofy antics of Ann Magnuson's *Made for TV*, or the nostalgic cache of Steve Hawley and Tom Steyger's *Science Mix*, it leaves no uncertainty about its politics. Moreover, because it is made to be presented within the confines of a classroom, it is unlikely the work will ever become neutralized by gallery display. *Appropriation of Culture* exemplifies the potential of critical appropriation within a pedagogical context.

There is one problem with this approach. The potential shortcoming of such directed interpretation lies in its negation of free reading. In telling students what to think of a text, one may be replicating yet another oppressive structure that student and teacher find themselves "inside." Moreover, there are limits to what can be accomplished in any classroom, for no matter how progressive or student-centered the teacher may be, the rules of institutional review, regulation, and assessment still apply. And to a certain extent there is no escape. As Burgin correctly points out, even leaving the confines of the educational establishment is rarely the answer, for upon entering another institutional sphere one may encounter many of the same structures and subject positions that one left behind. It is precisely this reason, however, that attention to texts, language, and discursive formations is insufficient in itself. Simply yielding to the existent structure of organizations and markets as givens forecloses changes at the level of social form that are so necessary in opening up new spaces for articulation.

INSTITUTIONS

Just as the Left needs radical texts, it also needs radical institutions. Such spaces can be created in at least three ways: subverting traditional institutions, as discussed above; enhancing progressive organizations currently at the margins; and creating new institutions and institutional forms. A healthy democracy requires a continual testing and reevaluation of social instruments. In part this is a function of the dynamic quality of all political relationships. Yet, it is an effect of capitalism, too, which, for all of its dehumanizing logic, is also a prime force of superstructural innovation and change. Capitalism constantly reinvents modes of consumption, desire, and their methods of reproduction. Because a market economy counts innovation as a virtue, it regularly creates openings for revision. In the previous chapter I focused on the work by cultural activists to subvert schools, museums, and other bureaucracies from the inside. What follows will emphasize models for developing new institutional forms and bringing marginal ones forward.

Popular Education

On a community level, there are many sites between the corporate state and the individual sphere where cultural workers can develop new audience configurations and discursive forms. This is a specifically local task that begins in the neighborhood, the workplace, or the school. Citizens otherwise disaffected from the political process are often willing to act passionately about issues that have a direct impact on their lives. This is an important phenomenon in breaking the shell of alienation that makes people feel that their opinions do not matter, that their voices will not be heard, that their votes do not really count.

On an institutional level cultural workers need to identify sites of maximum strategic value. For artists and writers conventional school itself has always been one of them. Unfortunately, such opportunities as residencies have become fewer and fewer in recent years, as conservative policymakers stress the primacy of "professional" teaching. For those inside the system the task is typically frustrating, as well. Conventional schooling begins the process of depersonalization and control by fragmenting knowledge into categories and units of measurement. Not only are the relationships among different ways of thinking removed, but learning is conceived as something that occurs only in school and at a specific point in one's life. In these and other ways, schooling positions teachers and students within what might be called "official culture." Young people are expected to respect this major instrument of socialization, even though it often denies the legitimacy of their own desire, experience, and cultural heritage.

Given the difficulty within the mechanisms of "formal" education, it is fortunate that a broad range of options exists. These fall under the rubric of popular education. More a generalized category than a specific type of schooling, popular education encompasses the range of social formations that have replaced the clubs and coffeehouses that nurtured grass-roots learning in past centuries. Some contemporary antecedents include community centers, local history societies, participatory research groups, health collectives, worker study programs, camera clubs, media access facilities, and other educational entities that people engage after their formal schooling. Considered as a whole they constitute a significant social and political resource. Moreover, "student" participation is generally voluntary and without direct economic motivation. This is exactly the type of organization in which genuine culture grows.

Worldwide, many linkages of political movements through popular education have developed in the modern era. Examples include the folk-high-school movement in Denmark, the Gaelic League in Ireland at the turn of the century, the Antigonism movement of the 1930s in Nova Scotia and, more recently, the Highlander Folk School in Tennessee.[17] During the last two decades Highlander has become an international focal point of popular education, providing a range of national and regional workshops on such topics as community organizing, literacy development, environmental activism, and cultural production. The axioms of Highlander are to "learn from the people and start education where they are" by educating "people away from the dead end of individualism into the freedom that grows from co-operation and collective solutions."[18]

Rather than seeking simply to relieve the suffering of the Appalachian poor, its goal is to harness their potential capabilities. Although Highlander was instrumental in bringing the trade union movement to Tennessee in the 1930s and the civil rights movement several decades later, the organization eschews a single ideology. As Tom Lovett explains, Highlander was deliberately vague in articulating its governing concepts: democracy, mutuality, and concerted community action. Highlander allowed "time and the people to define them more precisely. It quickly learnt that ideology, no matter how firmly grounded in objective reality, was of no value if it was separated from a social movement of struggling people.[19] Due to the dynamic quality of these social movements, the content as well as the form of education changes in the popular context. Phillip Wexler explains that

a mass educational politics implies, if not a single, unitary movement, then a popular articulation that directs attention to the fact that the common practices of these movements are what we now historically mean by education. Any popular educational movement now requires collective work to press toward articulation and realization. Not only will new sites of social communication need to develop, but even the goal of universal enlightenment will be historically redefined. The meaning of literacy in an information, semiotic society is not only that the artefacts (television, microcomputers, telecommunications) are new, but that the social relations to the artefacts also change. A new enlightenment aim of contemporary popular educational movements is consciously to appropriate and use various knowledge practices for collective aims.[20]

One place where this tradition lives is in the "workshop" model of nonhierarchical, nondegree-oriented schooling. Such alternative organizations throw into relief the structured domination that young people experience in traditional schooling. Most of today's schools identify students as passive recipients of knowledge while conveying conservative values based on fixed bodies of knowledge. As a model for subsequent social behavior, this institutionally determined relationship not only discourages student inquiry but also lessens the will toward public involvement that is necessary in a democracy. It becomes the task of the radical educator to devise strategies for reinstilling student voice in the system.

From 1979 to 1985 London's Cockpit Arts Workshop generated a series of programs that capitalized on media studies to develop curricula informed by student experience. As explained by Cockpit staff Andrew Dewdney and Martin Lister, "If you want to base work on valuing young people's culture then you have to offer them an acceptable and powerful form with which to do this."[21] Derived from the simple premise that students both consume and make contemporary culture, the program developed a unique series of models that combined critical media analysis and picture making. At the same time, Cockpit worked aggressively to undo what its founders saw as the regressive myths of conventional art. Instead, Dewdney and Lister encouraged young people to appropriate from mass media sources to either critique the media on its own terms or to integrate it into a student narrative.

> The gap between what was claimed as being art in schools and the lived realities of many pupils was vast. It is probably this experience of being with working class kids in the art rooms of inner city schools, and being alive to the irrelevance of what takes place to so many of them, that accounts for differences in our approach and that of photography and media teachers who are not so close to the institutional realities of art education.[22]

For this reason many of the early Cockpit lessons sought specifically to foreground the disparate relationship of fine art representation to the images made by young people themselves. From these acts of comparison, the lessons turned to analyses of the often-distorted images of young people (as "happy," "carefree," well-dressed, and white) in advertising, entertainment, and news media. How might young people resist such interpellation? How could they reassert their own identities in a chain of received subjectivities?

Through a series of carefully planned (but rather loosely executed) exercises, students were helped to understand both the strength of their own collectivity and the liberating potentials of its articulation. Specifically, the program linked student photography to self-representation of youth culture through an analysis of such stylistic indicators as clothing, cars, dance, and the accoutrements of popular music. This strategy assumes a great importance in an atmosphere of compulsory schooling, legal strictures, and parental control—one that all too often encourages students to reach for shortsighted or self-defeating forms of resistance. As Dewdney and Lister put it, of the many ways of organization "available to them, the most important from our point of view are through cultural and symbolic forms. These are ways in which positive identities are reasserted and celebrated."[23]

In encouraging students to critique the media, Dewdney and Lister were ever cautious to respect the truly popular—or "hip"—aspects of youth. Too frequently the elements of student culture most cherished by young people are overscrutinized in the progressive classroom, picked over for semiotic meaning, and sanitized by the powerful engines of the educational apparatus. Doing this removes the pleasure and creativity that such objects and rituals can offer. It fails to capitalize (and genuinely validate) significant elements of the student self. Thus a typical Cockpit exercise might involve the development of a diaristic album. What begins as a simple assemblage of snapshots becomes an index of cultural identity and value. Carried out in the context of a workshop, such peer group diagnostics can have a powerful effect. In giving validity to student culture, the teacher encourages young people to overcome feelings of resentment toward the learning process. Ultimately student dissatisfaction can be channeled into productive strategies for change.

Artists' Organizations and Media Centers

It should go without saying that cultural workers have another pedagogical resource waiting to be activated in nearly every city. Despite the damage done by conservative censorship and defunding efforts, the national network of over 400 visual artists' organizations and media centers holds dramatic potential for popular education. Designed in the 1970s with relative autonomy from corporate and government bureaucracies, these "alternative" organizations formed an important support base for community groups of many kinds.

In the current cultural environment, artists and their organizations are recognizing the need to challenge conventional definitions of art and break down the boundaries that separate different cultural spheres. At the same time, the current fiscal climate places these organizations under considerable financial strain to reach new constituencies. This obliges organizations to seek diverse and invigorating programs. Increasingly education is being recognized as a viable means of achieving these ends, with such prestigious institutions as Artists' Space (New York, NY), Los Angeles Contemporary Exhibits (Los Angeles,

CA), Southwest Alternative Media Project (Houston, TX), the DIA Foundation (New York, NY), and Film in the Cities (St. Paul, MN) recently sponsoring innovative educational programs.

Gaining most from these programs are the young people and adults who are afforded a type of pedagogical encounter often unavailable in traditional educational environments. Poised in the netherworld between school and museum, these organizations can offer types of adventurous education that more conventional organizations cannot tolerate. This is indeed what we mean by a new discursive territory. It is a field of possibility, where unconventional types of pedagogy can be allowed to grow.

In the I-Eye-I Video Workshops at New York's Henry Street Settlement, Branda Miller initiated a project with neighborhood adolescents addressing issues of sexuality. The resultant "Birth of a Candy Bar" series of video poems provided the teenagers an opportunity to speak openly and creatively about a topic typically suppressed by parents and other authorities: sex. Although the students' treatment of their subject matter is often ironic, the significance of the gesture should not be discounted. For many young people sex and sexuality constitute areas of considerable anxiety, particularly as these topics are aggressively promoted in movies, television, and magazine advertisements. At the same time, this very important element in the formation of student subjectivity is rarely, if ever, addressed in school. With the onslaught of conservative educational reform movements, the classroom has increasingly become a site of moral regulation. Crackdowns on AIDS education, a return to traditional gender roles, and an enforcement of compulsory heterosexuality are the legacies of the current educational system.

In these and other areas, entities like community media organizations, artists' spaces, and community cultural centers can begin to fill the discursive void. They can more openly give voice to student experience because they do not suffer the regulatory scrutiny of most schools. The "Birth of a Candy Bar" series was produced through a voluntary after-school pregnancy prevention program, and as such was afforded considerable leeway in its methods. One segment of tape dealt specifically with images of sex in the media. Appropriating footage from Budweiser commercials and popular films like *Top Gun*, the five-minute video incorporated a student-narrated voiceover detailing the many ways that sexuality is distorted on film and video.

> We know what television does for us, but we don't often really think about what it does to us. Television suggests that everyone does it and that casual sex is the norm. People are seen indulging in sex without worry or even thought. Whether in television, movies, or commercials, no one worries about disease or pregnancy.

Another, somewhat more whimsical "Birth of a Candy Bar" segment was a two-minute tape illustrated entirely by anthropomorphized candy bars. The spoken narrative went as follows:

On Payday, Mr. Goodbar wanted a Bit-O-Honey, so he took Miss
Hershey behind the Mars on the corner of Clark and 5th Avenue. He
began to feel her Mounds. That was pure Almond Joy and it made her
Tootsie Roll. He let out a Snicker and his Butterfinger went up her Kit
Kat and made a Milky Way. She screamed Oh Henry! as he squeezed
his Twix and made a Nestle's Crunch. Miss Hershey said you're better
than the Three Musketeers.

This is not the type of exercise one encounters in a typical high-school English
class, but perhaps it should be. By providing a forum for humorously addressing
its subject matter, the "Birth of a Candy Bar" tapes not only worked to reduce
student anxiety about discussing sex, but also presented remarkable exercises in
the exploration of figurative language through text/image juxtapositions. More
importantly, the tapes did something for the student producers that conventional
school does not. By asking the young people to use their own experience to create
didactic material for others, it placed them in positions of authority. As Miller has
explained, this reversed the traditional student/teacher dialectic by positioning the
teens as educators.[24] In doing so the process implied a productive value in being
a teenager, a student, and even in being a teen parent. It suggested that one's
knowledge (even of painful experiences) can be useful to others. Projects like
"Birth of a Candy Bar" demonstrate the pedagogical potential that alternative
environments such as artists' organizations can offer. Through such institutions
local community workers can begin to support the articulation of a new public
space for education and culture.

Clearly though, a broader level of collective strategizing will be needed
to effect large-scale political reform. This must entail the establishment or
strengthening of alliances among those groups that have always been the
backbone of progressive politics: trade unions, student groups, churches, ethnic
coalitions, peace and justice collectives, and environmental organizations. No
action on any level should be discounted. Models for large-scale cultural
organizing are relatively few, particularly when funding agencies encourage
only the most bureaucratic and politically ineffectual of such structures. Yet
one entity developing from the alternative media center movement seems to
hold promise.

By now the accomplishments of Deep Dish cable satellite network have
been well documented. The success of Deep Dish has lain in its ability to
structurally correct one of the major stumbling blocks of cable access: local
narrow casting. It should be remembered that in the 1960s atmosphere of
media utopianism, the promise of cable television, with its seemingly endless
number of channels, offered the possibility of breaking network hegemony
with unlimited viewer choice. In the interest of establishing opportunities for
citizen dialogue, municipalities across the nation required cable companies
to allow community groups program time on designated channels. But the
community access movement did not live up to expectations. Commercial cable

networks (CNN, MTV, VH-1, etc.) quickly emerged to fill the channel roster, overwhelming access programmers. Other problems dogged the movement, as well: low production values alienated viewers; sporadic programming was difficult for viewers to find; published listings ignored local productions. Except when copied and "bicycled" to another cable network, most local cable production failed to reach beyond a devoted grassroots following. This phenomenon in turn discouraged further production.

Things changed in 1986, when members of the Deep Dish distribution collective in New York City and Boston began renting time on the Westar Galaxy 1 television satellite (which also carried such services as the Nashville Network and the Disney Channel). With grant support to publicize the initial ten hours of programming, Deep Dish suddenly put community access (in the form of thematic programs gathered from producers nationwide) onto scores of cable networks and into the homes of the over 11 million satellite dish owners. In offering a program of subsidized satellite transponder time, Deep Dish has provided activist videomakers and community groups with a national system for cable access and home dish reception. As such it represents an important mechanism for intercommunity exchange outside the realm of corporate authorization.

Government Initiatives

Because implementing cultural pedagogy requires material and institutional support, a measure of political organizing is often needed. This means demonstrating to voters and legislators the social utility that art can embody. In a broader sense it also involves helping people to recognize that the market cannot be counted on to represent the interests of all citizens equally. Increasingly cultural workers are taking the initiative in this project. At a local level, artists and videomakers are finding employment in community health and welfare agencies: drug rehab centers, drop-out and pregnancy programs, AIDS clinics, and crime-prevention initiatives. In this way, they are proving that cultural matters need not be consigned to museum vaults or library stacks. They live in the daily lives of citizens.

Recently Don Adams and Arlene Goldbard have suggested the reinstitution of a broader program to utilize cultural workers as social-service providers. These proposals call for the reinstatement of such federal programs as the Roosevelt-era Federal One project (which incorporated the Federal Theater Project, the Federal Writers Project, and similar publicly supported programs in all arts) or the cultural components of the more contemporary Comprehensive Employment and Training Act (CETA) program.[25] To accomplish this, Adams and Goldbard suggest the adoption of some of the basic strategies that worked for the Left in the past:

> The task of the moment should be recognized as consciousness-raising and the goal should be to place questions of media and democracy

on the agendas of as many different organizations and communities
as possible, from teachers' unions to parent-teacher organizations,
from youth groups to senior centers, from civil rights organizations
to professional organizations. The first effect of a more widespread
concern with public policy for democratic media would be to open up
existing policy deliberations.[26]

Ironically, in this age of increasingly privatized philanthropy, one of the most
dramatic public incentives for progressive action has recently gone on line. In
1988, Congress responded to complaints from independent media producers
over the commercialized and unrepresentative character of public television.
Lawmakers created a new entity, the Independent Production Service, to receive
$6 million of production funds formerly administered by the Corporation for
Public Broadcasting. Now quietly functioning, this new entity has been specifically designed to create alternative models of media discourse. This means working
as much on the development of audiences as on the production of new programs.
As described by IPS advocate Lawrence Daressa, the entity is an endowment for
viewers who do not yet exist: "Instead of naturalizing a single point of view, it
makes point of view its overt subject matter."[27] Daressa's statement succinctly
articulates the responsibility facing activist artists: to create an environment in
which diversity and contest are encouraged rather than suppressed. Obviously,
this is not a new task, for progressive culture has always entailed a struggle by
the disenfranchised to gain a voice. But what is often overlooked in contemporary
artwork is the power of those voices when drawn together. That the IPS could be
brought into being is evidence that such structural revision is indeed possible.

SOCIAL FORMATIONS AND IDENTITIES

Alternative institutions are but the physical manifestation of new social
formations—new ways for citizens to come together in new understandings
of collectivity. I have already discussed some of the ways people establish
group identities through realizations of sameness and difference. What are
some other ways that community identity can be formed? Within the cultural
community precedents date to the 1930s, when a coalition briefly materialized
around the issue of antifascism. Assembled in 1936 through the auspices of the
American Artists' Congress (AAC) were groups and individuals with such diverse
concerns as racial inequality, poverty, government censorship, unemployment,
global armament, and unfair working conditions for artists. The initial call for
participation in the congress read in part:

This Call is to those artists, who, conscious of the need for action, realize
the necessity of collective discussion and planning, with the objective of
the preservation and development of our cultural heritage. It is for those
artists who realize that the cultural crisis is but a reflection of a world

economic crisis and not an isolated phenomenon . . . Dealers, museums, and private patrons have long ceased to supply the meager support they once gave. Government, State, and Municipally sponsored Art Projects are giving only temporary employment—to a small fraction of the artists. . . . Oaths of allegiance of teachers, investigations of colleges for radicalism, sedition bills aimed at the suppression of civil liberties, discrimination against the foreign born, against Negroes, the reactionary Liberty League and similar organizations, Hearst journalism, etc., are daily reminders of the fascist growth in the United States.[28]

Many well-known figures were drawn to the AAC—among them, Ansel Adams, Margaret Bourke-White, Alexander Calder, Adolf Gottleib, Isamu Noguchi, Jose Clement Orozco, Paul Strand, and Max Weber. For five years the congress initiated exhibitions, demonstrations, and other actions linking artistic production to other social concerns. The AAC grew directly from the John Reed Clubs that developed during the early 1930s for the purpose of unifying artists and writers with the working class. A year prior to the formation of the AAC, the John Reed Clubs organized a National Writers' Congress to address such problems as unemployment within the United States and the imprisonment of dissident writers overseas; it also argued in defense of the Soviet Union, against capitalistic aggression and for the preservation of civil liberties in order to strengthen the revolutionary labor movement.

Although the AAC repeatedly made clear that it eschewed any affiliation with any political group or clique of sectarian opinion, the majority of its members subscribed to the goals of the Soviet Union's Popular Front, introduced in August 1935 before the Seventh World Congress of the Communist International in Moscow. Simply put, the Popular Front shifted the public emphasis of international communism from the opposition between capitalism and socialism to more generally palatable debates of fascism versus democracy and war versus peace. Within the United States this strategy was deployed to unify the Left while garnering support among liberal and centrist groups.

At the same time, artists who typically had felt isolated from society were brought back into the mainstream. There could be little disagreement with Stuart Davis, the AAC's founding executive secretary, when he opened the congress with an attack on Italian futurist F. T. Marinetti, quoting his infamous remark, "War is the only world hygiene." Davis added that "increasing expression of social problems of the day in the new American art makes it clear that in times such as we are living in, few artists can honestly remain wrapped up in studio problems."[29] In an address entitled "The Social Bases of Art," Meyer Shapiro urged artists to abandon oppositional and elitist attitudes toward audiences, arguing that all too often cultural production becomes unnecessarily "cryptic, bizarre, something that we must solve as a conceit of the artist's mind." He concluded that in a society where citizens are "free individuals, individuality must lose its exclusiveness and its ruthless and perverse character.[30]

The demise of the congress occurred as it became more and more difficult to rationalize such Soviet behavior as Stalin's 1936–38 purge of the party hierarchy, his 1938 ban on modernist art, the 1939 nonaggression pact with Germany, and the subsequent Soviet invasion of Finland. By 1940, a group within the AAC headed by Shapiro and Davis led a protest of the pro-Stalinist faction within the AAC, ending in mass resignations among members. A year later the AAC's antiwar mission had clearly been overcome by history, and it soon splintered into various other groups: the Artists' Societies for National Defense, the Artists' Council for Victory, the Artists' Defense league, and United American Artists. A call in 1941 for what would be the AAC's final meeting contained the following premonitory passage:

> Today the fascist threat has come full circle. In a traditionally free and liberty loving America, Fascism comes in the name of Anti-Fascism. All the enemies of progress suddenly become defenders of democracy. Our liberties are destroyed to defend liberties and the policies to which our people are committed by our government, in the name of peace, border even closer to overt war.[31]

Recent decades have witnessed similar coalition efforts: the Art Workers' Coalition, the Alliance for Cultural Democracy, the Union for Democratic Communication, the Anti-Imperialism Cultural Union, the Association of American Cultures, the Association of Independent Video and Filmmakers, Bread and Roses, the Foundation for the Community of Artists, and Political Art Documentation/Distribution, among others. Yet despite this work a unified arena for oppositional practice has not materialized. The problem partly stems from the Left's failure to articulate a truly populist message or to structure a method of popular address. In the art world, for example, the Left has pitted its own avant-garde elitism against the canonical hagiography of the Right. At the same time, with a healthy suspicion of the tyranny a majority can impose on smaller groups, progressives have avoided the unidimensionality of a party line. Ironically, this has permitted the less reluctant (and equally heterogeneous) conservative camp to proffer a message of moral superiority. A decade of political advances has further allowed the Right to consolidate its authority in the primary institutions of socialization, culture, and law. As a result, the Left has been put on the defensive in a debilitating posture of response.

Polyvocal Alliance

How can we counter the forces that discourage agency and separate us on a collective level? To overcome these problems activist cultural workers can formulate discursive spaces that connect groups involved in similar struggles. Unfortunately the Left has always had difficulty accomplishing this. It has suffered from the fragmentation that accompanies a plurality of interests, and has failed to adequately unify the disenfranchised groups most sympathetic to its goals. Especially in the current post-Marxist era, the movement has studiously avoided totalizing paradigms that might elide the interests of its constituent groups. Ironically, conservatives have found no difficulty in labeling the entire panoply of progressive interests a threatening "other." The Right consolidated these various groups into a single enemy because they represent a threat to the very concept of a unified, centralized, and dominant monolith.[32] In the absence of a unified enemy, the Right has constructed one. The question one needs to consider is whether or not we want to respond in these terms.

Obviously a balance needs to be found between the central planning of a monolithic bureaucracy and ineffective balkanization of isolated struggle. This calls for a network of delicate linkages among groups. One model for this type of practice was recently developed in San Francisco by a small confederation of activist cultural organizations, youth groups, and social service organizations. "Project Mission: Who's the Landlord?" assembled a wide spectrum of community interests in a two-year project addressing urban problems. Rather than seizing upon one-dimensional explanations or remedies, the project sought to unravel the complex ways that homelessness, unemployment, and drug abuse are connected to gentrification, corporate greed, and government mismanagement. Yet despite its complexities, the project's unifying theme provided a common metaphor to bring together otherwise disparate groups.

The central component of "Project Mission" was a series of exhibitions held in artists' organizations, housing projects, and community centers throughout the Bay Area. The thematic shows were widely publicized as "forums" for artists and nonartists alike. One such assemblage, entitled "The Hidden Apparatus Is at Us," was intended, as its somewhat hyperbolic press materials stated, "to expose the 'War on Drugs' as a vile, repulsive and deceitful war on people, waged by a class of hypocritical political gangsters." Rather than a tightly curated selection of works, the display drew from a community-wide call for contributions. As a result the exhibition became a crazy quilt of photographs, children's drawings, newspaper clippings, Xeroxes, paintings, and home videos. In its nonhierarchial design and democratic scope the project exemplified the type of unifying practice necessary for cooperative social change.

Photographer Richard Bermack's work is a case in point. Straightforwardly documentary in the style of Eugene Richards or Milton Rogovin, Bermack's *Cracked Lives: Victims of the American Dream* (n.d.) matched portraits of a dealer and an addict, named Double $R and Goldie, respectively, with extensive transcribed accounts of their experiences on the streets. The resulting documents offered a layer of complexity by attempting to relate the drug dilemma to broader social problems. An accompanying wall label read:

> The real tragedy of the War on Drugs is not only the damage caused by
> police state measures, but that drugs and the causes of drug addiction are
> serious problems that require resources. Instead of spending billions

on jails, billions should be spent on improving a failing school system,
mental health programs, drug treatment centers, low income housing,
rebuilding the economy, and providing meaningful jobs.

Not that such gestures are without their contradictions. Within such polyvocal
alliances as "Project Mission" one must anticipate and tolerate conflicting
voices—even counterproductive ones. Although much of the work displayed
through the project came as a welcome change from the tight-lipped irony
associated with postmodern counterpractice, it occasionally fell into the trap
of validating semantic conventions and established roles of dominance and
repression. Even though we knew which side of the political fence the artist
occupied, the territory was described in a language of oppression in which
despotic leaders and invisible government remain the center of attention. The
purported rationale for this approach may be consciousness raising, but its mode
of address fails to construct a subjectivity of collective resistance. That role is
reserved for the socially alienated artist.

More often than not these latter difficulties were manifest in works that reified
fragments of the drug problem into stereotypes of binary opposition: rich/poor,
cops/criminals, government/citizenry. Such was the case with Montgomery
Powell's mixed media *Round Up the Usual Suspects* (n.d.), in which images
of dollar bills and U.S. flags were spattered with red paint amid portraits
of Manuel Noriega, Adolf Hitler, and George Bush. Similar sensibilities ran
through at least a dozen other pieces attempting, it seemed, to dramatize the
corruption of government power using signifiers of violence like guns, knives,
animal traps, and even urine. Given the disturbing expansion of drug-testing
policies, the use of this most ubiquitous symbol seemed quite logical. Positioned
near the entry of the gallery, Mason Byers's installation *Pissing in the Wind*
(n.d.) employed a high-powered fan that blew a continuous spray of yellow
liquid over the surface of the building's store front window. Numerous other
works made literal or figurative use of urine to underscore the erosion of civil
liberties.

Building on such prescriptions for change was an untitled and attributed
painting in the gallery's basement. The oversized diptych contrasted a crack-
smoking skeleton with a pair of black men clasping their hands above their
heads in a power salute. Across the top of the painting was the slogan "Take
the power not the pipe." In its uncomplicated affirmation of human agency this
painting provided an exhilarating counterpoint to the closure of many other works
on display. The issue of counterpoint and closure was essential to the success of
"The Hidden Apparatus," for rather than a monolith of unified opinion, the
exhibition offered a dialogic chorus of perspectives. In this way it demonstrated
that community consensus is more a matter of overlapping concern than virtual
agreement.

"The Hidden Apparatus" went an important step further, with direct educational
efforts at outreach, community dialogue, and coalition building among groups

touched by the drug war. The month-long series of events opened and closed with a sequence of widely publicized forums designed to air opinions about local problems and their possible solutions. The final session drew representatives from entities ranging from Refuse and Resist to the Revolutionary Communist Party to the National Organization for the Reform of Marijuana Laws (NORML), who jointly declared an economic and medical emergency around drug issues. In this spirit the organizers of the umbrella "Project Mission" effort designed a larger series of events, similar in grassroots orientation, intended to build upon one another. These included cable television programs, special inserts in neighborhood newspapers, and weekly art-making sessions conducted with children in San Francisco housing projects. This is exactly the sort of positive coalition building that progressive groups need to engage if their efforts are to make a difference.

Critical Consciousness

In recent years the beginnings of new coalition forms have already begun to emerge, which reflect responses to changing demographics and social conditions. Single-issue groups like ACT-UP and the Campaign for Freedom of Expression formed their bases of support in local communities and then unified on a national scale. Multiplying the advances of such groups is as much a technological event as a political one. For besides specific local actions, both groups have tapped into hitherto marginalized publics seeking to see themselves identified in the media. This is one of the reasons that analyses of media have an important role in the context of contemporary political strategizing.

A number of activist groups are currently at work to synthesize issues of community dialogue with coalition building through the all-important tools of representational analysis. One highly regarded media collective, the shoestring Paper Tiger Television Manhattan cable series, critiques magazines and newspapers in its weekly programs. With makeshift sets and a comical wraparound, each weekly episode opens with the question, "It's 8:30. Do you know where your brains are?"—a spoof on a local Group W news program that asks, "It's 10 P.M.: Do you know where your kids are?" Paper Tiger episodes feature scholars or artists (commentators have included Myra Bain, Winston, Serafina Bathrick, Joan Braderman, Alexander Cockburn, Herbert Schiller, and Ynestra King) deconstructing periodicals like *Cosmopolitan* or the *New York Times*. Consider this excerpt from Murray Bookchin's reading of *Time* magazine.

> *Time* makes time disappear. Everything is the same. There is no history. . . . The essence of *Time* is that it destroys the present, the past, and the future. Just like the hands of a clock keep turning around and around and give you no message, no perspective, no coordinates, no sense of direction. What *Time* does is relax you in time.[33]

In addition to discussing the periodicals as texts, Paper Tiger programs also provide information about the economic structure of the publication, its reader demographics, the composition of its board of directors, and so on.

Recently Paper Tiger has begun to participate in school programs with the Through Our Eyes Video and History Project. In *Torn Between Colors* (1989) students produced an analysis of racial bias in the media coverage of two widely reported crimes in the New York area: the murder of African-American teenager Josuf Hawkins by a group of Bensonhurst men and the Central Park assault on a white jogger by a group of Harlem youth. With blowups of headlines projected behind them, two student narrators focus on a pair of articles about the incidents in *New York* magazine. Written by the same reporter and using similar layouts and graphics, the stories offer markedly different descriptions of the suspects in each case. The white Bensonhurst youth are pictured in suits and ties and are referred to as "a group of friends" who were "hanging out." The Latino and black men from Harlem, shown dirty and bedraggled after their arrests, are called a "pack," a "gang" who were "wilding" in the park.

But the tape does not stop with these juxtapositions. After making its point about media stereotypes and internalized racism, it begins to suggest ways to approach the problem. Accompanying footage of rallies, demonstrations, and speeches, the voiceover states, "To learn what young people were doing about racism we spoke to youth from our school and around the city. We were glad to find that many felt strongly and had taken action to put an end to the vicious cycle of racial violence. We hope that after hearing these young people more youth will contribute to the fight against racism." This is followed by student interviews and scenes of Through Our Eyes producers at work with their cameras and microphones. In discussing the tape, media curator Chris Bratton has praised *Torn Between Colors* for reaching beyond the typical questions asked by most leftist media criticism of "who says what, how, to whom, and with what effect?" by also adding "for what purpose?"[34] In suggesting activism, the tape urges viewers to respond on more than a narrative level. This is not simply a text about a text. It is a call to action.

Yet despite its antihegemonic message, *Torn Between Colors*, like certain works described earlier in this chapter, is still bound by its form to replicate the relationship of one voice speaking to the many. Low-tech production values and multiple narration help correct this problem somewhat, but the effectiveness of the message is limited, nevertheless. Indeed it is a recurrent problem for many leftist media groups that even the most critically sophisticated fail to convey their radical critiques with an equally radical attitude toward the viewing subject.

Dialogic Production

One cannot correct this situation solely with in-kind responses to the challenges received. Nor will alternative texts and radicalized institutions alone accomplish the task. To meet the conservative assault, cultural activists need to work on the very ways people conceive their relationships to each other. This means locating the sources of analysis and judgment within us all. One needs to ask how cultural producers can evaluate ways of working that dislodge conventional roles of maker and viewer, in effect encouraging audiences to be active producers of texts rather than passive receivers of them. How can artists and writers help validate the culture that people produce in the course of their daily lives?

These are deeply political issues in that they involve the ability of citizens to speak—or not speak. But unfortunately the Left has often replicated regressive practices of address that discourage such voice. As Andrew Kopkind has put it, "The natural left—as opposed to small groups of self-conscious leftists—comprises an overwhelming majority of the world's population. It can't be that this force has no power to change things for itself, and for the better. For too long, however, the 'talking' leftists have been telling the natural left (what used to be called the 'masses') what to do and how to do it."[35] This requires thinking about how to listen to the "natural left." Clearly cultural workers' ability to assist in the development of a people's culture lies in creating conducive conditions for such articulation. Some precedents can be found in the efforts of the Canadian National Film Board (NFB), which during the 1960s initiated a series of experimental programs that had profound implications for media education. As part of the NFB's "Challenge for Change" program, producers used film and video to enable local groups to communicate to government leaders with minimal third-party mediation.

Based on earlier cinema verité and "consent film" efforts by producers like John Adair, Colin Low, George Stoney, and Sol Worth, NFB units attempted to confront the paternalistic notion that filmmakers could make objective statements about those photographed. They did this by engaging community members in the process of their own documentation—much in the way anthropologists conduct "participatory research." Dorothy Hénaut and Bonnie Klein applied these principles in a series entitled "VTR–St. Jacques" (1969) that involved a French-speaking community near Montreal. St. Jacques residents scripted, acted, shot, and critiqued a series of programs describing the issues facing their neighborhood. Hénaut and Klein found that citizens quickly gravitated to the idea of producing a tape about their civic concerns.

As the project moved to other Canadian towns it quickly demonstrated the enormous potential in creating new forums for popular speech. In group after group, it became apparent that vast storehouses of ideas and expression had been waiting for release. Of course, video was simply the catalyst. Although their techniques were widely adopted by other groups, Hénaut and Klein eventually became disturbed by the extent to which the enabling technology was romanticized. As Hénaut later explained, "A pernicious mythology grew up that video was somehow a miracle maker, that video was it. And of course, disappointment followed, because no amount of video can replace a good community organizer, no amount of video can make fuzzy thinking turn into clear social and political analysis."[36]

A more contemporary version of this practice occurs in Boomer, WV, where Terry Robbins mediates local disputes in 10 regional mining communities. Supported by a consortium of churches, Robbins documents confrontations among members of opposing factions who collaborate with him in the conceptualization of a finished tape. The programs are then screened in town meetings, for the dual purpose of publicizing the issues and helping community members to evaluate their interactions. In one instance, Robbins and the citizens of Minden, WV, (population 400) campaigned for the cleanup of a local toxic waste site. With Robbins's assistance the group took its case to local and state officials, and eventually to the Environmental Protection Agency. After months of investigation and bureaucratic red tape, the 15-year-old chemical dump was recognized as one of the five most dangerous sites in the country.

According to Robbins, many of the citizens who got involved in the Minden project had never experienced an organized community campaign. Thus Robbins's larger mission was one of educating community members to recognize the potentials of their own collective voice. It is this educational role that cultural workers must recognize. Like so many other aspects of community life, teaching and learning have become segregated from the everyday experience of most people. Artists, writers, and teachers can help restore the unity of education and community life. Particularly in the current era, this need for popular education exists outside, and even against, state schooling. It would seem that cultural workers and their alternative organizations are ideally situated to facilitate a renaissance of a people's pedagogy.

Recent debates over free speech have dramatically brought this point home. At the height of the congressional controversies over the National Endowment for the Arts, Massachusetts artist Richard Bolton assembled an installation entitled *The Emperor's New Clothes: Censorship, Sexuality, and the Body Politic* at the Photographic Resource Center on the Boston University campus. Occurring amid a flurry of free speech exhibitions (coinciding, in fact, with the Boston exhibition of the infamous Robert Mapplethorpe retrospective, "The Perfect Moment"), the show was conceived to encourage community dialogue. The installation juxtaposed three categories of erotic photographs—identified by Bolton as "Art, Fashion, and Pornography"—arranged on panels with written responses by prominent personalities in the censorship debate. "Art" images included a frame from Cindy Sherman's "Untitled Film Stills" (1978) series, an image from Larry Clark's *Teenage Lust* (1983), and pictures by Mapplethorpe, Joel Peter Witkin, and Ruth Berhnart, among others. "Fashion" meant Calvin Klein and Prince Matchabelli ads from *Vogue* and *Vanity Fair*, as well as a provocative shot of Madonna on the cover of *Interview* magazine. "Pornography" ranged from a *Playboy* centerfold to photos from magazines with names like *Big Dick* and *Lesbian Fever*.

In preparing the show, Bolton sent packages of images to 160 potential respondents on both sides of the political aisle, from Donald Wildmon of the American Family Association to censored artist Andres Serrano. Many

Installation view of Richard Bolton's series *The Emperor's New Clothes: Censorship, Sexuality, and the Body Politic* (1990). Used by permission.

responded to the invitation directly, such as ACT-UP member Aldo Hernandez ("Sooo bodacious and mmm . . . tasty"), Talking Heads leader David Byrne (who replied with an audiotape), feminist attorney Catherine MacKinnon ("a woman was tortured to make this picture"), as well as such notables as communications theorist Stewart Ewen, artist Leon Golub, and critic Carol Squiers. Others chose to make their comments elsewhere. Ultraconservative columnist James F. Cooper wrote in the pages of the *New York City Tribune* that he could not denigrate himself by responding to images with "so little artistic beauty."[37] When Nancy Sutton of Citizens for Family First received her package, her group registered a criminal complaint with the Boston police.

Visitors to the exhibit could respond as well with written comments or images that would be added to display panels. In this way the show evolved over the course of time, making public feedback part of the installation. As Bolton put it in the *Boston Globe*, "This is basically an attempt to create a forum in which to think about various relationships between art, sex, and obscenity. . . . It's a forum for members of the community to learn about issues and express their opinions. To think about obscenity, to analyze and then respond to these issues, a community first has to look at pictures."[38] As a consequence of both form and notoriety, "The Emperor's New Clothes" provided a public forum for censorship issues as few art exhibits do. Although originated by an individual, the installation relied from its inception on a multiplicity of voices to analyze the issues at hand. Occurring within a conventional gallery context, this gesture constituted a break with the traditional view of the artist-as-seer.

By incorporating the opinions of artists and nonartists, liberals and conservatives, Bolton redefined the function of the art gallery. Rather than a space of aesthetic contemplation, the Photographic Resource Center became a fulcrum for community debate. This point was underscored by the hundreds of written and visual comments added to the display by the public, as well as the way the exhibition was covered by the mass media. Few exhibitions of any kind have succeeded in quite this way. For not only did the show make a point, it posed questions to the community for evaluation and response. In doing so, "The Emperor's New Clothes" began to chip away at the certainty that we all come to expect from "experts," by suggesting that ultimate answers are often not that easy to come by. As David Joselit commented at the end of his review of the show:

> But perhaps more interesting, in light of Mapplethorpe's assertion of a sexual identity that is discontinuous, built from elements of both aggression and passivity, is the way some of Bolton's respondents identify with a variety of positions and fantasies. A lesbian artist talks about dicks, and what it feels like to be talking about them; a male gay activist gushed over a *Playboy* centerfold.
>
> As we read between the lines, these responses make us realize that the names we have for ourselves—straight, gay, etc.—are not

stable positions. Like Mapplethorpe's "perfect moments," or Bolton's "emperor's new clothes," they require constant redefinition, challenging the limits of our creativity.[39]

Significant in this statement is the acknowledgment of the dynamic character of meaning, of the way "The Emperor's New Clothes" calls for reassessment on the viewer's part. This is effected both intellectually (in the process of viewing the show) and literally (inasmuch as viewers are asked to participate).

A similar approach in activating viewer participation was taken by the circulating "Drawing the Line" exhibition by the Canadian Kiss and Tell collective of Vancouver. The show's primary focus is a series of 8-by-10-inch matted photographs created by Kiss and Tell members Emma Stoneridge, Susan Stewart, and Persimmon Blackbridge. The photographs were taken over the course of a year and depict two women in a variety of sexual activities, ranging from casual caresses to sadomasochistic role playing. Displayed in the gallery the images are arranged "from least to most controversial." The interactive aspect of the exhibition and its title derive from the open invitation to all gallery visitors to write comments about the exhibition—in effect, to "draw the line" at the point the pictures became difficult. Women were encouraged to write on the gallery walls around the photos; men were to put their remarks in a book nearby.

At venues in Vancouver, San Francisco, and elsewhere the exhibition has attracted considerable attention and, like "The Emperor's New Clothes," stimulated community discussion. Yet, the strategy of "Drawing the Line" was somewhat more pointed. Beyond inviting response, the exhibition articulated a continuum of choice upon which viewers were obliged to locate themselves. It asked people to answer and reflect upon questions of eroticism, pornography, morality, and acceptability. In every showing the walls immediately filled with commentary. What would typically be a blank space evolved into a dense (and often contradictory) text. As reported by Marusia Bociurkiw, a section of the Vancouver installation read:

This show has discouraged the cynicism about our traditionally anti-sex lesbian feminist community.

This is what the man who raped me said women like.

These pictures were not made by the man who raped you. They only remind you of what he said. *He* is the one to be angry with, not these photos.

These images represent choices.[40]

Choices for makers and viewers alike. Ultimately, "Drawing the Line" tells us that to a certain extent representation is what we choose to make of it, although we examine these processes all too infrequently. This message of critical analysis—of self and simulacrum—is the pedagogical point of the show.

Struggles and Crises

Perhaps the most powerfully transformative new discursive spaces are those resulting from human crises. Such ethically situated movements have the ability to call communities into existence and redefine social practices. For artists and teachers this lesson is especially important. As stated by Douglas Crimp in his introduction to *AIDS: Cultural Analysis/Cultural Activism*:

> Art does have the power to save lives, and it is this very power that must be recognized, fostered, and supported in every way possible. But if we are to do this, we will have to abandon the idealist conception of art. We don't need a cultural renaissance; we need cultural practices actively participating in the struggle against AIDS. We don't need to transcend the epidemic; we need to end it.[41]

More than any other issue, the AIDS crisis has demonstrated the need and potential of positive alliances, as it has mobilized cultural workers who never considered themselves political activists. The crisis has fostered forms of cultural practice of a directly pedagogical character, works that both disseminate public information and challenge the epidemic's discursive construction. The AIDS activism of such groups and individuals as Gran Fury, John Greyson, Jan Zita Grover, Sunil Gupta, Paula Treichler, the Testing the Limits Collective and Simon Watney has foregrounded ways that public knowledge of AIDS is produced through language and media. More dramatically, this work has frequently illustrated the often overlooked connection of such critically produced knowledge and material circumstance. As Crimp suggests, in addition to deploying alternative texts, this activist writing and picturemaking entails a critique of the way the cultural world participates in or resists representational conventions in both its own realm and society at large.

"WITH 42,000 DEAD, ART IS NOT ENOUGH. TAKE COLLECTIVE DIRECT ACTION TO END THE AIDS CRISIS." This statement by the activist collective Gran Fury appeared on a membership announcement of The Kitchen, a respected artists' space in New York City. Its message reflects the growing frustration of many cultural workers with the arts community's aestheticized insularity. As a figure for the hermetic closure that typifies all of academic culture, the Gran Fury poster makes a claim for a form of expression that reaches beyond the art world. But even more importantly, it links culture to everyday struggles. In this way the conventional discourse of art is cast into oblivion and replaced by a culture of use and relevance.

At a time when conservative politicians would legislate matters of life and death we can no longer cling to class-bound models of cultural elitism. All of us have an interest in promoting practices that give voice to the broadest number of people. This means making direct efforts to eliminate exclusionary tendencies that devalue the voices of nonartists. Beyond opening new discursive spaces, it also means closing old ones, for this is not a politically disinterested process. Rather than perpetuating forms of expression that tell people that everyday forms of culture lack value, we should try to find ways to develop these forms. When we become willing to recognize that art is made by people everywhere rather than handed to them by us, our work will begin to achieve the popular relevance it has been lacking. Upon this work we can forge the foundation of new political alliances.

NOTES

1. Ernesto Laclau and Chantal Mouffe, *Hegemony and Socialist Strategy: Towards a Radical Democratic Politics*, trans. Winston Moore and Paul Cammack (London: Verso, 1985), p. 189.

2. Carole S. Vance, "The War on Culture," *Art in America*, Sept. 1989, pp. 39–45.

3. Samuel Bowles and Herbert Gintis, *Schooling in Capitalist America: Educational Reform and the Contradictions of Economic Life* (New York: Basic Books, 1976), pp. 20–26.

4. Donna J. Haraway, *Simians, Cyborgs, and Women: The Reinvention of Nature* (New York: Routledge, 1991), p. 154.

5. Fred Glass, "Toward a Morphology of Labor Video," *Afterimage* 17, no. 2 (Sept. 1989): 12.

6. Andrew Kopkind, "The Rising of the Wretched," *Nation* 252, no. 7 (May 6, 1991): 586.

7. bell hooks, "Talking Back," in *Out There: Marginalization in Contemporary Cultures*, ed. Russell Ferguson, Martha Gever, Trinh T. Minh-ha, and Cornell West (Cambridge: MIT Press, 1990), p. 341.

8. See Nancy Fraser, "Rethinking the Public Sphere: A Contribution to the Critique of Actually Existing Democracy," *Social Text* 25/26 (1990): 56–80.

9. As cited in Michael Renov, "Early Newsreel: The Construction of a Political Imaginary for the New Left," *Afterimage* 14, no. 7 (Feb. 1987): 12–15.

10. Cornell West, "The New Cultural Politics of Difference," in *Out There*, ed. Ferguson, p. 32.

11. Pam Sporn, interview with author, February 1991.

12. Diane Neumaier, "Our People Are the Internal Exiles," in *Cultures in Contention*, ed. Douglas Kahn and Diane Neumaier (Seattle: Real Comet Press, 1985), p. 73.

13. Ibid.

14. See Abigail Solomon-Godeau, "Living with Contradictions: Critical Practices in the Age of Supply-side Aesthetics," in *Universal Abandon? The Politics of Postmodernism*, ed. Andrew Ross (Minneapolis: University of Minnesota Press, 1989).

15. Raymond Williams, *Marxism and Literature* (New York: Oxford University Press, 1977), p. 114.

16. Victor Burgin, *The End of Art Theory: Criticism and Postmodernity* (Atlantic Highlands, NJ: Humanities Press, 1986), p. 190.

17. Tom Lovett, "The Challenge of Community Education in Social and Political Change," *Convergence II*, no. 1 (1978): 47–48.

18. Ibid, p. 47.

19. Ibid.

20. Philip Wexler, *Social Analysis of Education: After the New Sociology* (New York: Routledge and Kegan Paul, 1987), p. 183.

21. Andrew Dewdney and Martin Lister, "Youth and Photography," *Ten* 8, no. 21 (1986): 12.

22. Andrew Dewdney and Martin Lister, *Youth, Culture, and Photography* (London: Macmillan, 1988), p. 5.

23. Ibid.

24. Interview with author, February 1991.

25. Don Adams and Arlene Goldbard, "Social Studies: Public Policy and Media Literacy," *Independent* 12, no. 7 (Aug./Sept. 1989): 36–38.

26. Ibid., "Learning to Read the World," *exposure* 28, no. 1/2 (1991): 14.

27. Lawrence Daressa, "The Politics of Distribution," *Afterimage* 15, no. 2 (September 1987): 8–9.

28. Matthew Baigell and Julia Williams, eds. *Artists against War and Facism: Papers of the First American Artists' Congress* (New Brunswick, NJ: Rutgers University Press, 1986), p. 47.

29. Ibid., p. 65.

30. Ibid., p. 113.

31. Ibid., p. 34.

32. Joan Wallach Scott, "History in Crisis? The Other Side's Side of the Story," *American Historical Review* 94, no. 3 (June 1989): 689.

33. Deedee Halleck, "Paper Tiger Television," in *Cultures in Contention*, ed. Kahn and Neumaier, p. 35.

34. Chris Bratton, "Teaching TV: Toward Media Literacy," gallery notes (New York: Artists' Space, 1990), n.p.

35. Kopkind, "Rising of the Wretched," p. 588.

36. Dorothy Todd Hénaut, "Asking the Right Questions: Video in the Hands of Citizens" (unpublished manuscript, National Film Board of Canada, 1975).

37. James F. Cooper, "Real Issue in the NEA Battle: Artistic Merit," *New York City Tribune*, July 15, 1990.

38. Mark Munro, " 'X-Rated' Photo Exhibit Aims to Raise Eyebrows—and Issues," *Boston Globe* Aug. 3, 1990.

39. David Joselit, "The Body (Im)politic," *Boston Phoenix*, sec. 3, Aug. 10, 1990.

40. Marusia Bociurkiw, "The Transgressive Camera," *Afterimage* 16, no. 6 (Jan. 1989): 19. Documentation of Kiss and Tell exhibitions has recently been collected in Susan Stewart, Persimmon Blackridge, and Lizard Jones, *Drawing the Line: Lesbian Sexual Politics on the Wall* (Vancouver: Press Gang Publishers, 1991).

41. Douglas Crimp, "AIDS: Cultural Activism/Cultural Analysis," *October* 43 (Winter 1987): 6–7.

6

Changing the Subject:
Pedagogy and Citizenship

Democracy is a relative term. Like any other expression, its meaning is a matter of interpretation, debate, and contest—and in recent years it is a word we have heard a great deal: from the "democratic" reforms in Nicaragua to the suppression of democratic protest in China's Tiananmen Square, to the democratic revolutions throughout Eastern Europe, to the democratic liberation of Kuwait. In light of these propitious events and the presumed role of the United States in their occurrence, George Bush termed his first year in office "the year of democracy." Yet despite such historic circumstances on the international front, the domestic state of democracy could not be more in question. As detailed by Brian Wallis:

> At home democracy had been inverted. If democracy meant equal rights for all citizens, the attack on the welfare system and the systematic transfer of wealth from the poor to the rich signaled a fundamental reconsolidation of the power of the elite. If democracy meant participation of the citizenry in decision making, the perpetuation of policies opposed by a majority of the public (such as the illegal funding of the contras) signaled an expansion of presidential powers and an increase in the rule of the state. If democracy meant freedom of the press, Americans were faced with media that were increasingly owned by a small minority of corporations. And if democracy meant the enfranchisement of all voters, the 22.7 percent of the population that actually voted for Reagan's successor in 1988 signaled the disinterest of most of the population in the democratic process.[1]

While totalitarian regimes and oppressive bureaucracies tumbled across the globe, within the United States the military-industrial complex consolidated its grip through a decade of conservative assistance. As the 1980s advanced, the aggressiveness of this program intensified, and by decade's end conservatives had moved beyond the realm of conventional politics. In the words of former Reagan director of communications Patrick Buchanan, "While the Right has been busy winning primaries and elections, cutting taxes, and funding anti-communist guerrillas abroad, the Left has been quietly seizing all the commanding heights of American art and culture."[2]

With a program of moral fundamentalism and unproblematic patriotism, the Right has recognized the strategic value of cultural politics and has seized the high ground in both education and the art world. With its emphasis on tradition rather than emancipatory memory, canonical literature rather than multiple literacies, censorship rather than free expression, conservatives have enforced a view of the arts and humanities that privileges particular forms of history and community over others.

This vision of culture would deny the voices of culturally diverse groups in favor of a regressive monolith inscribed in Eurocentrism, racism, and compulsory heterosexuality. For the most part, progressives have been unprepared, disorganized, and fragmented in response to the Right's cultural campaign. They have permitted conservatives to capitalize on the issue of difference in assaulting the Left on multiple fronts. Worse still, the Left has often responded to the conservative assault on its own terms, in effect validating the very frame of the opposing position.

In what follows I will discuss the implications of this struggle for redefining the structure of progressive response. At the heart of the issue lies the need for a new form of coalition politics within the Left that will allow it to build upon people's individual strengths and to gain (rather than suffer) from our differences. To do this requires a recognition of the common challenges facing all cultural workers involved in these debates, whether they work in the school, the gallery, the studio, or the office. It means recognizing the importance of broadening such concepts as education and artistic practice into a more integrated category of cultural writing that produces a new paradigm of activist practice. These principles should be attached to the culture of everyday life.

In sketching these interwoven political and pedagogical agendas I will organize these proposals within the framework of a radical democratic imaginary that speaks in the tradition of history's great emancipatory struggles. As described by Chantal Mouffe, such a practice rejects the conservative deployment of "liberty" as an excuse for exploitation and self-interest, and restores its true meaning as a value that "while belonging to the individual, can only be exercised collectively and presuppose the existence of equal rights for others."[3] Such a political philosophy requires a pedagogy that supports the production of diverse knowledge as a prerequisite for an egalitarian civic order. While honoring difference, it recognizes that democracies are noisy and clamorous affairs.

In the context of cultural struggle, this involves a critical reexamination of the way textual signification is constructed, as well as an acknowledgment of the frequent indeterminacy of narrative representations. Yet, while rejecting modernism's claim of rationality, it is important to salvage its most idealistic impulses. If anything has been learned from recent debates over identity and difference, it is that human agency does not vanish in the presumed absence of the humanist subject or the presence of decentered identities. In broadening this notion of education, the Left can develop mutually supportive practices for contesting forms of cultural dominance wherever people shape their identities and their relations to the world. Finally this chapter will review the implications of this broadened practice within various sites of cultural production and examine what it might mean for future alliances and forms of solidarity among artists, educators, and other cultural workers.

THE CONSERVATIVE ASSAULT

Although cultural workers in different arenas face particularized challenges, they share a common estrangement from power that comes from a discourse that establishes itself as central and all else as marginal. There are, as well, distinct similarities in the ways that different voices are discredited and excluded from that discourse. In both the educational and cultural worlds conservative reformers have consistently cautioned against the anarchistic implications of unbridled democracy.

In the area of schooling, the conservative vanguard has quite unapologetically stated that the drive to egalitarianism and the encouragement of social critique have been the major reasons for the decay of the American academy. In calling for a tightening of curricula around a certified list of "great books" and a crackdown on academic "permissiveness" and "relativism," Allan Bloom has become the standard-bearer in the conservative movement to legislate its own hegemony. This position is written in more specificity in the work of E. D. Hirsch, Jr., who has mapped out the particulars of the "common culture" to be enforced. More dogmatic than Bloom in his view of history, Hirsch would wrench selected names, dates, and ideas from their times and circumstances and render them ritualistic monuments to the dominant regime. This philosophical program is being carried forward at the level of state curricula in New York and California by front-line conservative activists like Diane Ravitch and Chester Finn, among others.

These efforts in the educational realm are but fragments of a broader and more heterogeneous pattern of conservative activism. During the past decade this movement has assumed many forms, from the religious fundamentalism of groups like the American Family Association to the "trickle-down" economic theories promoted by the Reagan administration to the assaults on affirmative action and reproductive rights enacted by the new Supreme Court. These actions have contributed to an atmosphere on both the Right and the Left of heightened political consciousness, which has induced a new emphasis on culture—a heightened belief that social and political events can be influenced through interventions in the realm of public representation.

On the cultural front, the assaults on democracy have been waged by a multitude of conservative reactionaries launching both independent and coordinated volleys. Beginning with the infamous *Mandate for Leadership* Reagan transition, we were told that "as a true friend of democracy," the federal cultural apparatus should "teach the nation the limits of egalitarian impulse."[4] This meant developing a cultural program implemented through the National Endowments for the Arts and Humanities that would reimpose "standards" and "quality" into a system deemed to have run amok with "social crusades, political action, or political education as demanded by narrowly partisan interests."[5] The covert cultural oppression of the 1980s evolved in the overt acts of censorship, defunding, arrest, and harassment of the 1990s.

During this period politicians have increasingly searched for pragmatic rationales for cultural spending that could be equated (at least theoretically) with economic gain: a more intelligent citizen, a more perceptive worker, a more discriminating consumer of goods. Such logic has been reinforced by functionalist views of social adaptation held in place by an obliteration of any distractions. This attitude toward culture both excludes other perspectives and ignores its own self-justifying tendencies. Gayatri Spivak argues that this blindness is endemic to all dominant social speech, because "when a narrative is constructed, something is left out. When an end is defined, other ends are rejected, and one might not know what those ends are."[6]

These conceptions of knowledge fail to acknowledge that stories and images change when viewed in different social contexts and at different times. They cannot recognize that reception is an inherent part of the process and that signification is therefore always local and contextual. Instead they offer a pedagogy of pessimism, disengagement, and a failure of human agency. Manuel Alvarado and John O. Thompson identify three categories through which this negative cultural interpellation functions:

de-skilling: abilities, know-hows, sensitivities are subtracted rather than added to the audience-members' repertoire (Leaving them with less Liberty to act than they might have had);

self-denigration: the audience-members' pleasure is made dependent on thinking systematically less well of themselves, and of those like themselves, than the Equality and Fraternity (sic) considerations would suggest was desirable;

contempt for others: pleasure derives from fictional resolution of audience worries via some sort of scapegoating or "containment" or worry-inducing groups.[7]

CULTURAL WORKERS AND EDUCATIONAL ACTIVISM

The cultural conservativism of the last decade has not gone unchallenged. Increasingly artists, writers, and teachers argue that culture cannot be reduced to a single narrative, that texts cannot be removed from histories and contexts, and that the separation of high and low culture is itself a fabrication. Indeed a massive movement has been slowly gaining strength to counter the conservative will to cultural homogeneity, as manifest in battles in universities nationwide over the canon, the demands within local school districts for more diverse curricula, the revolt of arts groups against the repression of the NEA, and the overt challenges to conservative authority from recording artists.

Within the last few years, we have seen artists joining with school people to assert a more activist stance on issues of pedagogy. From last year's "Democracy: Education" program organized in New York City by Group Material to the more recent "Magnetic Youth" video compilation at LACE in Los Angeles to the practices of groups like Artists/Teachers Concerned, Rise and Shine Productions, and Tim Rollins + Kids of Survival, cultural workers in the studio and the classroom are recognizing the imperative of cooperative practice. For artists this reflects a further dissatisfaction within Kantian models of aesthetic transcendence that separates art from life. Increasingly cultural workers are recognizing the limits of gallery-bound avant-gardism in a world of lived homophobia, racial oppression, and escalating economic inequity. More and more they see the importance of getting involved beyond a theoretical or textual level with the political exigencies that affect their lives.

From across the occupational spectrum artists, teachers, writers, and other cultural workers are recognizing their responsibilities as active agents in combatting the tyranny of cultural conservatism. Moreover, they are recognizing that this is largely a pedagogical process that takes place as individuals come to know the means through which they are ideologically constituted. This is what activates human agency, as it begins to tell people that their actions can make a difference, that their voices can be heard. It means deconstructing the repressive myths that would objectify individuals into faceless masses of "the public." It means challenging debilitating beliefs in the intractability of rationalized government bureaucracies and corporate oligarchies; it means revealing the discursive myths that perpetuate an endless psychic self-dissatisfaction that can only be cured through systemic obedience and consumption.

Cultural workers can also find common ground in understanding their roles as what Henry Giroux has termed "transformative intellectuals."[8] This is an activist sensibility that motivates cultural workers to become involved with their communities and break through the shells of academic discourse. At the same time it is an identity that leaves behind totalizing claims of authenticity, originality, or objectivity.

This represents a view of cultural workers as "bearers of dangerous memory" who combine a sense of their own partiality with a commitment for justice and an attempt to overcome human exploitation. Most importantly, this is not a call for cultural workers to become wedded to some abstract totalizing ideal that removes them from everyday life, that turns them into prophets of perfection and certainty; on the contrary, it represents a call for artists and teachers to undertake social criticism not as outsiders but as public and concerned educators who address the most pressing social and political concerns of their neighborhood, community, and society, as individuals who have an intimate knowledge with the workings of everyday life, who make organized connections with the historical traditions that provide themselves, audiences, and students with a voice, history, and sense of individual freedom and democratic community.[9]

Central to this position is the understanding of the productive character of knowledge. This is the realization that learning is not dependent on transmission models of master/servant dialectics, but rather an active process generated between sender and receiver. Audiences, viewers, and students construct knowledge from the materials presented to them. Although cultural workers can exert considerable influence over that process, such influence is always partial.

Acknowledging the role of the "learning subject" in the construction of culture, we affirm processes of agency, difference, and, ultimately, democracy. We suggest to students and audiences that they have a role in the making of their world and that they need not accept positions as passive spectators or consumers. This is a position that recognizes and encourages the atmosphere of diverse and contradictory opinions so dreaded by the conservative proponents of a "common culture." It functions on the belief that a healthy democracy is one that is always being scrutinized and tested.

FROM RESISTANCE TO PRODUCTION

How then are these productive theories put into practice? Considerable recent attention has been focused on resistance as an indication of student agency. Research conducted during the last decade, most notably at Great Britain's Birmingham Center for Contemporary Cultural Studies, has demonstrated that mechanisms of social and cultural reproduction are never complete and are usually met with some degree of opposition. In their studies of teenage subcultural groups, proponents of contemporary "resistance theory" have concluded that within any environment of dominant authority, there remains room for the refusal, rejection or reconfiguration of ideological codes. Although its existence is undeniable, this revolutionary populism has a limited tactical effect. For example, radical appropriations of vestmentary styles are almost immediately co-opted by the fashion industry.[10] Similarly the agencies of resistance that stymie cultural reproduction often contribute to a process that locks students into an underclass role. The most common resistances to oppressive schooling (nonperformance, truancy, disruptive behavior) generally culminate in academic failure, thus giving the system the last word. It is precisely for this reason that progressive educators have a role to play in helping students to understand and articulate their own critical power.

The teacher's job, then, becomes one of unraveling motivations for student behavior in order to facilitate a productive revolution. This can be explained in psychoanalytic terms as a means of channeling unsatisfied desire. Ideology is not so much a matter of "false consciousness" as it is an individual's operative "unconscious." Shoshana Felman describes a process whereby the teacher functions as an analyst to help students find their own wisdom.

> Through the analytic dialogue the analyst, indeed, has first to learn where to situate the ignorance: where his [sic] own textual knowledge is resisted. It is, however, out of this resistance, out of the patient's active ignorance, out of the patient's speech which says more than it itself knows, that the analyst will come to learn the patient's own unconscious knowledge, that knowledge which is inaccessible to itself because it cannot tolerate knowing that it knows; and it is the signifiers of this constitutively a-reflexive knowledge coming from the patient that the analyst returns to the patient from his different vantage point, from his non-reflexive, asymmetrical position as an Other.[11]

The question that even such an "analytical" approach leaves begging is the extent to which teachers project themselves (often unintentionally) into their students' work. Here again lies the danger of reproducing the same roles one seeks to undermine. Liberal educators can think they are producing a more open situation when in fact they are creating a more insidious and covert relationship of surveillance and control.[12] The much-celebrated liberal ethic of "process" or of "learning how to learn" can be simply another method of regularizing behavior. What we conceive of as individuality is clearly formulated within the apparatuses of social determination. Students are encouraged to express themselves, explore their environments, and learn through doing—but only in such a manner as the teacher approves.

In theoretical terms, this condition of learning is termed "transference," in reference to the way students transfer to teachers the emotional attachments once reserved for their parents. Young people (children in particular) seek affection and approval from figures of authority, and because teachers are presumed to possess knowledge, they easily assume parental roles. Not surprisingly, institutionalized teaching often encourages this imaginary relationship as a device for reproducing social norms. Because of this, teachers frequently exploit transference phenomena rather than pressing students to move toward subjective autonomy.

In most discussions of educational practice the delicate interplay of authority and agency is frequently reduced to an either/or question—with little consideration of the middle ground. This is similar to the problem that arises in the art community in defining the roles of makers and audiences. The rarely examined emotional relationship between pedagogical subject and object informs a work by New York video artist Sarah Drury. In the deceptively brief *Helen Keller Knows She's There* (1989), Drury reflects on the learning process through a montage of pictorial, written, and spoken elements. The eight-minute work weaves textual fragments into a disjunctive voice-over adapted from Keller's book *The Story of My Life* (1954). Although one might expect this to entail a recap of Keller's struggle with deafness and blindness, Drury opts for a more impressionistic rendering that focuses on passages dealing with Keller's acquisition of language. The tape comprises a series of close-ups, intercut with long blackouts, that follow a solitary figure on a walk (perhaps a search) through an area of beach and tall grass. The blackouts evoke sensations of blindness that heighten one's attention to the halting voice of a woman reading from Keller's text. The voice-over is similarly punctuated by long silences that suggest the inability to hear.

As the tape progresses, themes emerge of representational ambiguity and psychic doubt. As Keller's perceptual capacities cause her to question the world around her, she writes, "I cannot be quite sure of the boundary line between my ideas and those I find in books. I suppose that may be because so many of my impressions come to me through the medium of others' eyes and ears. . . . What I read becomes the very substance of my own mind." Extending these motifs of simulacral displacement, the Keller narration moves to a description of the teaching transaction. In a series of passages that might have come from a psychoanalytic textbook, Keller writes of her identification with her tutor Ann Sullivan (to whom she often referred simply as "Teacher"), stating, "I can scarcely think of myself as apart from her. I feel that her being is inseparable from my own and that the footsteps of my life are in hers."

Following Jacques Lacan, Constance Penley has delineated the close correspondence between a relationship of learning and one of love. "Teaching proceeds by way of seduction," Penley writes. "The student wants to learn because he or she loves the teacher insofar as he or she presumes that the teacher *knows*."[13] *Helen Keller Knows She's There* conveys this quality with a variety of subtle and not-so-subtle references that derive in part from Keller's lyrical writing style. Late in the tape Keller recounts an episode in which the vulnerability of the invalid, the student, and the lover converge. "Suddenly my ecstasy gave way to terror, for my foot struck against a rock. And in the next instant there was a rush of water over my head. The good firm earth had slipped from my feet and everything seemed shut out from this strange all-enveloping environment: life, earth, air, and love." Engulfed by the swirling water, Keller is infantilized by powers over which she has no control. Finally, "the sea, as if weary of its new toy, threw me back to the shore. And in another instant I was clasped in my teacher's arms. Oh the comfort of the long tender embrace."

Through its dual messages of subjective ambiguity and pedagogical attraction, the tape suggests that Keller is undergoing the process of unconscious transformation by which the teacher's very way of thinking passes to the student. In this way the child represses his or her own impulses and internalizes the controlling superego of the adult, often suffering the side effects later in life. What passes to the student is more a set of codes or styles than a cohesive body of ideas. It is what Gregory Ulmer has termed an implicit pedagogy of "total knowledge."[14] As the tape concludes, Keller seems unable to transcend her need for Teacher, and the two remain together for life. As a consequence Sullivan remains the object of unexamined transference, a character of the archetypical pedagogue.

Obviously this is not a typical student/teacher relationship, but the lesson it provides is an important one. Within an atmosphere of pedagogical transference the essence of teaching is seen to inhere within a knowledgeable person, rather than in something that happens between the teacher and student.[15] Such a treatment is tolerable within the logic of *Helen Keller Knows She's There*, for to unmask the structure of the relationship would be to defuse the emotional tension of the tape. At the same time the story provides a lesson for the radical educator in learning when to exert (and yield) power in the educational event. In the final analysis the teacher can neutralize transference by revealing its presence through a self-critical approach to pedagogy.[16]

According to Freirian methodology, one avoids such an overdetermined relationship by working toward a "dialogic" exchange in which the teacher and student work as partners. Again, Felman is instructive in explaining that the pedagogic relationship

> is not a substance but a structural dynamic: it is not contained by any individual but comes about out of the mutual apprenticeship between two partially unconscious speeches which both say more than they know. Dialogue is thus the radical condition of learning and of knowledge, the analytically constitutive condition through which ignorance becomes structurally informative; knowledge is thus irreducibly dialogic.[17]

Clearly this is an impossibility in absolute terms, considering the institutional contexts in which teaching occurs, its compulsory legal status, and the implicit parent-child relationships implied. We can mediate this paradox, however, by becoming aware of it and by critically examining the work done in schools. Like analysis, education is an interminable project, and the best teachers are those who learn from and with students.

BEYOND INDIVIDUALISM

Regrettably in the reified atmosphere of textbook debates and the quantifiable curriculum, knowledge is rarely treated as anything more than an exchangeable currency. A society predicated on self-interest and competition fosters a retreat to a banking concept of education. In such an environment many of the Left's most important messages have failed to engage the mainstream of cultural and political life. The task facing progressive culture is to devise a counterstrategy for popularizing its radical critique of society. This will not be accomplished by competitive individualism, because it entails the rendering of disparate needs into collective action. The program will also require more than ideological proselytizing via "alternative" films, tapes, and photography. It will involve nothing less than a renegotiation of sending and receiving roles, for democracy hinges on the active participation of all citizens.

How, then, is this dynamic put into motion in practical terms? The Right has recognized the importance of education as a site of ideological contest, because in the classroom both text and audience can be contained. Progressive cultural workers need to take back that terrain with a program that weakens its controlling grip, while encouraging subjective critique. Using the classroom as a laboratory, the contemporary women's movement developed a variety of practical approaches to both expose and correct the oppression of women. These strategies were implemented through efforts to restructure the actual classroom experience through such devices as circular arrangements of chairs, small-group sessions, calling instructors by first names, journal keeping, and interactive modes of teaching.[18] The limitation of this approach is that unless measures are taken to extend consciousness-raising exercises beyond the classroom, the larger hierarchies outside remain intact. As discussed earlier, production exercises can promote such outreach by extending lessons beyond school premises. In effect, we can use the classroom as a laboratory to encourage the evolution and development of everyday forms of culture. It would be a grave mistake, though, to vest too much credit in the form of what is actually an exercise in community interaction. Such dynamics cannot be forced. After all, school is but a *partially* consensual environment at best.

Hunter College education professor Herb Perr describes a series of approaches in which students produce such works as murals, gardens, or window displays in their own neighborhoods.[19] According to Perr, most kids start out liking art, but the more time they spend in school the less satisfying the experience becomes. What was once a form of creative play is transformed through institutionalized education into a rigid system of rules and rewards. As in most conventional pedagogies, the underlying mission in art education is the socialization of students into roles of work and consumption. Benefits accrue only to those who can satisfy the authoritarian demands of a teacher. Frequently those demands are little more than idiosyncratic interpretations of a market aesthetic alien to the lives of most people. As Perr explains, "Participatory activity of benefit to the community is not considered a primary objective. And for all of the rhetoric about educating the young to be thoughtful citizens who care for their fellow beings, private gain over public good is recurrently the message received."[20]

Central to Perr's approach are the collective processes of nonindividualized production and a dialogue with the audience. For example, in preparing the window display, students first tour the local community to study, sketch, and photograph representative samples, often interviewing both shopkeepers and passersby in the process. They then discuss conventional uses of shop windows (as promotional sites for products) versus noncommercial applications (such as artists' installations). Next, four to seven students come together in a production meeting. Each member of the team is encouraged to offer suggestions, and all remarks are recorded by a group note taker. When a consensus is reached on the direction of the project, the team selects a site and gets permission for its use. Securing consent necessitates contact not only with the owner or proprietor, but with workers, customers, or others who might be affected. Production crew members then volunteer for specific tasks and execute the plan. On completion of the project, students, teachers, and other classes examine the work—and again people who use and travel by the window are interviewed. In this way school cultural production is directly linked to nonschool forms of production and use.

To sidestep the alienating consumerism of conventional art studies, Perr's assignments often draw upon student cultural experience. By stressing the group process involved in executing an ephemeral project like a sidewalk chalk drawing or a parade, the lessons prevent excess preoccupation with finished objects. At the same time, emphasis is subtly shifted from traditional forms of high culture to more immediate forms of daily culture. Other exercises involve analyses of particular cultural forms such as television, newspapers, or even children's board games. Students are encouraged to examine the relationship between mass media fictions and their own lives. "Do the pictures of people and places remind you of your family, friends, and community?" Perr asks in a magazine critique. "Would you like to be like the people in these pictures?"

After analyzing the manipulative potentials of representational systems, youngsters are directed to use the same tools and vocabularies toward more humanitarian ends. For example, in a project entitled "Totem Pole for Social Change," students place images illustrating community problems on one side of a column, then counter them with visions of utopian possibility on the opposite side. As a final step classes are always encouraged to analyze their work and the processes involved. Is each participant satisfied with the finished piece? How successfully did the group interact? What did members learn from each other? Was the process democratic? By asking these questions the primacy of student experience is renewed, thus encouraging participation in the educational process. This, in turn, fosters a willingness to engage in the activity of civic decision making necessary for a democratic society.

A similar approach is taken by the Chicago Community TV Network (CTVN) (formerly the Alternative Schools Network Video Project), an organization that has involved more than 800 youths, mostly teenagers from low-income neighborhoods, in television production classes. In this instance the exercise takes the important next step in the pedagogy of everyday culture. It encourages students to apply their productive capabilities to a pressing local problem. CTVN places its emphasis on education and community action, based on the simple proposition that people working together actually can effect change. The approach is micropolitical, focusing on particular elements of local student experience (drug usage, vandalism, gang membership) via peer interviews. In producing *Think Twice* (1980), for example, teenage women tape-recorded their own discussions of contraception and pregnancy—supplementing this material with commentary from friends, male and female.

In the view of CTVN executive director Denise Zaccardi, what the students learn in making tapes is as important as the messages conveyed to others. For each personal problem or community crisis identified, producers document solutions or people seeking them. Zaccardi explains the overriding premise of CTVN to show "that people working together can make a positive difference and that these people are right in the neighborhood. (All heroes are not in Hollywood.)"[21] Programs like ones described above begin to demonstrate ways that activist educators and cultural workers can begin to reach beyond the realm of the classroom, the gallery, or the museum to make cultural education a more integrated part of community life. Ultimately they function to build bridges between people by encouraging everyday cultural production as a means of empowerment. In making tapes, organizing meetings, mounting exhibits or displays, citizens begin reaching out to each other. This is the stuff of democratic public life.

TOWARD DEMOCRACY

Much of this book has been devoted to redefining education and artistic practice as components of a larger unified cultural project. Eminently political in character, this project constructs human subjectivity along a continuum that ranges from the passive recipient to the active production of knowledge. Within this context schooling is both a practical instrumentality and a metaphoric construction for locating individuals on that continuum. It is the powerful mechanism of socialization that we all encounter for the better part of our early lives, as well as a process of growth that we carry with us ever after. Wherever we encounter it, schooling is a primary mechanism through which we understand how to be in the world. It is also how we learn to make the world, and to change it if we wish. In short, schooling is a model through which notions of public life and citizenship are acquired.

Democracy is a process that depends on participation—the willingness and belief that the actions, voices, and votes of individuals can have an effect on the collective totality. In part this constitutes an exercise in political imagination; in part it is a consequence of positive agency that convinces an active citizenry that its constituents are their own rulers. To a large extent, what makes this process of democracy work is a faith in its fairness, in a belief that participation is unstymied by such inequity and injustice. This is what gives the practice of democracy its moral character—not a belief in a common culture that supplants all other, not a faith in an unproblematic form of patriotism that blindly follows symbols, not a reverence for a dehistoricized heritage.

Democracy achieves its moral dimension in its demand for participation from all quarters and by necessity in its resistance to racism, homophobia, commodification, sexism, and all other forms of objectifying, colonizing, and dehumanizing behavior. Within this moral environment pedagogy has a dual function. It is both the means by which the oppressed come to know their oppression and the vehicle through which they struggle to find methods for change.

NOTES

1. Brian Wallis, "Democracy and Cultural Activism" in *Democracy: A Project by Group Material*, ed. Brian Wallis (New York: DIA Art Foundation, 1990), p. 5.

2. Patrick Buchanan, "In the War for America's Culture, the 'Right' Side Is Losing," *Richmond News Leader*, June 24, 1989.

3. Chantal Mouffe, "Radical Democracy: Modern or Postmodern?" in *Universal Abandon? The Politics of Postmodernism*, ed. Andrew Ross (Minneapolis: University of Minnesota Press, 1988), p. 42.

4. Michael S. Joyce, "The National Endowments for the Humanities and the Arts," in *Mandate for Leadership*, ed. Charles L. Heatherley (Washington, DC: Heritage Foundation, 1981), pp. 1040–41.

5. Ibid., p. 1041.

6. Gayatri Chakravorty Spivak, *The Post-Colonial Critic: Interviews, Strategies, Dialogues*, ed. Sarah Harasym (New York: Routledge, Chapman, and Hall, 1990), p. 19.

7. Manuel Alvarado and John O. Thompson, "Introduction," in *The Media Reader*, ed. Manuel Alvarado and John O. Thompson (London: British Film Institute, 1990), p. 4.

8. See Henry A. Giroux, *Schooling and the Struggle for Public Life* (Minneapolis: University of Minnesota Press, 1988).

9. Henry A. Giroux and David Trend, "Cultural Workers, Pedagogy, and the Politics of Difference: Beyond Cultural Conservatism," *Cultural Studies* (forthcoming).

10. Dick Hebdige, *Subculture: The Meaning of Style* (New York: Methuen, 1979).

11. Shoshana Felman, "Psychoanalysis and Education: Teaching Terminable and Interminable," *Yale French Studies* 63 (1982): 33. This issue of *Yale French Studies*, edited by Barbara Johnson and entitled "The Pedagogical Imperative: Teaching as a Literary Genre," also contains articles on education by Joan de Jean, Paul de Man, Jacques Derrida, Jane Gallop, Barbara Guetti, Neil Hertz, Barbara Johnson, Jean-François Lyotard, Andrew McKenna, Angela S. Moger, Michael Ryan, Richard Terdiman, and Steven Ungar.

12. Valerie Walkerdine, "Progressive Pedagogy and Political Struggle," *Screen* 27, no. 5 (Sept.–Oct. 1986): 54–61.

13. Constance Penley, "Teaching in Your Sleep: Feminism and Psychoanalysis," *Theory in the Classroom*, ed. Cary Nelson (Chicago: University of Illinois Press, 1986), p. 132.

14. Gregory Ulmer, *Applied Grammatology: Post(e)-Pedagogy from Jacques Derrida to Joseph Beuys* (Baltimore: Johns Hopkins University Press, 1985), p. 170.

15. See Jane Gallop, *Reading Lacan* (Ithaca, NY: Cornell University Press, 1985), pp. 27–30.

16. This is not to suggest an exclusive method of shifting pedagogical roles or revealing inherited power relationships, but to note one of many scenarios.

17. Felman, "Psychoanalysis and Education," p. 33.

18. Marilyn Boxer, cited in Paula A. Treichler, "Teaching Feminist Theory," in *Theory in the Classroom*, ed. Nelson, p. 69. Treichler proceeds to qualify the quotation by acknowledging the dissension within segments of the women's movement over the efficacy of these techniques. The issues are taken up at greater length in a subsequent essay in the same volume: Penley, "Teaching in Your Sleep," pp. 129–48. Penley elaborates on tendencies of the feminist classroom to mask deeper power structures that remain unchanged by classroom consciousness-raising exercises.

19. Herb Perr, *Making Art Together: Step-by-Step* (San Jose, CA: Resource Publications, 1988).

20. Ibid., p. 2.

21. Denise Zaccardi, *Liberatory Education Curriculum in TV Production for Inner City Young Adults* (Chicago: CTVN, 1984), p. 1.

Selected Bibliography

Adair, Jon, and Sol Worth. *Through Navajo Eyes*. Bloomington: Indiana University Press, 1972.

Adams, Don, and Arlene Goldbard. *Crossroads: Reflections on the Politics of Culture*. Ukiah, CA: Institute for Cultural Democracy, 1990.

————. "Learning to Read The World." *exposure* 28, no. 1/2 (1991): 14.

————. "Social Studies: Public Policy and Media Literacy," *Independent* 12, no. 7 (Aug./Sept. 1989): 36–38.

Adams, Parveen, and Beverley Brown. "The Feminist Body and Feminist Politics." *m/f* 3 (1979).

Althusser, Louis. *For Marx*. Trans. Ben Brewster. New York: Vintage Books, 1970.

————. "Ideology and Ideological State Apparatuses (Notes toward an Investigation)." In *Lenin and Philosophy and Other Essays*, trans. Ben Brewster. London: New Left Books, 1971.

Alvarado, Manuel, and John O. Thompson, eds. *The Media Reader*. London: British Film Institute, 1990.

American Association of Museums. *Museums for a New Century*. Washington, DC: AAM, 1984.

————. *Museums: Their New Audiences*. Washington, DC: AAM, 1972.

Anderson, Perry. *In the Tracks of Historical Materialism*. London: Verso, 1983.

Apple, Michael. W. *Education and Power*. Boston: Routledge and Kegan Paul, 1982.

————. *Teachers and Texts: A Political Economy of Class and Gender Relations in Education*. New York: Routledge, 1989.

Araeen, Rasheed. "From Primitivism to Ethnic Arts." *Third Text* 1 (Autumn 1987): 6–24.

Arnstine, Donald. "Art, Aesthetics, and the Pitfalls of Discipline-Based Art Education," *Educational Theory* 40, no. 4 (Fall 1990): 412–22.

Aronowitz, Stanley. *The Politics of Identity: Class Culture, Social Movements*, New York: Routledge, 1992.

Aronowitz, Stanley, and Henry A. Giroux. *Education under Seige: The Conservative, Liberal and Radical Debate over Schooling*. South Hadley, MA: Bergin and Garvey, 1985.

———. *Postmodern Education: Politics, Culture and Social Criticism*. Minneapolis: University of Minnesota Press, 1990.

Ashcroft, Bill, Gareth Griffiths, and Helen Tiffin, eds. *The Empire Writes Back: Theory and Practice in Post-Colonial Literatures*. New York: Routledge, 1989.

Aufderheide, Pat. "Charting Cultural Change: The Role of the Critic." In *Reimaging America: The Arts of Social Change*, ed. Mark O'Brien and Craig Little. Santa Cruz, CA: New Society Publishers, 1990.

Bagdikian, Ben J. *The Media Monopoly*. 3rd ed. Boston: Beacon Press, 1990.

Baigell, Matthew, and Julia Williams, eds. *Artists against War and Fascism: Papers of the First American Artists' Congress*. New Brunswick, NJ: Rutgers University Press, 1986.

Bailey, David A. "Re-Thinking Black Representations: From Positive Images to Cultural Photographic Practices." *Ten* 8, no. 31 (Winter 1988): 36–50. Reprinted in *exposure* 27, no. 4 (Fall 1990): 37–46.

Bakhtin, Mikhail. *The Dialogic Imagination*. Austin: University of Texas Press, 1981.

Ball, Stephen J. *Foucault and Education: Disciplines and Knowledge*. New York: Routledge, 1990.

Banfield, Edward C. *The Democratic Muse: Visual Arts and the Public Interest*. New York: Basic Books, 1984.

Barthes, Roland. *Camera Lucida: Reflections on Photography*. Trans. Richard Howard. New York: Hill and Wang, 1981.

———. *The Grain of the Voice: Interviews 1962–1980*. Trans. Linda Coverdale. New York: Hill and Wang, 1985.

———. *Image/Music/Text*. Trans. Stephen Health. New York: Hill and Wang, 1977.

———. *Mythologies*. Trans. Annette Lavers. New York: Hill and Wang, 1972.

Baudrillard, Jean. *For a Critique of the Political Economy of the Sign*. Trans. Charles Levin. St. Louis: Telos Press, 1975.

———. *Simulations*. New York: Semiotext(e), 1983.

Becker, Howard S. *Doing Things Together*. Evanston, IL: Northwestern University Press, 1986.

Benjamin, Walter. "A Short History of Photography." Trans. Stanley Mitchell. *Screen* 13, no. 1 (Spring 1972): 5–26.

———. "The Work of Art in the Age of Mechanical Reproduction." In *Illuminations*, trans. Harry Zohn. New York: Schocken Books, 1969.

Bennett, Tony. "Popular Culture: A Teaching Object." *Screen Education* 34 (1980); 18–20.

Bennett, Tony, Colin Mercer, and J. Woollacott, eds. *Popular Culture and Social Relations*. Philadelphia: Open University Press, 1986.

Bennett, William J. *James Madison High School: A Curriculum for American Students*. Washington, DC: U.S. Dept. of Education, 1986.

———. *Our Children and Our Country: Improving America's Schools and Affirming the Common Culture*. New York: Simon and Schuster, 1988.

Berger, John. *Ways of Seeing*. London: British Broadcasting Company, 1972.

Bhabba, Homi K. "Of Mimicry and Man: The Ambivalence of Colonial Discourse." *October* 28 (Spring 1984): 125–33.

———. "Representation and the Colonial Text." In *Theory of Reading*, ed. Frank Gloversmith. Sussez: Harvester Press, 1984.

Bloch, Ernst, Georg Lukács, Bertolt Brecht, Walter Benjamin, Theodor Adorno. *Aesthetics and Politics*. London: New Left Books, 1977.

Bloom, Allan, *The Closing of the American Mind*. New York: Simon and Schuster, 1987.

Boffin, Tessa, and Sunil Gupta, eds. *Ecstatic Antibodies: Resisting the AIDS Mythology*. London: Rivers Oram Press, 1990.

Bolton, Richard. "The Cultural Contradictions of Conservatism." *New Art Examiner* 17, no. 10 (June 1990): 26.

———. "Enlightened Self-Interest: The Avant-Garde in the '80s." *Afterimage* 16, no. 7 (February 1989): 12–18.

Bourdieu, Pierre. *Outline of a Theory of Practice*. Cambridge and New York: Cambridge University Press, 1977.

———. *Reproduction in Education, Society, and Culture*. London and Beverly Hills, CA: Sage Publications, 1977.

Bowles, Samuel, and Herbert Gintis. *Democracy and Capitalism: Property, Community and the Contradictions of Modern Social Thought*. New York: Basic Books, 1986.

———. *Schooling in Capitalist America: Educational Reform and the Contradictions of Economic Life*. New York: Basic Books, 1976.

Brecht, Bertolt. *Brecht on Theatre: The Development of the Aesthetic*. Ed. and trans. John Willett. London: Methuen, 1964.

Brett, Guy. *Through Our Own Eyes*. Philadelphia: New Society, 1987.

Bright, Deborah. "Confusing My Students, Eating My Words." *exposure* 26, nos. 2/3 (1988): 14–18.

Brooker, Peter, and Peter Humm. *Dialogue and Difference: English into the Nineties*. New York: Routledge, 1989.

Brosio, Richard A. "Teaching and Learning for Democratic Empowerment: A Critical Evaluation." *Educational Theory* 40, no. 1 (Winter 1990): 69–81.

Buchanan, Patrick. "In the War for America's Culture, the 'Right' Side Is Losing." *Richmond News Leader*, June 24, 1989.

Burger, Peter. *Theory of the Avant-Garde*. Minneapolis: University of Minnesota Press, 1984.

Burgin, Victor. *The End of Art Theory: Criticism and Postmodernity*. Atlantic Highlands, NJ: Humanities Press, 1986.

Burnett, Linda R., and Frederick Goldman. *Need Johnny Read? Practical Methods to Enrich Humanities Courses Using Films and Film Studies*. Dayton, OH: Pflaum, 1971.

Carnegie Forum of Education and Economy. *A Nation Prepared: Teachers for the 21st Century*. New York: Carnegie Foundation, 1986.

Carnoy, Martin. *Schooling and Work in the Democratic State*. Stanford, CA: Stanford University Press, 1985.

Carr, Cynthia, *Lesbians and Art*. Special issue, *Heresies* 3, vol. 1, no. 3 (1977).

Cheney, Lynne V. *American Memory: A Report on the Humanities in the Nation's Schools*. Washington, DC: National Endowment for the Humanities, 1988.

Clarke, I. E. *Art and Industry, Instruction in Drawing Applied to Industrial and Fine Arts*. Washington, DC: U.S. Government Printing Office, 1884.

Clifford, James. *The Predicament of Culture*. Cambridge: Harvard University Press, 1988.

Conde, Carole, and Karl Beveridge. *First Contract: Women and the Right to Unionize*. Toronto: Between the Lines, 1986.

———. *Words and Images/Mots et Images*. Ottawa: Photo Gallery, 1980.

Crimp, Douglas, ed. "AIDS: Cultural Activism/Cultural Analysis." *October* 43 (Winter 1987).

———. *AIDS Demographics*. Seattle: Bay Press, 1990.

———. "Pictures." Catalog essay, p. 3. Committee for the Visual Arts, 1977.

Culkin, John M., and Anthony Schillaci, eds. *Films Deliver*. New York: Citation Press, 1970.

Culler, Jonathan. *Structuralist Poetics: Structuralism, Linguistics and the Study of Literature*. Ithaca, NY: Cornell University Press, 1975.

Daressa, Lawrence. "The Politics of Distribution." *Afterimage* 15, no. 2 (September 1987): 8–9.

de Castell, Suzanne, Allan Luke, and Carmen Luke, eds. *Language, Authority, and Criticism: Readings on the School Textbook*. London: Falmer Press, 1989.

De Lauretis, Teresa. *Alice Doesn't*. Bloomington: Indiana University Press, 1984.

———. *Technologies of Gender*. Bloomington: Indiana University Press, 1987.

Deleuze, Gilles, and Felix Guattari. *Anti-Oedipus: Capitalism and Schizophrenia*. New York: Viking Press, 1977.

Dennett, Terry, and Jo Spence. "Photography, Ideology, and Education." *Screen Education* 21 (Winter 1976/77): 42–69.

Derrida, Jacques. *Writing and Difference*. Trans. Alan Bass. Chicago: University of Chicago Press, 1978.

de Tocqueville, Alexis. *Democracy in America*. 1835; reprint, New York: Schocken Books, 1961.

Dewdney, Andrew, and Martin Lister. "Youth and Photography." *Ten* 8, no. 21 (1986).

———. *Youth, Culture, and Photography*. London: Macmillan Education, 1988.

Dewey, John. *Democracy and Education*. New York: Macmillan, 1916.

Diamond, Robert M., ed. *A Guide to Instructional Media*. New York: McGraw-Hill, 1964.

Dorfman, A., and Armand Mattelart. *How to Read Donald Duck*. International General, 1975.

D'Sousa, Dinesh. "The National Endowment for Pornography." *Policy Review* (Spring 1982).

Dyer, Richard, ed. *Gays and Film*. New York: New York Zoetrope, 1984.

Eagleton, Terry. *The Function of Criticism*. London: Verso, 1984.

———. *Literary Theory: An Introduction*. Minneapolis: University of Minnesota Press, 1983.

Eco, Umberto. "Can Television Teach?" *Screen Education* 31 (Summer 1979).

Eisner, Elliot W. "Discipline-Based Art Education: Conceptions and Misconceptions." *Educational Theory* 40, no. 4 (Fall 1990).

———. *The Role of Discipline-Based Art Education in America's Schools*. Los Angeles: Getty Center for Education in the Arts, 1987.

Ellsworth, Elizabeth. "Critical Media Analysis, Radical Pedagogy, and MTV." *Feminist*

Teacher 2, no. 1 (1986): 8–13.

———. "Educational Media, Ideology, and the Presentation of Knowledge through Popular Cultural Forms." In *Popular Culture, Schooling, and Everyday Life*, ed. Henry A. Giroux and Roger Simon, pp. 47–90. New York: Bergin and Garvey, 1989.

———. "Why Doesn't This Feel Empowering? Working Through the Repressive Myths of Critical Pedagogy." *Harvard Educational Review* 59, no. 3 (August 1989): 297–323.

Emerson, Ralph Waldo. "The American Scholar" (1837). In *Selected Essays, Lectures and Poems of Ralph Waldo Emerson*, ed. R. E. Spiller. New York: Simon and Schuster, 1965.

Enzensberger, Hans Magnus. "Constituents of a Theory of the Media." In *The Consciousness Industry*, trans. Stuart Hood. New York: Seabury Press, 1974.

Evans, Brendan. *Radical Adult Education: A Political Critique*. New York and London: Croom Helm, 1987.

Ewen, Stewart. *All Consuming Images: The Politics of Style in Contemporary Culture*. New York: Basic Books, 1988.

———. *Captains of Consciousness*. New York: Seabury Press, 1974.

Fanon, Franz. *The Wretched of the Earth*. New York: Grove Press. 1968.

Feistritzer, C. Emily. *The Condition of Teaching: A State by State Analysis*. Princeton, NJ: Princeton University Press, 1986.

Feld, A. M., and J.M.D. Schuster. *Patrons Despite Themselves: Taxpayers and Arts Policy*. New York: New York University Press, 1983.

Felman, Shoshana. "Psychoanalysis and Education: Teaching Terminable and Interminable." *Yale French Studies* 63 (1982).

Ferguson, Russell, Martha Gever, Trinh T. Minh-ha and Cornell West, eds. *Out There: Marginalizaton and Contemporary Culture*. Cambridge: MIT Press, 1990.

Fish, Stanley. *Is There a Text in This Class? The Authority of Interpretive Communities*. Cambridge: Harvard University Press, 1980.

Fiske, John. *Reading the Popular*. Boston: Unwin Hyman, 1989.

———. *Television Culture*. London: Methuen, 1987.

Fleming, Martha. "The Production of Meaning: An Interview with Carole Conde and Karl Beveridge." *Afterimage* 10, no. 4 (Nov. 1982): 10–13.

Foster, Hal. *The Anti-Aesthetic*. Port Townsend, WA: Bay Press, 1983.

———. *Recodings: Art, Spectacle, Cultural Politics*. Port Townsend, WA: Bay Press, 1985.

———. ed. *Discussions in Contemporary Culture: Number One*. New York: DIA Art Foundation, 1988.

Foucault, Michel. *The Order of Things: The Archaeology of the Human Sciences*. New York: Vintage. 1970.

———. "Politics and Ethics: An Interview." Trans. Catherine Porter. In *The Foucault Reader*, ed. Paul Rabinow. New York: Pantheon, 1984.

Fraser, Nancy. *Unruly Practices: Power, Discourse, and Gender in Contemporary Social Theory*. Minneapolis: University of Minnesota Press, 1989.

———. "Rethinking the Public Sphere: A Contribution to the Critique of Actually Existing Democracy." *Social Text* 25/26 (1990): 56–80.

Freire, Paulo. *Literacy: Learning to Read the Word and the World*. South Hadley, MA: Bergin and Garvey, 1987.

————. *Pedagogy of the Oppressed*. Trans. Myra Bergman Ramos. New York: Continuum, 1970.

————. *Politics of Education: Culture, Power, and Liberation*. South Hadley, MA: Bergin and Garvey, 1985.

Friedman, John S., and Eric Nadler. "Hard Right Rudder at the NEH." *Nation,* April 14, 1984, p. 448.

Fusco, Coco. "Fantasies of Oppositionality." *Afterimage* 16, no. 5 (December 1988): 6–9.

Gabriel, Teshome H. *Third Cinema in the Third World: The Aesthetics of Liberation.* Ann Arbor, MI: UMI Research Press, 1982.

Gallop, Jane. "The Pleasures of the Phototext." *Afterimage* 12, no. 9 (April 1985): 16–18.

————. *Reading Lacan.* Ithaca, NY: Cornell University Press, 1985.

Garrels, Gary, ed. *Amerika: Tim Rollins + KOS.* New York: DIA Art Foundation, 1989.

Gates, Henry Louis. *"Race," Writing, and Difference.* Chicago: University of Chicago Press, 1986.

————. *The Signifying Monkey.* New York: Oxford University Press, 1989.

Geertz, Clifford. *The Interpretation of Cultures.* London: Hutchenson, 1975.

Getty Center for Education in the Arts. *Beyond Creating: The Place for Art in America's Schools.* Los Angeles: Getty Center for Education in the Arts, 1985.

Gever, Martha, ed. "The Next Generation: Media Education." Special issue of *The Independent* 12, no. 7 (Aug./Sept. 1989).

Gever, Martha, and Nathalie Magnan. "The Same Difference: On Lesbian Representation." *exposure* 24, no. 2 (1986): 27–56.

Giroux, Henry A. *Border Crossings: Cultural Workers and the Politics of Education.* New York: Routledge, 1992.

————. *Schooling and the Struggle for Public Life.* Minneapolis: University of Minnesota Press, 1988.

————. *Theory and Resistance in Education: A Pedagogy for the Opposition.* South Hadley, MA: Bergin and Garvey Press, 1983.

Giroux, Henry A., and Peter McLaren, eds. *Critical Pedagogy, the State, and Cultural Struggle.* Albany: SUNY Press, 1988.

Giroux, Henry A., and David Trend. "Cultural Workers, Pedagogy, and the Politics of Difference: Beyond Cultural Conservatism." *Cultural Studies* (Winter 1992).

Glass, Fred. "Toward a Morphology of Labor Video." *Afterimage* 17, no. 2 (Sept. 1989): 12.

Glueck, Grace. "Arts Endowment Begins Broad School Program." *New York Times,* May 19, 1986, sec. C, p. 14.

Goffman, Erving. *Gender Advertisements.* New York: Macmillan, 1979.

Gomez-Pena, Guillermo. "The Multi-cultural Paradigm: An Open Letter to the National Arts Community." *High Performance* 47 (Fall 1989): 18–27.

Goodman, Jesse. "Education for Critical Democracy." *Journal of Education* 171, no. 2 (1989): 88–116.

Gramsci, Antonio. *Selections from the Prison Notebooks.* Ed. and trans. Quintin Hoare and Geoffrey Nowel Smith. New York: International Publishers, 1971.

Grossberg, Lawrence, and Cary Nelson, eds. *Marxism and the Interpretation of Culture.* Chicago: University of Illinois Press, 1988.

Grover, Jan Zita. "The Subject of Photography in the Academy." *Screen* (Sept./Oct. 1986).

Gutman, Amy. *Democratic Education*. Princeton, NJ: Princeton University Press, 1987.

Habermas, Jürgon. "Modernity versus Postmodernity." *New German Critique* 22 (1981).

Hall, Stuart. "The Emergence of Cultural Studies and the Crisis of the Humanities," *October* 53 (Summer 1990).

———. "Encoding/Decoding." In *Culture, Media, Language*, ed. Stuart Hall et al., pp. 128–39.

Hall, Stuart, Dorothy Hobson, Andrew Lowe, and Paul Willis, eds. *Culture, Media, Language*. London: Hutchenson, 1980.

Hall, Stuart, and Tony Jefferson. *Resistance through Rituals: Youth Subcultures in Post-War Britain*. London: Unwin Hyman, 1976.

Halleck, Deedee. "Paper Tiger Television." In *Cultures in Contention*, ed. Douglas Kahn and Diane Neumaier. Seattle: Real Comet Press, 1986.

Hanhardt, John, ed. *Video Culture*. Visual Studies Workshop Press, 1986.

Haratonik, Peter, and Kit Laybourne, eds. *Video and Kids*. New York: Gordon and Breach, 1974.

Haraway, Donna J. *Simians, Cyborgs, and Women: The Reinvention of Nature*. New York: Routledge, 1991.

Hebdige, Dick. *Hiding in the Light: On Images and Things*. New York: Comedia/Routledge, 1988.

———. *Subculture: The Meaning of Style*. New York: Methuen, 1979.

Hecter, Michael. *Principles of Group Solidarity*. Los Angeles: University of California Press, 1987.

Hirsch, E. D., Jr. *Cultural Literacy: What Every American Needs to Know*. Boston: Houghton Mifflin, 1987.

Hoggart, Richard. *The Uses of Literacy*. New York: Penguin, 1958.

hooks, bell. *feminist theory: from margin to center*. Boston: South End Press, 1985.

———. *talking back: thinking feminist, thinking black*. Boston: South End Press, 1989.

hooks, bell, and Cornell West. *Breaking Bread: Black History and Cultural Work*. Boston: South End Press, 1991.

Horkheimer Max, and Theodor Adorno. *The Dialectic of Enlightenment*. Trans. John Cumming. New York: Herder and Herder, 1972.

Huntington, Samuel P. *The Crisis of Democracy: A Report on the Governability of Democracies to the Trilateral Commission*. New York: New York University Press, 1975.

Iser, Wolfgang. *The Act of Reading: A Theory of Aesthetic Response*. Baltimore, MD: Johns Hopkins University Press, 1978.

Jacoby, Russell. *The Last American Intellectuals: American Culture in the Age of Academe*. New York: Basic Books, 1987.

Jameson, Fredric. *The Political Unconscious*. Ithaca, NY: Cornell University Press, 1981.

———. "Postmodernism and Consumer Society." In *The Anti-Aesthetic: Essays on Postmodern Culture*, ed. Hal Foster, pp. 111–25. Port Townsend, WA: Bay Press, 1983.

Jhally, Sut, and Ian Angus, eds. *Cultural Politics in Contemporary America*. New York: Routledge, 1989.

Johnson, Richard. "Cultural Studies and Educational Practice." *Screen Education* 34 (Spring 1980): 5–29.

Joyce, Michael S. "The National Endowments for the Humanities and the Arts." In *Mandate for Leadership*, ed. Charles L. Heatherley, pp. 1040–41. Washington, DC: Heritage Foundation, 1981.

Julien, Isaac, and Kobena Mercer, eds. *The Last 'Special Issue' on Race?* Special issue, *Screen* 29, no. 4 (Autumn 1988).

Kahn, Douglas, and Diane Neumaier, eds. *Cultures in Contention*. Seattle: Real Comet Press, 1985.

Kaprow, Allan. "The Education of the Un-Artist." *Artnews*, Feb. 1971.

Kenny, Lorraine. "The Birds and the Bees: Teen Pregnancy and the Media." *Afterimage* 16, no. 1 (Summer 1988): 6–8.

Kolodny, Annette. "Dancing through the Mine Field: Some Observations on the Theory, Practice, and Politics of a Feminist Literary Criticism." *Feminist Review* 6 (Spring 1980): 1–25.

Kramer, Hilton. "A Note on the New Criterion." *New Criterion* 1, no. 1 (September 1982): 7.

Kruger, Barbara, and Phil Mariani, eds. *Remaking History: Discussions in Contemporary Culture No. 4*. Seattle: Bay Press, 1989.

Kuhn, Annette. "Ideology, Structure, Knowledge," *Screen Education* 27 (Summer 1978): 34–41.

Lacan, Jacques. *Ecrits: A Selection*. Trans. Alan Sheridan. New York: Norton, 1977.

Laclau, Ernesto, and Chantal Mouffe. *Hegemony and Socialist Strategy: Toward a Radical Democratic Politics*. Trans. Winston Moore and Paul Cammack. London: Verso, 1985.

Larson, Gary O. *The Reluctant Patron: The United States Government and the Arts, 1943–1965*. Philadelphia: University of Pennsylvania Press, 1983.

Leavis F. R., and Thompson, Denys. *Culture and Environment*. London: Chatto and Windus, 1933.

Leonard, Stephen T. *Critical Theory in Political Practice*. Princeton, NJ: Princeton University Press, 1990.

Lerner, Ruby. *Comprehensive Organizational Assistance for Artists' Organizations*. Washington, DC: National Association of Artists' Organizations, 1988.

Lipman, Samuel. "Art, Patronage, and Education." *Design for Arts Education* (July/August 1986): 32–38.

Lippard, Lucy R. *Get the Message? A Decade of Art for Social Change*. New York: Dutton, 1984.

———. *Mixed Blessings: New Art in Multi-Cultural America*. New York: Pantheon, 1990.

Livingstone, David, et al. *Critical Pedagogy and Cultural Power*. South Hadley, MA: Bergin and Garvey, 1987.

Lloyd-Kolkin, Donna, and Kathleen Tyner. *Media and You: An Elementary Media Literacy Curriculum*. San Francisco: Strategies of Media Literacy, 1991.

Lord, Catherine. "Bleached, Straightened, and Fixed." *New Art Examiner* 18, no. 6 (February 1991): 25–27.

Lourde, Audre. *A Burst of Light: Essays*. Ithaca, NY: Firebrand Press, 1988.

Lovett, Tom. "The Challenge of Community Education in Social and Political Change." *Convergence II*, no. 1 (1978): 47–48.

Lowrey, W. McNeil, ed. *The Arts: Public Policy in the United States*. Englewood Cliffs, NJ: Prentice Hall, 1984.

Lusted, David. "Why Pedagogy? An Introduction to the Issue." *Screen* 27, no. 5 (Sept.–Oct. 1986): 2–15.

Lyotard, Jean-François. *The Postmodern Condition: A Report on Knowledge*. Minneapolis: University of Minnesota Press, 1984.

Marcuse, Herbert. *The Aesthetic Dimension: Toward A Critique of Marxist Aesthetics*. Boston: Beacon Press, 1978.

———. *An Essay on Liberation*. Boston: Beacon Press, 1969.

Marshall, Brenda. *Teaching the Postmodern*. New York: Routledge, 1992.

Marx, Karl, and Freidrich Engels. *The German Ideology*. New York: International Publishers, 1956.

Masterman, Len. *Teaching the Media*. London: Comedia, 1985.

Mattick, Paul, Jr. "Art and the State: The NEA Debate in Perspective." *Nation* 251, no. 10 (Oct. 1, 1990).

McCabe, Colin, ed. *High Theory, Low Culture*. Manchester: Manchester University Press, 1986.

McLaren, Peter. *Life in Schools: An Introduction to Critical Pedagogy in the Social Foundations of Education*. New York: Longman, 1989.

———. ed. *Postmodernism, Postcolonialism, and Pedagogy*. Albert Park. Australia: James Nicholas, 1992.

———. *Radical Pedagogy: Postcolonial Politics in a Postmodern Age*. New York: Routledge, forthcoming.

———. *Schooling as Ritual Performance: Toward a Political Economy of Educational Symbols and Gestures*. New York: Routledge and Kegan Paul, 1986.

McLuhan, Marshall. *Understanding Media: Extensions of Man*. New York: McGraw-Hill, 1964.

McRobbie, Angela. *Feminism for Girls: An Adventure Story*. London and New York: Routledge and Kegan Paul, 1981.

Mercer, Colin. "A Poverty of Desire: Pleasure and Popular Politics." In *Formations of Pleasure*, ed. Formations. London: Routledge and Kegan Paul, 1983.

Mesa-Bains, Amalia. "Meeting the Challenge of Cultural Transformation." *FYI* 5, no. 3 (Fall 1989): 1.

Mitchell, Candace, and Kathleen Weiler, eds. *Rewriting Literacy: Culture and the Discourse of the Other*. New York: Bergin and Garvey, 1991.

Modleski, Tania, ed. *Studies in Entertainment: Critical Approaches to Mass Culture*. Bloomington: Indiana University Press, 1986.

Mohr, Richard D. "Gay Studies as Moral Vision." *Educational Theory* 39, no. 2 (Spring 1989): 121–32.

Mooney, Michael. *The Ministry of Culture: Connections among Art, Money, and Politics*. New York: Wyndham Press, 1982.

Morely, David. *Family Television: Cultural Power and Domestic Leisure*. London: Comedia, 1986.

Morris, Meaghan. "Banality in Cultural Studies." *Block* 14 (1988): 15–26.

———. *The Pirate's Fiancée: Feminism, Reading, and Postmodernism*. London and New York: Verso, 1988.

Mouffe, Chantal. "Radical Democracy: Modern or Postmodern?" In *Universal Abandon: The Politics of Postmodernism*, ed. Andrew Ross. Minneapolis: University of Minnesota Press, 1988.

National Commission on Excellence in Education. *A Nation at Risk: The Imperative for*

Educational Reform. Washington, DC: U.S. Government Printing Office, 1983.

National Endowment for the Arts. *The National Endowment for the Arts: Five Year Plan, 1986–1990*. Washington, DC: National Endowment for the Arts, 1986.

————. *Toward Civilization: A Report on Arts Education*. Washington, DC: U.S. Government Printing Office, 1988.

Neff, Thomas, and Tony Fredericks. "Teaching Photography." Special issue, *exposure* 18, nos. 3/4 (1980).

Nelson, Cary, ed. *Theory in the Classroom*. Urbana and Chicago: University of Illinois Press, 1986.

Netzer, Dick. *The Subsidized Muse: Public Support for the Arts in the United States*. New York: Cambridge University Press, 1978.

Nichols, Bill. *Ideology and the Image*. Bloomington: Indiana University Press, 1981.

Ontario Ministry of Education. *Media Literacy Resource Guide*. Toronto: Ontario Ministry of Education, 1989.

Owens, Craig. "The Allegorical Impulse: Toward a Theory of Postmodernism." *October* 12 (Spring 1980): 67–86. Reprinted in *Art after Modernism: Rethinking Representation*, ed. Brian Wallis, pp. 203–37. New York: David Godine and the New Museum, 1984.

————. "The Discourse of Others: Feminists and Postmodernism." In *The Anti-Aesthetic*, ed. Hal Foster, pp. 57–83. Port Townsend, WA: Bay Press, 1983.

————. "Outlaws: Gay Men in Feminism." In *Men in Feminism*, eds. Alice Jardine and Paul Smith. New York and London: Methuen, 1987.

Pankratz, David B. "Aesthetic Welfare, Government, and Educational Policy." *Design for Arts Education*, 87, no. 6 (July/August 1986).

Pearson, Tony. "Teaching Television." *Screen* 24 (1983): 35–43.

Penley, Constance. "Teaching in Your Sleep: Feminism and Psychoanalysis." *Theory in the Classroom*, ed. Cary Nelson. Chicago: University of Illinois Press, 1986.

People for the American Way. *The American Public's Perspective on Federal Support for the Arts, and the Controversy over Funding for the National Endowment for the Arts*. Washington, DC: People for the American Way, 1990.

Perr, Herb. *Making Art Together: Step-by-Step*. San Jose, CA: Resource Publications, 1988.

Photography Workshop. *Photography/Politics One*. London: Photography Workshop, n.d.

Pindell, Howardina. "Art (World) and Racism: Testimony, Documentation, and Statistics." *Third Text* 3/4 (Spring/Summer 1988): 157–90.

Pollock, Griselda. "Art, Art School, Culture: Individualism after the Death of the Artist." *exposure* 24, no. 3 (1986).

Raven, Arlene, ed. *Art in the Public Interest*. Ann Arbor, MI: UMI Press, 1989.

Ravitch, Diane. *The Schools We Deserve: Reflections of the Educational Crises of Our Time*. New York: Basic Books, 1985.

Renov, Michael. "Early Newsreel: The Construction of Political Imaginary for the New Left." *Afterimage* 14, no. 7 (Feb. 1987): 12–15.

Risatti, Howard, ed. "Are Art Students Educated? If Not, Why Not?" Special issue, *New Art Examiner* 17, no. 1 (September 1989).

Robinson, John P. "Assessing the Artist's Condition: Some Quantitative Issues." In *The Modern Muse: The Support and Condition of Artists*, ed. Richard Swaim. New York: American Council for the Arts, 1989.

Rosenberg, Harold. *The Tradition of the New*. New York: Horizon Press, 1959.

Rosler, Martha. "Lookers, Buyers, and Makers: Thoughts on Audience." In *Art after Modernism: Rethinking Representation*, ed. Brian Wallis, pp. 311–40. New York: New Museum of Contemporary Art, 1984.

Ross, Andrew, ed. *Universal Abandon? The Politics of Postmodernism*. Minneapolis: University of Minnesota Press, 1989.

Said, Edward W. *Covering Islam: How the Media and the Experts Determine How We See the Rest of the World*. New York: Pantheon Books, 1981.

———. *The World, the Text, and the Critic*. Cambridge: Harvard University Press, 1983.

Schiller, Herbert I. *Communications and Cultural Domination*. White Plains, NY: International Arts and Sciences Press, 1976.

———. *Culture, Inc.: The Corporate Takeover of American Expression*. New York: Oxford University Press, 1988.

Scott, Joan Wallach. "History in Crisis? The Other Side's Side of the Story." *American Historical Review* 94, no. 3 (June 1989).

Sekula, Allan. "School Is a Factory." In *Photography against the Grain: Essays and Photo Works, 1973–1983*, pp. 197–234. Halifax: Nova Scotia College of Art and Design, 1984.

Simon, Roger. *Teaching against the Grain: A Pedagogy of Possibility*. New York: Bergin and Garvey Press, 1991.

Simon, Roger I., Don Dippo, and Arleen Schenke. *Learning Work: A Critical Pedagogy of Work Education*. New York: Bergin and Garvey, 1991.

Simonson, Rick, and Scott Walker, eds. "Multi-cultural Literacy: The Opening of the American Mind." Special issue, *Graywolf Annual* 5 (1988).

Sims, Lowrey Stokes. "The Mirror/The Other: The Politics of Esthetics." *Artforum* 28, no. 7 (March 1990): 111–15.

Smith, Page. *Killing the Spirit: Higher Education in America*. New York: Viking, 1990.

Solomon-Godeau, Abigail. *Photography at the Dock*. Minneapolis: University of Minnesota Press, 1990.

Sontag, Susan. *On Photography*. New York: Penguin, 1979.

Spence, Jo, and Patrical Holland. *Family Snaps: The Meanings of Domestic Photography*. London: Virago, 1991.

SPE Women's Caucus. "Survey of Women and Persons of Color in Post-Secondary Photographic Education." *exposure* 26, nos. 2/3: 41–87.

Spivak, Gayatri Chakravorty. *In Other Worlds: Essays in Cultural Politics*. New York and London: Routledge, 1987.

———. *The Post-Colonial Critic: Interviews, Strategies, Dialogues*. Ed. Sarah Harasym. New York: Routledge, Chapman and Hall, 1990.

Stern, Simon. "Lesbian and Gay Studies: A Selected Bibliography." *Yale Journal of Criticism* 3, no. 1 (1989): pp. 253–60.

Swaim, C. Richard. *The Modern Muse: The Support and Condition of Artists*. New York: American Council on the Arts, 1989.

Sykes, Charles. *Profscam: Professors and the Demise of Higher Education*. New York: St. Martin's Press.

Tompkins, Jane. *Reader-Response Criticism: From Formalism to Post-Structuralism*. Baltimore, MD: Johns Hopkins University Press, 1980.

Treichler, Paula A. "Teaching Feminist Theory." In *Theory in the Classroom*, ed. Cary Nelson. Chicago: University of Illinois Press, 1986.

Trend, David. "Changing the Subject: From Reproduction to Resistance in Media Education." *Afterimage* 16, no. 4 (November 1988): 10–14.

———. "Photography and Education." Special issue, *exposure* 28, nos. 1/2 (1991).

Trinh T. Minh-ha. *Women Native Other*. Bloomington: Indiana University Press, 1989.

Ulmer, Gregory L. *Applied Grammatology: Post(e)-Pedagogy from Jacques Derrida to Joseph Beuys*. Baltimore, MD: Johns Hopkins University Press, 1985.

U.S. Department of Education. *The Nation's Report Card*. Washington, DC: U.S. Government Printing Office, 1987.

Vance, Carole S. "Reagan's Revenge: Restructuring the NEA." *Art in America* 78, no. 11 (Nov. 1990): 49–55.

———. "The War on Culture." *Art in America* 77, no. 9 (Sept. 1989): 39–45.

Walkerdine, Valerie. "Progressive Pedagogy and Political Struggle." *Screen* 27, no. 5 (Sept.-Oct. 1986): 54–61.

Wallace, Michelle. *Invisibility Blues: From Pop to Theory*. New York: Routledge, Chapman, and Hall, 1990.

Wallis, Brian, ed. *Democracy: A Project by Group Material*. New York: DIA Art Foundation, 1990.

Watney, Simon. "Photography—Education—Theory." *exposure* 24, no. 1 (1986): 13–16.

West, Cornell. *The Ethical Dimensions of Marxist Thought*. New York: Monthly Review Press, 1991.

———. "The New Cultural Politics of Difference." *October* 53 (Summer 1990).

Wexler, Philip. *Social Analysis of Education: After the New Sociology*. New York: Routledge, 1987.

Williams, Raymond. *Marxism and Literature*. New York: Oxford University Press, 1977.

———. *Resources of Hope*. London: Verso, 1989.

———. "Television and Teaching." *Screen Education* 31 (1979): 5–14.

———. *Television: Technology and Cultural Form*. London: Fontana, 1974.

Williamson, Judith. *Consuming Passions: The Dynamics of Popular Culture*. New York: Marion Boyers, 1985.

———. "How Does Girl Number Twenty Understand Ideology? *Screen Education* 40 (Autumn/Winter 1981/82): 80–87.

———. "Woman Is an Island: Femininity and Colonization." In *Studies in Entertainment: Critical Approaches to Mass Culture*. ed. Tania Modleski, pp. 100–101. Indianapolis, Indiana University Press, 1986.

Willis, Paul. *Common Culture: Symbolic Work at Play in the Everyday Cultures of the Young*. San Francisco: Westview Press, 1990.

———. *Learning to Labor: How Working Class Kids Get Working Class Jobs*. New York: Columbia University Press, 1981.

Wolf, Constance. "The Multicultural Debate: Challenges of the 1990s." *exposure* 28, nos. 1/2 (1991).

Zaccardi, Denise. *Liberatory Education Curriculum in TV Production for Inner City Young Adults*. Chicago, CTVN, 1984.

FILMS AND VIDEOTAPES

Bread and Roses Cultural Project. *Take Care*. New York: Local 1199 Drug, Hospital, and Health Care Workers' Union. 1989.

Chicago Community Television Network. *Think Twice*. Chicago: CTVN. 1980.

Drury, Sarah. *Helen Keller Knows She's There*. New York: Sarah Drury, 1989.

Goodman, Steve. *2371 Second Avenue: An East Harlem Story*. New York: Educational Video Center, 1986.

Lamb, Gina. *Textbook Mystery: Oral History*. Los Angeles: Jefferson High School Humanitas Program, 1990.

Miller, Branda. *Birth of a Candy Bar*, New York: I-Eye-I Video Workshop, Henry Street Settlement, 1989.

————. *Talkin' 'bout Droppin' Out*. Boston: Madison High School, 1988.

————. *What's Up?* Los Angeles: Masada Placement Community Day Center Humanitas Program, 1987.

Newsreel, *Columbia Revolt*. New York and San Francisco: Newsreel, 1968.

————. *Summer '68*. New York and San Francisco: Newsreel, 1968.

Paper Tiger Television. *Murray Bookchin Reads Time*. New York: Paper Tiger Television, 1984.

Papson, Steve. *Appropriation of Culture: The IBM Tramp*. Canton, NY: St. Lawrence University, 1985.

Sopher, Sharon. *Witness to Apartheid*. New York: Women Make Movies, 1986.

Sporn, Pam. *The Road to Mississippi: Reclaiming Our History*. Bronx, NY: Through Our Eyes Video and History Project, Bronx Satellite Academy, 1990.

————. *Torn Between Colors*. Bronx, NY: Through Our Eyes Video and History Project, Bronx Satellite Academy, 1989.

Index

ABOUT THE AUTHOR

DAVID TREND most recently served as codirector of programs at the Capp Street Project, a nonprofit alternative arts organization based in San Francisco. He spent five years as editor of *Afterimage*, an award-winning progressive visual arts publication, and continues to lecture nationally on media and culture. He has written over 90 articles on these subjects in such periodicals as *Afterimage*, *Art in America*, *Artweek*, *Cultural Studies*, and *exposure*. He holds an MFA in visual studies from SUNY at Buffalo.